DISCUSSIONS OF LITERATURE

Discussions of

SHAKESPEARE'S

SONNETS

Edited with an Introduction by
BARBARA HERRNSTEIN
Bennington College

D. C. HEATH AND COMPANY
BOSTON

CONTENTS

INTRODUCTION

It has been observed that, after a certain point, repetition without progression is comical. With a glance at the accumulation of commentary that has been published on Shakespeare's *Sonnets,* one could add that after it has become comical, it becomes depressing. The selective bibliography provided in the *New Variorum* edition of the *Sonnets* lists over seven hundred books and articles and constitutes, for the most part, a record of three hundred years of folly, futility and fanaticism. There are, to be sure, perfectly legitimate reasons for the sheer abundance of this material; the same is more or less true of all Shakespeare's works. Our own admiration is combined, on the one hand, with the inexhaustible richness and subtlety of his achievement and, on the other, with ever-increasing sources of information and ever-changing ideas and attitudes concerning poetry, man and the world. There are, however, some special reasons for the nature as well as the quantity of commentary on the *Sonnets.*

For one thing, the text of the *Sonnets* comes to us with a host of attendant mysteries. The 1609 quarto is our only edition of the complete sonnets and it is, in many ways, an unreliable or unsatisfactory one. The date of publication is not as informative as we should like, for it tells us only that the sonnets were written sometime before 1609; over what period and in what order, we do not know. Since the dedication to Mr. W. H. is both unconventional in form and obscure in substance, it would seem almost calculated to invite speculation. The sequential arrangement of the poems is a particular source of consternation: it appears at some points to be thematic and at others to be chronological. But sonnets which would in either case apparently belong together are separated, and several seem to be juxtaposed for obviously spurious reasons. Each reader finds himself privately (or publicly) rearranging them to make more sense as a coherent work of art or a consistent record of events.

Certain concerns are unique to the criticism of the *Sonnets* primarily because, among Shakespeare's works, these are the most obviously or directly personal with respect to both the poet and the reader. Although we do not know to what extent we may confidently regard the sonnets as autobiographical (and controversy over the sincerity or conventionality of the poems accounts for another sizeable portion of the commentary), many of them seem to be occasioned by specific events in the poet's life and to address or allude to specific people. The temptation to give more substance to these events and identity to these people has apparently been hard to resist.

Finally, certain critical problems which arise in connection with all Shakespeare's work are more troublesome in the sonnets because they are non-dramatic poems. In the plays, obscurities of language and intention can often be elucidated by the plot, the dramatic situation of the speaker, the replies and reactions of other characters, and so forth. To a certain extent, many of the sonnets do create their own dramatic context, as plot, character and scene seem to spring into existence. And yet interpretations which depend upon a presumed "story" are likely to be circular in their argument, for one's perception of the story will depend, in turn, upon one's interpretation of the individual poems. Many of the sonnets, however, invite this kind of interpretation (that is, through cross-reference to and inter-annotation of the other sonnets) because they are so obviously oblique and circumspect. The meanings may be precise but private, known only to the poet and a special audience, perhaps only to the poet himself. They may allude to situations not only beyond our recovery, but beyond our surmise. We could, of course, regard such poems as ultimately inexplicable, as presenting more problems than we have the means to solve. Such seemingly ignoble confessions of critical impotence, however, though we are often enough racked for them, are rare.

As we know, it is in the deserts of ignorance that theories are most likely to proliferate and flourish. And yet one sometimes wishes that these problems were even more clearly and absolutely insoluble; for, as it is, we do not know enough to say anything conclusive and we know too much to keep ourselves from speculating. (It is perhaps for this reason that the *Sonnets* have attracted more than their share of attention from the lunatic fringe of the scholarly world. There is probably no imaginable hypothesis concerning the identities of the dark lady, the fair youth and the rival poet—to give these *personae* their familiar names —that has not, at some time, been solemnly proclaimed and duly documented. We have had Mr. W. H. as William Himself, the lady as a negro courtesan, the rival poet as the Roman Church, and the whole sequence as the record of Shakespeare's struggle to overcome alcoholism.) Moreover, it seems to be a law of human nature—and not restricted to the study of literature—that agnosticism is an unstable creed:

it constantly teeters toward fideism in one direction or another. Thus we are rarely satisfied merely to affirm our ignorance; and every serious reader of the *Sonnets* finds himself assuming, even if not publishing, certain solutions to many of the mysteries.

The commentaries in the present volume were not chosen as representative samples of the history of *Sonnet* criticism; such a collection would be of little value to the student or reader of the poems. The selections in Section II must suffice to represent the sort of speculative controversy which comprises about ninety percent of the literature. Hotson's famous essay suggests the methods and concerns of such pursuits, and Bateson's retort raises some of the critical and scholarly issues involved. The reader may find himself wondering whether Bateson's alternative explication of the crucial Sonnet 107 is not as vulnerable in the rigidity of its assumptions as Hotson's is in its relentless single-mindedness. If so, he will be in a good position to understand how the basic ingredients for the familiar stew are brought together, and what keeps the pot boiling.

The selections in the first section—assessments of and reactions to the *Sonnets* from the seventeenth through the nineteenth centuries—should not be read as a capsule view of the reputation of the poems over that period. There has always been more variability and less continuity than such a scanty culling could summarize adequately. Benson's preface is suspect in intention, since his "anthology" of the *Poems* is a shameless piece of editorial scissors-work and general skulduggery—apparently designed to deceive a gullible public. The very possibility of his observations, however, make it of interest, and it is perhaps an ironically appropriate introduction to our volume. Steevens' notorious animadversions represent a frequent reaction to Shakespeare's non-dramatic poetry in the eighteenth century. The selections from Coleridge and Keats catch both writers in somewhat casual moments, and reveal the way in which Shakespeare reveals his readers. We find Coleridge—haunted by the nature of Shakespeare's relationship to the person presumably addressed in the sonnets—moving in thirty years from wishful rationalization to willful blindness while, in the period between, Keats—blithely unconcerned with (or unaware of) questions of moral depravity—is reading the *Sonnets* as the admired achievement of a fellow-poet. Hallam's commentary, with its combination of reverence for the poet and embarrassment at his poetry, is a fair sample of an early Victorian's response to the *Sonnets*.

The selections in the last three sections bring us to the center of contemporary criticism, where it is difficult to avoid self-congratulation. The interpretation of the *Sonnets* in recent years has tended to transform them from a set of riddles or the fragmentary notes for an unwritten autobiography to a group of poems by a recognizable human being. The essays in Section III cover, among them, most of the major themes in the sonnets, and were chosen to complement rather than to oppose each other. Thus the reader is as likely to be impressed by the richness and brilliance of Knight's comprehensively correlated readings as by the solidly informed, yet sensitive, interpretations offered by Lever.

It will be clear from many of the selections (especially those by Hubler, Cruttwell and Lever), that we are growing self-consciously aware of the fact that the *Sonnets* were not handed down to us from the empyrean, but were written in a particular world of events, ideas and assumptions, and by a poet who responded to certain literary conventions and traditions. But since literary scholarship may have the double effect of removing the veil of ignorance only to replace it with the wall of alienation, the student is often left in a state of paralyzed awe at the spectacle of Shakespeare's poetry restored to its "context." The critics and scholars represented in this volume are notable for having recognized that our reading of the sonnets is still likely to bring us closest to Shakespeare when we allow them to be closest to ourselves: when, responding to the personal appeal and challenge of the poems, we interpret them also through our own feelings about time and beauty, and through our own experiences of love, friendship, jealousy and guilt.

Most of the contemporary essays reprinted here do not discriminate the literary value of the sonnets with respect to each other or to any other body of poetry, or do so only incidentally. This is partly a matter of each man doing only one job at a time. To the extent, however, that it suggests a general axiomatic assumption of the *Sonnets'* value, the articles in Section IV can be seen as representing a sort of "emperor's new clothes" attitude toward this estimation. Both Ransom and Winters are highly and rather cantankerously critical of Shakespeare's achievement in the sonnets, and for similar reasons: their supposed breakdown of structure and the violations of logical coherence in their imagery and syntax.

Mizener's reply to Ransom's objections is more than a piece of polemics; it contains some of the most valuable observations on Shakespeare's characteristic imagery that we have. Other articles in the final section suggest how our understanding and appreciation of the *Sonnets* have profited from the finer-grained descriptions and distinctions of contemporary critical methods. Empson's explications enshrined the term "ambiguity" for modern criticism and introduced an analytic approach to the *Sonnets* which continues to be fascinating and fruitful. (In the original edition of *Seven Types of Ambiguity*, Empson acknowledged the Riding-Graves analysis of Sonnet 129 as his model, and it will be seen that his readings share with theirs the tendency to pursue the ingenious even unto the perverse and outrageous.) Mrs. Nowottny's article is another attempt to deal with the apparent incoherence of Shakespeare's images, here in terms of their "formal integrity" within a sequence of six related sonnets. Readers may find the analysis somewhat too strained to be entirely convincing, but that is nothing remarkable in *Sonnet* criticism; the central point is well worth consideration, especially in conjunction with Mizener's observations. Barber's essay presents a good general description of Shakespeare's sonnet-structure, and is particularly interesting in emphasizing the importance of sound-patterns as an organizing principle in individual sonnets.

As the section headings suggest, this volume was designed to provide the reader with a variety of approaches to the *Sonnets:* to the themes, attitudes and experiences which the poems reflect, to their value as literary achievements and to their characteristics as poetic art. Taken together, however, the selections incidentally reveal why, in recent years, the criticism of the *Sonnets* has become substantially less of an imposition on and embarrassment to the literary world.

Notes and Suggestions for Further Reading

The most valuable reference for students of the *Sonnets* is *The New Variorum Edition,* edited by Hyder Edward Rollins (1944). Volume I contains the 1609 text, along with the record of its editorial emendations and the history of critical and scholarly comments on each poem, passage and punctuation mark. Volume II consists of a series of appendices which amount to a comprehensive survey of commentary, controversy and speculation on the *Sonnets,* arranged by topics (e.g. "The Dedication and Master W. H.," "The Dark Lady," "The Rival Poet"). Each appendix contains representative extracts from hundreds of books and articles.

Among the books published after the appearance of *The New Variorum Edition,* several have made notable contributions to the critical literature on the *Sonnets.* The following list may provide a brief guide to their contents and concerns.

Elizabethan Poetry: A Study in Conventions, Meaning, and Expression, by Hallett Smith (Cambridge, Mass., 1952). The section on the *Sonnets* contains analyses and interpretations of several poems, and general observations on the relation of Shakespeare's style to the conventions of Elizabethan poetry.

The Sense of Shakespeare's Sonnets, by Edward Hubler (Princeton, 1952). An examination of some of the themes, attitudes and ideas in the *Sonnets*, with an appendix on the question of Shakespeare's alleged homosexuality.

The Shakespearean Moment: and its Place in the Poetry of the 17th Century, by Patrick Cruttwell (New York, 1955). A study of the literary, social and intellectual climate in seventeenth-century England. Chapter I considers the *Sonnets* as a barometer of the changes which were reflected, during the following decades, in the characteristic work of the metaphysical poets.

The Mutual Flame: on Shakespeare's Sonnets and The Phoenix and the Turtle, by G. Wilson Knight (London, 1955). Part I considers the *Sonnets* as a "semi-dramatic expression of a clearly defined process of integration pointing towards the realization of a high state of being." The mysticism is patent, and Knight's extrapolations are often extravagant, but the interpretations are bold, original, and always fascinating.

The Elizabethan Love Sonnet, by J. W. Lever (London, 1956). A study of the English sonnet from Wyatt to Shakespeare: its sources, development and achievement. Lever's observations are perceptive and informative throughout the book, and the long chapter on Shakespeare's *Sonnets* is probably the most comprehensive and thorough reading of the poems ever published.

Themes and Variations in Shakespeare's Sonnets, by J. B. Leishman (London, 1961). Observations on the development and modifications of several themes, particularly those involving Time, from classical literature to the *Sonnets*. Along the way, Leishman makes some intriguing comparisons between Shakespeare and such diverse figures as Sophocles, Michelangelo, Chaucer, Swift, Mozart, and Rilke.

The Riddle of Shakespeare's Sonnets (New York, 1962). This volume includes the text of the *Sonnets*, Oscar Wilde's semi-fictional *Portrait of Mr. W. H.*, and interpretive essays by Edward Hubler, Northrop Frye, Leslie A. Fiedler, Stephen Spender and R. P. Blackmur. It exhibits modern criticism in some of its most exhibitionist and irrelevant forms, but the essay by Spender may be recommended without qualification, particularly for its sympathetic insights concerning Shakespeare's relationship to that fair young man.

Barbara Herrnstein

notes on the

CONTRIBUTORS

C. L. Barber has taught at Harvard and at Amherst and is now at the University of Indiana. He is the author of *Shakespeare's Festive Comedy* (1959), and is engaged on a study of Marlowe's *Tamburlaine* and *Doctor Faustus*.

F. W. Bateson has been University Lecturer in English Literature at Corpus Christi College, Oxford, since 1946. He is founder and editor of the quarterly *Essays in Criticism*, and editor of the *Cambridge Bibliography of English Literature*. Among his many critical works are *English Comic Drama 1700–1750* (1929), *English Poetry and the English Language* (1934), and *Wordsworth: a Re-interpretation* (1954).

John Benson was a seventeenth-century London printer, publisher and literary pirate.

Samuel Taylor Coleridge (1722–1834), English poet and critic: Coleridge's lectures on Shakespeare fairly revolutionized the appreciation of his plays and poetry during the nineteenth century, and remain, along with the *Biographia Literaria* (1817), among the most important works of English literary criticism.

Patrick Cruttwell teaches English at the University, Exeter, England. He has published critical articles on diverse literary subjects and is the author of two novels, *A Kind of Fighting* (1960) and *A Matter of Succession* (1962).

William Empson, English poet and critic, teaches at Sheffield University. His critical studies include *Seven Types of Ambiguity* (1930), *Some Versions of Pastoral* (1935), *The Structure of Complex Words* (1951), and *Milton's God* (1961). His *Collected Poems* were published in 1955.

Robert Graves is an eminent and prolific poet, novelist, critic and translator. His principal works include *Goodbye to All That* (1929), *I, Claudius* (1934), *The White Goddess* (1948), and *The Greek Myths* (1955). A new edition of his *Collected Poems* appeared in 1961.

Henry Hallam (1777–1859), English historian, wrote works dealing with Medieval Europe and English constitutional history. He was the father of the poet, Arthur Henry Hallam.

Leslie Hotson, Canadian-born scholar, is now at King's College, Cambridge, England. He has presented the results of his investigations into Elizabethan literary history in a number of books, which include *The Death of Christopher Marlowe* (1925), *Shakespeare's Motley* (1952), *The First Night of Twelfth Night* (1954), and *Shakespeare's Wooden O* (1959).

John Keats (1795–1821): in recent years, it has been recognized that Keats's literary achievement includes his letters as well as his poetry. His admiration for Shakespeare was profound, and the literary and temperamental affinities of the two poets have been widely noted.

G. Wilson Knight, English-Canadian critic and scholar, has published a series of interpretive studies of Shakespeare's plays, including *The Wheel of Fire* (1930), *The Imperial Theme* (1931), *The Shakespearean Tempest* (1932), and *The Crown of Life* (1947). His studies of other English poets include *The Burning Oracle* (1939) and *The Starlit Dome* (1941).

J. W. Lever teaches English at Durham University, England. He is the editor of the new Arden edition of *Measure for Measure*.

Arthur Mizener is Professor of English at Cornell University. He is the author of numerous critical articles and *The Far Side of Paradise: A Biography of F. Scott Fitzgerald* (1951).

Winifred M. T. Nowottny teaches English at University College, London. She is the author of *The Language Poets Use* (1962).

John Crowe Ransom, prominent American critic and poet, is now at The School of Letters, Indiana University. He is editor of the quarterly *The Kenyon Review*, and his critical works include *God without Thunder* (1930) and *The New Criticism* (1941). In 1950, he received the Bollingen Prize for poetry; a new edition of his *Selected Poems* appeared this year (1963).

Laura Riding, American poetess and essayist, is the author of several books, including *Trojan Ending* (1937) and *Lives of Wives* (1939). Her *Collected Poems* were published in 1938.

George Steevens (1736–1800) devoted his professional life to the preparation and annotation of various eighteenth-century editions of Shakespeare's works.

Yvor Winters, distinguished poet and critic, is Professor of English at Stanford University. His critical works include *Edward Arlington Robinson* (1946), *In Defense of Reason* (1947), and *The Function of Criticism* (1957). His *Collected Poems* received the Bollingen Prize in 1952.

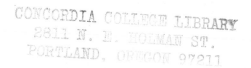

JOHN BENSON

A Preface

To the Reader.

I Here presume (under favour) to present to your view, some excellent and sweetely composed Poems, of Master *William Shakespeare,* Which in themselves appeare of the same purity, the Author himselfe then living avouched; they had not the fortune by reason of their Infancie in his death, to have the due accomodation of proportionable glory, with the rest of his everliving Workes, yet the lines of themselves will afford you a more authentick approbation than my assurance any way can, to invite your allowance, in your perusall you shall finde them *Seren,* cleere and eligantly plaine, such gentle straines as shall recreate and not perplexe your braine, no intricate or cloudy stuffe to puzzell intellect, but perfect eloquence; such as will raise your admiration to his praise: this assurance I know will not differ from your acknowledgement. And certaine I am, my opinion will be seconded by the sufficiency of these ensuing Lines; I have beene somewhat solicitus to bring this forth to the perfect view of all men; and in so doing, glad to be serviceable for the continuance of glory to the deserved Author in these his Poems.

I. B.

From *Poems: Written by Wil. Shake-speare. Gent.;* printed 1640.

GEORGE STEEVENS

A Note on Shakespeare's Sonnets, &c.

WE HAVE not reprinted the Sonnets, &c. of Shakespeare, because the strongest act of Parliament that could be framed, would fail to compel readers into their service; notwithstanding these miscellaneous Poems have derived every possible advantage from the literature and judgement of their only intelligent editor, Mr. Malone, whose implements of criticism, like the ivory rake and golden spade in Prudentius, are on this occasion disgraced by the objects of their culture.—Had Shakespeare produced no other works than these, his name would have reached us with as little celebrity as time has conferred on that of Thomas Watson, an older and much more elegant sonnetteer.

From the preface to *The Plays of William Shakespeare*, 1793.

SAMUEL TAYLOR COLERIDGE

On Shakespeare's Sonnets

(1) I can by no means subscribe to the above pencil mark of W. Words-worth;[1] which, however, it is my wish should never be erased. . . . These sonnets thou, I trust, if God preserve thy life, Hartley![2] thou wilt read with a deep interest, having learnt to love the plays of Shakespeare, co-ordinate with Milton, and subordinate only to thy Bible. To thee, I trust, they will help to explain the mind of Shakespeare, and if thou wouldst understand these sonnets, thou must read the chapter in Potter's *Antiquities*[3] on the Greek lovers. . . . This pure love Shakespeare appears to have felt—to have been in no way ashamed of it—or even to have sus-pected that others could have suspected it. Yet at the same time he knew that so strong a love would have been made more completely a thing of permanence and reality, and have been blessed more by nature and taken under her more especial protection, if this object of his love had been at the same time a possible object of desire—for nature is not soul only. In this feeling he must have written the twentieth sonnet; but its possibility seems never to have entered even his imagination. It is noticeable that not even an allusion to that very worst of all possible

---

(1) From Coleridge's marginalia on his copy of R. Anderson's *British Poets*, dated Novem-ber 2, 1803. Reprinted from *Coleridge's Miscellaneous Criticism*, edited by Thomas Middle-ton Raysor (London, 1936), pp. 454–55, by permission of Constable & Company, Ltd. and Professor Raysor.
(2) From Coleridge's "Table-Talk," May 14, 1833. Reprinted from *Coleridge's Shake-spearean Criticism*, edited by Thomas Middleton Raysor (Cambridge, Mass., 1930), II, 355–56, by permission of Professor Raysor.

1 [Wordsworth had written as follows: "These sonnets beginning at CXXVII to his mistress, are worse than a puzzle-peg. They are abominably harsh, obscure, and worthless. The others are for the most part much better, have many fine lines and passages. They are also in many places warm with passion. Their chief faults—and heavy ones they are—are same-ness, tediousness, quaintness, and elaborate obscurity." (Text from *Coleridge's Miscellane-ous Criticism*, p. 454.) Cf. Wordsworth's sonnet beginning "Scorn not the Sonnet; Critic, you have frowned,/Mindless of its just honours; with this key/Shakespeare unlocked his heart . . ."—Ed.]
2 [His eldest son, Hartley Coleridge—then seven years old.—Ed.]
3 *Archaeologia Graeca or the Antiquities of Greece*, by John Potter, D.D., 1804. The author, Archbishop of Canturbury, argued that the Greek custom of love of men for boys was entirely spiritual. [From T. M. Raysor's note.]

vices (for it is wise to think of the disposition, as a *vice*, not of the absurd and despicable act, as a *crime*) not even any allusion to it [occurs] in all his numerous plays—whereas Jonson, Beaumont and Fletcher, and Massinger are full of them. O my son! I pray fervently that thou may'st know inwardly how impossible it was for a Shakespeare not to have been in his heart's heart chaste. I see no elaborate obscurity and very little quaintness—nor do I know any sonnets that will bear such frequent reperusal: so rich in metre, so full of thought and *exquisitest* diction.

(2) I believe it possible that a man may, under certain states of the moral feeling, entertain something deserving the name of love towards a male object—an affection beyond friendship, and wholly aloof from appetite. In Elizabeth's and James's time it seems to have been almost fashionable to cherish such a feeling; and perhaps we may account in some measure for it by considering how very inferior the women of that age, taken generally, were in education and accomplishment of mind to the men. . . . I mention this with reference to Shakespeare's sonnets, which have been supposed, by some, to be addressed to William Herbert, Earl of Pembroke, whom Clarendon calls the most beloved man of his age, though his licentiousness was equal to his virtues. I doubt this. I do not think that Shakespeare, merely because he was an actor, would have thought it necessary to veil his emotions towards Pembroke under a disguise, though he might probably have done so, if the real object had perchance been a Laura or a Leonora. It seems to me that the sonnets could only have come from a man deeply in love, and in love with a woman; and there is one sonnet[4] which, from its incongruity, I take to be a purposed blind. These extraordinary sonnets form, in fact, a poem of so many stanzas of fourteen lines each; and, like the passion which inspired them, the sonnets are always the same, with a variety of expression,—continuous, if you regard the lover's soul—distinct, if you listen to him, as he heaves them sigh after sigh.

These sonnets, like the Venus and Adonis, and the Rape of Lucrece, are characterised by boundless fertility and laboured condensation of thought, with perfection of sweetness in rhythm and metre. These are the essentials in the budding of a great poet. Afterwards habit and consciousness of power teach more ease—*praecipitandum liberum spiritum.*

---

[4] [Probably the twentieth—which, however, he interprets otherwise above.—Ed.]

JOHN KEATS

from the Letters

. . . . One of the three Books I have with me is Shakespear's Poems: I neer found so many beauties in the sonnets—they seem to be full of fine things said unintentionally—in the intensity of working out conceits —Is this to be borne? Hark ye!

> When lofty trees I see barren of leaves
>   erst
> Which [not] from heat did canopy the he[a]rd,
> And Summer's green all girded up in sheaves,
> Borne on the bier with white and bristly beard.[1]

He has left nothing to say about nothing or anything: for look at Snails, you know what he says about Snails, you know where he talks about "cockled snails"[2]—well, in one of these sonnets, he says—the chap slips into—no! I lie! this is in the Venus and Adonis: the Simile brought it to my Mind. [Here he quotes lines 1033–1038 from *Venus and Adonis* beginning: "Or as the snail, whose tender horns being hit. . . ." etc.] He overwhelms a genuine Lover of Poesy with all manner of abuse, talking about—

>   "a poets rage
> And stretched metre of an antique song"[3]—

Which by the by will be a capital Motto for my Poem[4]—wont it?—He speaks too of "Time's antique pen"—and "aprils first born flowers"—and "deaths eternal cold"[5]. . . .

From the letter to John Hamilton Reynolds, November 22, 1817. Reprinted by permission of the publishers from *The Letters of John Keats, 1814–1821*, edited by Hyder Edward Rollins; Cambridge, Mass.: Harvard University Press, Copyright, 1958, by The President and Fellows of Harvard College.

[1] Sonnet 12, lines 5–8. [The footnotes are from Rollins' edition. The brackets ([]) in the text enclose portions crossed out by Keats.—Ed.]
[2] *Love's Labor's Lost*, IV. iii.338, "the tender horns of cockled snails."
[3] Sonnet 17, lines 11 f.
[4] It appears on the title-page of *Endymion*.
[5] Sonnets 19, line 10 ("thine antique pen"); 21, line 7; 13, line 12.

HENRY HALLAM

Sonnets of Shakespeare

. . . . These sonnets were long overlooked: Steevens spoke of them with the utmost scorn, as productions which no one could read: but a very different suffrage is generally given by the lovers of poetry; and perhaps there is now a tendency, especially among young men of poetical tempers, to exaggerate the beauties of these remarkable productions. They rise, indeed, in estimation, as we attentively read and reflect upon them; for I do not think that at first they give us much pleasure. No one ever entered more fully than Shakespeare into the character of this species of poetry, which admits of no expletive imagery, no merely ornamental line. . . . They may easily be resolved into several series, according to their subject: but, when read attentively, we find them relate to one definite, though obscure, period of the poet's life; in which an attachment to some female, which seems to have touched neither his heart nor his fancy very sensibly, was overpowered, without entirely ceasing, by one to a friend; and this last is of such an enthusiastic character, and so extravagant in the phrases that the author uses, as to have thrown an unaccountable mystery over the whole work. It is true, that in the poetry as well as in the fictions of early ages we find a more ardent tone of affection in the language of friendship than has since been usual; and yet no instance has been adduced of such rapturous devotedness, such an idolatry of admiring love, as one of the greatest beings whom nature ever produced in the human form pours forth to some unknown youth in the majority of these sonnets. . . .

Notwithstanding the frequent beauties of these sonnets, the pleasure of their perusal is greatly diminished by these circumstances; and it is impossible not to wish that Shakespeare had never written them. There is a weakness and folly in all excessive and misplaced affection, which is not redeemed by the touches of nobler sentiments that abound in this long series of sonnets. But there are also faults of a merely critical

Reprinted from *Introduction to the Literature of Europe in the Fifteenth, Sixteenth, and Seventeenth Centuries* (New York and Boston, 1863), III, 253–56. First published in 1839.

nature. The obscurity is often such as only conjecture can penetrate; the strain of tenderness and adoration would be too monotonous, were it less unpleasing; and so many frigid conceits are scattered around, that we might almost fancy the poet to have written without genuine emotion, did not such a host of other passages attest the contrary.

LESLIE HOTSON

Shakespeare's Sonnets Dated

EVEN IN this age of ours, Science—good luck to it—has no corner in discovery. History, Biography, Literature: these, too, hold important secrets which may still be brought to light. And for the general reader, the processes of discovery in these fields are more interesting than those of science, both because he can more readily follow them, and because their results are more human.

Here we shall look over the shoulder of the master poet of the modern era, Shakespeare, as he views stirring events as they pass, and transmutes them into literature. We shall discover his response to his world's narrow escape from total destruction; to the crucial naval battle of the century; to the most signal triumph of engineering; to the assassination of the King of France.

Stranger still, in doing so we shall uncover something the world has never suspected: the fact that Shakespeare's poetic powers were full-grown when he was no more than twenty-five years old. It will be an adventure of discovery in History, Biography, and Literature rolled into one.

In not a few of the Sonnets we find a supreme beauty and power of emotion clothed in thought; and since in them we feel drawn closer to the heart of Shakespeare than anywhere in his plays, these poems have aroused enormous interest, almost as much as *Hamlet* has done. But questions about them have also produced volumes of diverse comment, and a perplexing library of conflicting theories. The Sonnets have been called a maze, a labyrinth, the most intricate puzzle in Shakespeare. "There are many footprints around the cave of this mystery, none of them pointing in the outward direction." Such is the grim warning of Professor Raleigh.

Just before the War, the danger was pictured for me in a more personal way in Chelsea by Logan Pearsall Smith, whose sane and sensitive

From *Shakespeare's Sonnets Dated: And Other Essays* by Leslie Hotson. Rupert Hart-Davis, Ltd. and Oxford University Press, Inc., 1949. Reprinted by permission.

judgment is now lost to us. He cautioned me to steer clear of the problem of the Sonnets—a Wandering Wood, he said: an Error's Den. And in his delightful essay *On Reading Shakespeare* he went farther. Here it is not merely "the Serbonian sonnet-bog, in which armies whole have sunk," but a region of inky night where not a soul but feels a fever of the mad:

> For listen! the fanatic followers of no less than five ghostly, resurrected Elizabethan Earls are shouting at each other, the two bands of Pembrokians and Southamptonites, each vociferating that their Lord was the inspirer of the Sonnets, while three other bands proclaim the more glorious boast . . . that Lord Derby, or Lord Rutland, or Lord Oxford, was the author of them. . . . And then, faint and far, as the wind shifts, we hear the ululations of those vaster herds of Baconian believers, as they plunge squeaking down the Gadarene slope of their delusion.

We have been warned! Yet if in the face of all friendly dissuasives we insist on risking our sanity in a fresh attempt, we may draw courage from the remarks of John Benson, on republishing the Sonnets in 1640. Benson was born in Shakespeare's lifetime, before theories about the Sonnets had been invented. And he told his readers, "You shall find them serene, clear, and elegantly plain; . . . no intricate or cloudy stuff to puzzle intellect, but perfect eloquence." We should also remember that Shakespeare was no mystifier. Both he and his audience knew what he was talking about. George Santayana assures us that the comprehensive poet, such as Shakespeare, "would be a poet of business. He would have a taste for the world in which he lived, and a clean view of it."

To begin, then, with the first "mystery": when were the Sonnets written? No agreement has been reached on this primary question. If we could fix that date, we should have a standpoint from which perhaps to decide what (if anything) there is in the rival theories which see in Shakespeare's friend either the Earl of Southampton or the Earl of Pembroke. We might make a better guess at the identity of the Rival Poet. Above all, what is infinitely more important than anything else, by finding out where the Sonnets belong in the story of Shakespeare's development, we might correct and enlarge our understanding of the greatest poet of the modern world.

Shakespeare has not left us without clues to work upon. Two or three of his sonnets are recognized as carrying external or topical references. Under the influence, however, of diverse preconceptions about their date, critics cannot agree on what events Shakespeare is pointing at. This being so, it is curious that no one has carefully compared these references with the news: that is, with the emergent occurrences of the Europe in which Shakespeare lived as the Soul of the Age—to discover to what notable events between 1585 and 1605, grouped fairly closely together in time, the topical sonnets refer. Possibly historians have not been sufficiently interested in Shakespeare. Or perhaps the literary folk have not troubled to go back to the living contemporary history. Whatever the reason, this obligatory job of collation has not been done.

In comparing the facts of his times with the poet's references, we must begin without a theory, and be ready to follow where the evidence leads. "If you wish to see the meaning of a thing, look directly into it; for if you think about it, it is altogether missed." To look directly into the years marching to the close of the Sixteenth Century means for us to look into them so far as we can from Shakespeare's point of view, with Elizabethan anxieties, beliefs, and prejudices. Only in this way shall we see his topical references plain.

I. THE MORTALL MOONE

107

Not mine owne feares, nor the prophetick soule,
Of the wide world, dreaming on things to come,
Can yet the lease of my true loue controule,
Supposde as forfeit to a confin'd doome.
The mortall Moone hath her eclipse indur'de,
And the sad Augurs mock their owne presage,
Incertenties now crowne them-selues assur'de,
And peace proclaimes Oliues of endlesse age.
Now with the drops of this most balmie time,
My loue lookes fresh, and death to me subscribes,
Since spight of him Ile liue in this poore rime,
While he insults ore dull and speachlesse tribes.
    And thou in this shalt finde thy monument,
    When tyrants crests and tombs of brasse are spent.

This is the chief "dating sonnet," and it has been called the most difficult of all. And here I think we shall find that the world has been led down a false trail by assuming that *the mortall Moone* means Queen Elizabeth, and that *hath her eclipse indur'de* means either that she is dead, or that she has survived a dangerous crisis in her life.

To read it as "the Queen is dead" would place this sonnet in 1603. Beyond the unnatural callousness of writing "*the* Moone" instead of "*our* Moone," there are other serious objections to this interpretation. For the Elizabethan vogue of sonnet-writing, 1603 is too late. It is also too late in Shakespeare's career to suit with the style and tone of his sonnets, in one of which he describes himself as a beginner, wielding a "pupil pen." Most critics have therefore taken the second meaning—that *the mortall Moone* is the living Queen.

But this theory will not stand the test of the times. All the English poets write of their beloved Queen in terms approaching adoration. She is a goddess come to earth, a heaven-born Astræa. "This is that Queen, as writers truly say, That God had marked down to live for aye." She is Diana. "Time weares her not . . . Mortalitie belowe her orbe is plaste." Her word is *Ever the Same*. Her loyal subjects neither wish nor dare to remind her that she is mortal. "Wee are afraid," says John Donne, "to speake to the great men of this world of their death, but nourish in them a vaine imagination of immortality." Loathing the advances of creeping Time, Elizabeth carries her aversion to the mention of death to strange lengths. Informed by the unwary Lord North that a certain covered pie is called a "coffin," she bursts out in anger, "And are you such a fool, to give a pie such a name?"

Mortal, moreover, bears a meaning even more hideous, and one equally common in Shakespeare's works: *deadly, death-dealing*. "Mortal poison," "mortal murders," "mortal butcher," "mortal rage." To fancy Shakespeare deliberately writing of his "imperiall Votresse" not only that she is *mortal*, but that she has been obscured by an eclipse, is to imagine him a greater fool than Lord North.

If it cannot be Elizabeth, what then is this *mortall Moone*? For more than three centuries the answer has vainly stared us in the face. It is the *deadly Spanish Armada of 1588*—the mightiest floating army that the world had ever seen—which in its menacing moon-shaped line of battle appeared in the English Channel, only to be shattered by the drum-fire of Elizabeth's heavy guns, and driven northward away before an irresistible gale into ignominy, disaster, and eclipse.

> *The Spanish Fleet did flote in narrow Seas*
> *And bend her ships against the English shore.*
> Theodore Beza, *Ad Serenissimam Elizabetham*
> *Angliae Reginam*, 1588.

. . . their fleete was placed in battell araie, after the maner of a Moone cressant, being readie with her horns & hir inward circumference to receiue either all, or so manie of the English nauie, as should giue her the assault.
Petruccio Ubaldino, *A Discourse concerninge the Spanish fleete*, 1588.

> *Don Pedro.* Cast our Fleet
> Into a wide, and Semi-circled Moone:
> And if we can but once incompasse them,
> Wee'll make the Sea their Graues.
> Thomas Heywood, *If you know not me*, Part 2,
> (1606) (published 1632).

> *That fleet, which with the Moone for vastnesse stood,*
> *Which all the earth, which all the sea admires,*
> *Amaz'd to see on waves a Moone of wood.*
> Phineas Fletcher, *The Locusts*, 1627.

. . . like your invincible Armado's, which in their first appearance make a mighty Moone, but are burnt and confounded in the end.

> Richard Carpenter, *Experience, Historie, and Divinitie,* 1642.

. . . a horned Moone of huge and mighty shippes. . . . But all is vaine: for the breath of the Lords mouth hath dimmed the brightnesse of her Moone, and scattered those proud shippes.

> J[ames] L[ea], *The Birth, Purpose and mortall Wound of the Romish holie League,* 1589.

The mortall Moone hath her eclipse indur'de. That Shakespeare, like James Lea in his triumphant political cartoon,[1] is here in Sonnet 107 celebrating the eclipse suffered by the deadly "Moone of huge and mighty shippes" now appears, as John Benson might say, serene, clear, and elegantly plain.

But if in any mind there lingers a doubt, it is set at rest by Shakespeare himself. For in his dealing with another great sea-fight which likewise marked a turning-point in history, we now discover him repeating his metaphor of an eclipsed moon for a defeated fleet. This was the Battle of Actium on the Ionian Sea, in which the huge heavy galleys of Antony and Cleopatra, crowded with people and not well manned, were beaten by the smaller, nimbler, battle-wise craft of Octavius and Agrippa. Like every Englishman reading his Plutarch, Shakespeare would mark that historic parallel with the Armada fight.

The ranked fleets of beaked galleys faced each other in curving line-abreast. After Agrippa had lured out Antony's left wing from its well-nigh impregnable position and the fierce struggle had been joined, Cleopatra and her Egyptian contingent of sixty huge ships, shamefully followed by her enslaved Antony, "fled From that great face of Warre, whose seuerall ranges Frighted each other." The brave remnant fought on to defeat.

> *Enobarbus.* Alacke, alacke.
> *Canidius.*   Our Fortune on the Sea is out of breath,
>   And sinkes most lamentably.

This anguished avowal is later echoed by the "noble ruin," Antony. Plunged in black remorse over their ominous defeat, he cannot hear Cleopatra:

> *Cleo.* Haue you done yet?
> *Ant.*   Alacke our Terrene Moone is now Eclipst,
>   And it portends alone the fall of *Anthony.*

Terrene is a short form of *Mediterranean,* favourite with the geographer Ortelius and the dramatist Marlowe: "not far from Alexandria, Whereas

---

[1] [This cartoon and two other contemporary illustrations of the Armada appear in Hotson's book.—Ed.]

the Terrene and the Red Sea meet." The mighty battle-crescent of their Mediterranean fleet has suffered eclipse, giving infallible omen of Antony's fall.

The *mortall Moone* sonnet, then, is Shakespeare on the Armada. If this capital fact is now evident, we should also find in the poem some reference to the fatal and wonderful year, 1588: the menacing, long-prophesied Eighty-Eight, ever memorable in the world's mind for the destruction of the Invincible Fleet. For in retrospect the two were inseparable:

> *The miraculous victory atchieved by the English Fleete . . . upon the Spanish huge Armada sent in the yeere 1588.* Having in part declared the strange and wonderfull events of the yeere eightie eight, which hath bene so long time foretold by ancient prophesies; we will now make relation of the most notable and great enterprise of all others which were in the fore-said yeere atchieved.
>
> Emanuel van Meteren, *History of the Low Countries,* ch. XV (1602).

And whereas the aduersaries made no small accompt of that Astrologicall prediction, & perhaps trusted in it . . . we may now safely declare the accomplishment, by adding a Pentameter, and say

> *Octogesimus octauus mirabilis annus,*
> *Clade Papistarum, faustus vbique pijs.*
> [Fifteen Eighty-Eight, that fatal and wonderful year,
> Papists' defeat; to the godly, joy everywhere.]
>
>> Dr. William Fulke's dedication to Queen Elizabeth of
>> his *Text of the New Testament,* 1589.

But Thou, Lord . . . madest the year of greatest expectation, even '88, marvellous by the overthrow of thine . . . enemies.

> Anthony Rudde, Bishop of St. David's, prayer in sermon at Court,
> April 9, 1596.

The Prediction of Regiomontanus; *Octogesimus octauus mirabilis Annus;* Was thought likewise accomplished, in the sending of that great Fleet, being the greatest in Strength, though not in Number, of all that euer swamme vpon the Sea.

> Francis Bacon, "Of Prophecies," *Essayes,* 1625.

Octogesimus Octauus Annus, That same terrible 88. which came sayling hither in the Spanish Armado.

> Thomas Dekker, *The Wonderfull Yeare,* 1603.

. . . with the Spanish vndoubted hope of Englands conquest, in the dread-full yeare of 1588.

> Anthony Mundy, *A Briefe Chronicle,* 1611.

A.D. 1588. We are now come to that fatall yeare, which the *Astrologers* called the *Marveilous yeare;* some said it was the *Climactericall* yeere of the world. And they that trust not in the *liuing God* . . . tooke the opportunitie of this *fatall* yeare as they supposed, now vtterly to overthrow the *Church* of *England* and *State*. Which before they could not doe. The *Pope* and *Spanyard* layd vp all their hopes vpon this yeares *destiny*.

George Carleton, Bishop of Chichester, *A Thankfull Remembrance*, 1624.

Witness that admirable year eighty-eight. . . . It was a year of strange *expectation*, before it came, and of *admiration*, when it was come. Some designed it to be the end of the world, but were deceived. Others designed it to be the doomsday of England, the ruin of our Church and religion, and the funerals of our prince, people, and kingdom, all on one day: but these also through the great mercy of God were deceived.

Thomas Taylor, "Eighty Eight," a sermon, 1631.

The year of universal apprehension, in which the world expected the day of doom, or at the least miracles full of peril—such was the year 1588. It had loomed for more than a century, ever since that "most notorious prophesie" of 1475, attributed either to Johann Stoffler or to Johann Müller of Königsberg (Regiomontanus), and taken up and repeated by Melanchthon:

> Tausent fünffhundert achzig acht,
> Das ist das Jar das ich betracht:
> Geht in dem die Welt nicht vnder,
> So geschiet doch sonst grosz mercklich Wunder.

These "Germanical Rhythmes" were expanded into Latin verses, of which the following was one English version:

> *When from the Virgin Birth a thousand yeares*
> *With full five hundred be compleat and told,*
> *The Eightie Eighth a famous yeare appeares,*
> *Which brings distresse more fatall then of old.*
> *If not in this yeare all the wicked world*
> *Do fall, and land with sea to nothing come;*
> *Yet Empires must be topsie turvie hurl'd,*
> *And extream grief shall be the common summe.*

As the time foretold inexorably drew near, this was regarded as "the onely prophesie of the world." The embattled Protestants worked out 1588 as the world's "grand climacterical"—the end of ten cycles of sevens —as follows:

the Captiuitie of Babylon endured 70. yeares, which may be thought too prefigure the Captiuitie of the Gospel in these latter dayes: for from the yeare of our Lord 1518. in the which Martine Luther began truely to preach Gods word, which forthwith became captiue with fire, sworde, and all crueltie, too 1588, are iust .70. yeares, in the whiche yeare .1588. according as *Iohannes Regiomontanus*, . . . *Schonerus, Leouitius,* and other greate learned men agree, some greater thing shall bee done.[2]

---

[2] James Sandford, *Houres of Recreation*, 1576.

Ominous corroboration came from the astronomers. They pointed to 1588's threatening conjunction of the planets Saturn, Jupiter, and Mars; and "in the selfsame yeere 88 . . the Sunne shall be eclipsed the 16. day of *February* at the change; and shortly after, at the very next full, namely the second day of *March* there shall follow a Totall Eclipse of the Moone." On top of this, there would be a second "vniuersall *Eclipse* of the Moon this 88. to befall the 26. day of August." Three eclipses in one year! And the renowned Hermes Trismegistus had laid it down that "there insue manifold mischiefes in the world when the Sun, and Moone are both eclipsed in one moneth."

Alarm was so deep and general that books had to be written to combat the auguries of dread. John Harvey devised a discourse "especially in abatement of the terrible threatenings, and menaces, peremptorily denounced against the kingdoms, and states of the world, this present famous yeere, 1588. supposed the *Greatwoonderfull*, and *Fatall* yeere of our Age." Ministers were preaching repentance before Judgment, as a "Preparation against the prognosticated dangers of this yeare 1588." Broadside ballads and books were printed "Of the end of the world." For everything clearly pointed to a present fulfillment of the Gospel prophecy of the Last Day:

> *And there shalbe signes in the sunne and in the moone, & in the starres: and vpon the earth trouble among the nations, with perplexitie. The sea and the water shall rore.*
> *And mens heartes shal fayle them for feare, and for loking after these thinges which shall come on the world.*
>
> Luke 21:25, 26.

Leonard Wright sums it up:

> who hath not read or hard what wonderful strange eclips of sun & moon, terrible blazing stars, glistering comets, dreadful coniunctions of planets, strange flashing of fire in the elements, & alteration of the heauens, resembling as it were the countenance of the angry Iudge?[3]

Such were the universal fears and auguries of 1588. And the arrogant Spaniards, "Who by report through all the world, had won The name of conquest ere the fight begun," assumed that the prophecy would be fulfilled by the fall of England under the blows of their military might. To advertise their purpose, and to strike terror into *los lutheranos*, they painted their England-bound battleships black, and flew great "pennons tragicall" bearing "sad ostents of death and dismall feare." One such displayed a sun and moon, with a menacing legend in Spanish to this effect: *Yesterday the Full, but Today the Wane.*

Now let us read again the beginning of Shakespeare's sonnet:

[3] *A Summons for Sleepers*, 1589.

> *Not mine owne feares, nor the prophetick soule,*
> *Of the wide world, dreaming on things to come,*
> *Can yet the lease of my true loue controule,*
> *Supposde as forfeit to a confin'd doome.*

His plays amply show Shakespeare as a man of his age, believing in signs and portents. He and the world he lived in had every reason to fear what 1588 might bring. And that the soul in sleep could see into the future was another belief commonly held: "any person going to his rest . . . his Soule (in sleeping) may fore-see many thinges to come."[4] The doom prophesied would have put a "confine," a limit or end, to the life of the world with everything in it, including the poet's love for his friend.

But Eighty-Eight with all its terrors and eclipses has come—and gone! The apprehensions of doomsday have proved baseless:

> *The mortall Moone hath her eclipse indur'de,*
> *And the sad Augurs mock their owne presage . . .*

The Invincible Armada has suffered defeat: an event, writes Professor Trevelyan, "which all Europe at once recognized as a turning point in history." Instead of cataclysm, 1588 brought to England, and to all Protestant Europe with her, the rejoicing dawn of certain deliverance. The relief was indescribable. And in his treatise against astrology (1601) John Chamber has the prophets of a black 1588 mocking their own presage:

> It were well that all of that trade had those two figures .88. seared in their foreheads, that when they meet, they might laugh one at another, as did the *Aruspices* in olde time. Howsoeuer they might laugh, it was no laughing matter to the Catholike king, and his inuincible Nauie, who will be famous for that exploit till 88 come againe.

> *Incertenties now crowne them-selues assur'de,*
> *And peace proclaimes Oliues of endlesse age.*

Here is where the modern historian leads us astray. He likes to call the Armada fight the beginning of Elizabeth's formal hostilities with Philip, leaving us to think that Shakespeare's countrymen now knew they were at war. How totally different was the view of the man on the spot! For him, the victory of '88 brought not war, but the certain assurance of *peace* for England. There would be no invasion and butchery, such as the Low Countries suffered under Alva. No savage civil wars of religion, like those torturing France. Throughout her reign, whatever forces she might dispatch to fight her enemies abroad, Elizabeth was incessantly extolled for keeping her land at peace.

---

[4] Pedro Mexia and others, *Treasurie of auncient and moderne Times* (tr. T. Milles), 1613, I. 476*b*.

Tom Nashe and Robert Greene give us the characteristic post-Armada sentiment. Nashe writes, "the Prayers of the Church of England flie vppe into heauen for her Maiestie, and returne againe with Oliue-branches in their mouthes . . . to bring tydings of peace and long life vnto her highnesse." And he calls his Queen "heauenborne *Elizabeth*, . . . a subiect of wonder, & Peace."[5] In his triumphant and thankful *Spanish Masquerado* (entered 1 February 1589) Greene borrows from the Bible to exclaim,

> Let Englishmen then, shrouded vnder the wings of the most highest, not feare what thousands can doe against them: nay let them giue thanks to God who hath blest vs with such a Prince as makes vs eate fruites of our own vineyard, and drinke water of our owne welles: our Cities are full of ioy, and our children are seene sporting in the streetes: peace and plentie flourisheth in *England* . . . our mercifull God maketh *ENGLAND* like *EDEN,* a second Paradice.

Elizabeth's great astrologer, Dr. John Dee, addresses her from Bohemia to thank God for "this wunderfull triumphant Victorie, against your mortall enemies," and to thank her Majesty for "calling me . . . hoame, into your British Earthly Paradise, and Monarchie incomparable."[6] And Francis Bacon, looking back over Elizabeth's reign, saw the Armada "first beaten in a battle, and then dispersed and wasted in a miserable flight with many shipwrecks; while on the ground and territories of England, peace remained undisturbed and unshaken."[7]

> *Now with the drops of this most balmie time,*
> *My loue lookes fresh, and death to me subscribes,*
> *Since spight of him Ile liue in this poore rime,*
> *While he insults ore dull and speachlesse tribes.*
> *And thou in this shalt finde thy monument,*
> *When tyrants crests and tombs of brasse are spent.*

The drops of this most balmie time—after the eclipse of the deadly Spanish "Moone"—have brought life revived and fresh out of the shadow of doom. Balm is the biblical Balm of Gilead or Balsam of Mecca, the prime life-restoring elixir. Its source is the Eastern balsam tree, "out of which issueth a Gumme of excellent swiftnesse." As Othello says, "Drops teares as fast as the Arabian Trees Their Medicinable gumme." Books were written on the magical healing powers of the drops of balm. Shakespeare often mentions it: "balme, Earth's soueraigne salue," "drop sweet Balme in *PRIAMS* painted wound," "balme to heale their

---

5 *The Returne of the renowned Caualiero Pasquil of England*, 1589; *The Anatomie of Absurditie*, entered 19 September, 1588.
6 B.M. MS. Harley 6986, f. 28 (45).
7 *In Felicem Memorian Elizabethae* (tr. James Spedding), *Works* (1855) vi. 295, 309.

wounds," "Balme of hurt Mindes." It is frequent in his fellow-authors: "the drops of balsamum, that salveth the most dangerous sores" (Dr. Thomas Lodge). "The tree of life . . .

> From that first tree forth flowd, as from a well,
> A trickling streame of Balme, most soueraine . . .
> Life and long health that gratious ointment gaue,
> And deadly woundes could heale, and reare againe
> The senselesse corse appointed for the graue."
>
> (Spenser)

"*Elizabeth*, who with her English balme, Then much the poysnous biting of that *Spanish* aspe did calme" (Warner). "The time! O blessed time! Balme to our sorrow!" (Dekker).

Now that the Elizabethans have given us the indispensable background, we are better equipped to attempt a running comment on the thought of Sonnet 107, as follows:

The poet's fear, shared with the whole Protestant world, of the dread cataclysm foretold for 1588, has not been able to put an end to his love. The foe's "invincible" battle-crescent has, however, met disaster; and the prophets of doom are laughing at their recent fears. Danger of invasion and civil war has vanished as if blown away with the storm that wrecked the beaten Armada. Elizabeth's Englishmen find themselves joyfully gazing down far vistas of assured peace.

To minds hurt by cruel apprehension and suspense, the miraculous passing of 1588 not only in safety but crowned with victory has come as a life-restoring balm. In this blessed time of deliverance love has renewed its youth. Death, shorn of his terrors, now submits to the poet, whose verse is his passport to immortality. The poet's friend, the subject of his lines, will be remembered when the blazoned crests and tombs of the defeated tyrants Philip and Sixtus are long gone into oblivion.

It is deeply satisfying to find that long before he sang the glory of Agincourt, Shakespeare had begun by recording with his "pupil pen" the overthrow of the Invincible Armada, the eclipse of the Spanish dream of world dominion. To the insatiable monarch—whose inflated motto *The Whole World is Not Enough* Drake found so amusing—Shakespeare gave England's answer, quiet and conclusive:

> *The mortall Moone hath her eclipse indur'de.*

The naval historian may now see Shakespeare's line great with meaning: an utterance proclaiming the death of the old order and the birth of the new. For he tells us that the Armada fight spelled the eclipse of the ancient naval tactics. The Spaniards' fleet was still ranged line-abreast in the *falange*, "a battle like a halfe Moone," like the warships at Actium. Their classic aim was to fight ship against ship, grapple, board, and settle the issue hand to hand. But the nimbler English never gave them the chance. Howard and Drake, coming down a-weather on them in line-ahead, "crossing their T," concentrating crushing broadsides of heavy metal on a selected target, brought not only the eclipse of the "Moone," but also the dawn of the modern era at sea.

As soon as we locate the spiritual landscape—the passing of 1588— in which it was written, Shakespeare's "most difficult" sonnet becomes clear and plain. We see what events he has turned into ideas; and, for the first time, we understand. May not other sonnets that still seem puzzling or obscure behave in the same way? . . .

IV. CONCLUSIONS

So much for the more obvious allusions we have discovered in Sonnets 107, 123, and 124.[8] Against the modern subjective criticism which treats these sonnets as difficult or obscure, John Benson's opinion in 1640 that they will be found clear and plain stands vindicated by the simple expedient of looking into the leading events of Shakespeare's Europe.

"The great poet," remarks Mr. T. S. Eliot, "in writing himself, writes his time." If Shakespeare, the Soul of the Age, writes his time, his meanings are not hidden from his contemporaries. To them, his *Moone* is more than a poetic figure: it is an accurate and familiar description of the Armada's battle-formation. And this *Moone* was literally *mortall* or deadly. It killed a hundred Englishmen, and it meant to kill thousands more. To them, again, *pyramyds* is not metaphor for "any modern marvels of architecture," but the common name for certain particular and world-famous obelisks being set up by Pope Sixtus in Rome. Finally, for them there is no vagueness or generality about *the childe of state* who *suffers in smilinge pomp* and *falls Vnder the blow of thralled discontent*. This is plainly and exclusively the murdered Henry of Valois, King of France.

As for the date of these sonnets, we have seen that the *mortall Moone* was written in 1589, after the close of the Wonderful Year. The *pyramyds* sonnet, 1587–9, most probably in 1589. *The blow of thralled discontent* puts Sonnet 124 in 1589, after the beginning of August.

What do these discoveries reveal about the date of the rest of the Sonnets? In the 1609 arrangement as printed by Thomas Thorpe, these three all stand near the close of the "first series" of 126 sonnets. And most of the proposed rearrangements likewise regard them as belonging near the end of the group.

Here is a fact of cardinal importance. It indicates that *Shakespeare completed this main group of his sonnets by 1589.*

8 [Sonnets 123 and 124 are examined in Sections II and III, respectively, of Hotson's essay, here omitted. The allusions in the following paragraph are to these two sonnets.—Ed.]

The evidence has led us to a revolutionary conclusion. Heretofore, theory has put the completion of the Sonnets anywhere from 1596 to 1603—from Shakespeare's thirty-third to his fortieth year. To realize the implications of placing his later sonnets as early as 1589—this will demand heroic efforts in casting off notions of Shakespeare long and fondly held.

The grand point which now rises to dwarf all else is the new knowledge—since the Sonnets unquestionably embody some of his highest poetry—that *Shakespeare's power had reached maturity by the time he was no more than twenty-five years old.* Yet strictly speaking he was still a beginner. Now at length we see that he is quite literal in writing in Sonnet 16 of his "pupil pen." Like Keats, Shakespeare sprang to maturity in his youth. Had Logan Pearsall Smith known the true date of the Sonnets, he would never have been forced by the mannered narrative poems to conclude that "of all that wealth of poetic emotion seeking to find expression, that mass of brooding thought we are aware of in young poets like Shelley and Keats, there is no trace." He would certainly have discovered a profusion of it in the Sonnets, which we may now study as an eloquent portrait of the artist as a young man: a young man expressing in his own person the very movements of the soul and the height of feeling which were later to appear in his plays.

We have long imagined that Shakespeare "followed the vogue of sonnet-writing." Rounding out a series of sonnets as a young man in 1589, we find him on the contrary setting rather than following the fashion; and outdoing the lamented leader, Sir Philip Sidney.

Other carefully fabricated structures of theory about Shakespeare's development as a poet must now be drastically altered. For example, *Venus and Adonis* and *Lucrece* were published in 1593 and 1594, and one of the articles of Shakespearean faith has been that they are "more youthful work" than the Sonnets. What shall we say now?

One need not adopt Hazlitt's description of these two narrative poems as a "couple of ice-houses" to recognize their striking inferiority to the profound and masterly work Shakespeare had already achieved four or five years earlier in his unpublished "Sonnets among his private friends." But how to account for it? The answer must lie in the sort of market for which they were prepared. *Venus* and *Lucrece* were the very stuff required to please the sophisticated taste of the wealthy patron to whom they were offered: that vain, fantastical, amorous, and hare-brained young sprout of the New Nobility, Southampton. As such they were a notable success; for the enthusiastic Gullios of the age exclaimed, "Let this duncified worlde esteeme of Spencer and Chaucer, I'le worshipp sweet Mr. Shakspeare, and to honoure him will lay his Venus and Adonis under my pillowe." But to peer into them for guide-posts to Shakespeare's "development" is to look for what is not there.

And the poet's fair friend? What have our discoveries done with him? In Sonnet 104 Shakespeare tells us that he has known him for three years. If that disclosure belongs to 1589, the acquaintance was formed in 1586, when the poet was twenty-two. We may now assume that he had already begun his stage career by that date. And the marvellous poetic accomplishment growing out of the young player's friendship with "W. H." at last gives us work of the highest importance to put into the so-called "lost years" of his life between 1585 and 1592.

As for the Dark Lady, we can now put her back where she belongs—with the mistresses of Jack Donne—in the poet's youth.

What must we now say of the noble candidates who have so long been pushed forward for the role of the young friend, "Mr. W. H."—the Earls of Pembroke and of Southampton? In 1586 Pembroke was, alas, but six years old. Under the circumstances he may be allowed to withdraw. And as for Southampton, late in the same year he began his second academic year at Cambridge and achieved his thirteenth birthday. This would make him all of sixteen when Shakespeare was finishing his Sonnets. Hardly as yet a man who has "pass'd by the ambush of young days," or one who at the outset of the Sonnets must be urged to marry and beget a son before it is too late. It looks as though we should have to give up Southampton too.

This is a welcome relief. How could anyone seriously expect us to believe that the publisher's dedication of 1609 to "the onlie begetter of these insuing sonnets" as "*Mr. W. H.*" could possibly be taken as addressed to a right honourable peer of the realm? Not even a left-wing publisher of today would be guilty of so glaring a breach of manners. And for a Jacobean publisher, seeking a gift of money from the dedicatee,—utterly unthinkable. It is high time to lay away the Cinderella story about Shakespeare's imaginary intimacies with the nobility. To tell the truth, it was an ignorant fancy gotten by Bardolater out of Snobbery.

With the earls cleared away, we perhaps begin to see that if "Mr. W. H." means anything, it means what it undoubtedly meant in 1609: a gentleman or an esquire with those initials, generally known as the friend of Shakespeare who as a youth some twenty-odd years earlier inspired the writing of the Sonnets. Need I add that I am grooming a candidate for this position? But to propose him here would be premature and would make a tale too long for these pages.

F. W. BATESON

ELEMENTARY, MY DEAR HOTSON!
A Caveat for Literary Detectives

DR. LESLIE HOTSON's identification of Shakespeare's "mortall Moone" (sonnet cvii, line 5) with the crescent formation popularly believed to have been adopted by the Spanish ships in the Armada has, as he has himself noted, "met with very general acceptance."[1] For example, the reviewer in the *Times Literary Supplement* of Hotson's book *Shakespeare's Sonnets Dated and Other Essays* (in which the suggestion was originally elaborated) found the particular argument "convincing," and the essay as a whole perhaps "the most significant contribution to Shakespeare studies of recent years." And the notice by Dr. J. G. McManaway in *Shakespeare Survey*, an even more august and responsible organ, was to the same effect, if more temperately expressed ("I think he is right").[2] The incident provides a nice example of the limitations of pure scholarship.[3] As long as sonnet cvii is considered merely as a historical document, the phrase can no doubt bear the sense that Hotson attributes to it. Although the Armada did not in fact assume a crescent formation, the references collected by Hotson and others make it clear that it was thought to have done so at the time. And the general illusion may well have been shared by Shakespeare. But, of course, the sonnet is only *incidentally* a historical document. Primarily it is a poem, a very beautiful poem by the greatest of all poets, and the final criterion in a disputed passage in such a poem ought never to be the plausibility of a historical allusion. The criterion must be a literary one. Does the proposed interpretation make good poetry or bad poetry? Or, to put it more precisely, does the meaning now assigned to the particular phrase or

Reprinted from *Essays in Criticism*, I (1951), 81–88, by permission of Basil Blackwell, publisher.

[1] "The Date of Shakespeare's Sonnets," *Times Literary Supplement*, June 2nd, 1950.
[2] No. 3 (1950), p. 31.
[3] It has been noticeable in the lengthy correspondence that has been going on in the *Times Literary Supplement* that, whereas the amateurs have occasionally dared to question Hotson's conclusions, the professionals, like John Sparrow and I. A. Shapiro, have only corrected points of detail.

passage reinforce or contradict the poetic argument of the work as a whole? It must be said that by this test the Hotson interpretation, ingenious though it is, hasn't a leg to stand on.

As printed in the first edition of 1609 the sonnet reads as follows:

> Not mine owne feares, nor the prophetick soule,
> Of the wide world, dreaming on things to come,
> Can yet the lease of my true loue controule,
> Supposde as forfeit to a confin'd doome.
> The mortall Moone hath her eclipse indur'de,
> And the sad Augurs mock their owne presage,
> Incertenties now crowne them-selues assur'de,
> And peace proclaimes Oliues of endlesse age.
> Now with the drops of this most balmie time,
> My loue lookes fresh, and death to me subscribes,
> Since spight of him Ile liue in this poore rime,
> While he insults ore dull and speachlesse tribes.
>> And thou in this shalt finde thy monument,
>> When tyrants crests and tombs of brasse are spent.

Although there are local obscurities, the sonnet's general meaning is clear enough. The framework round which it is organized is a *parallel,* terminating in the final couplet in a *contrast,* between Shakespeare's private world and the public Elizabethan world of which he was a member. The first quatrain describes the private world. Shakespeare's "true love" —i.e. either Mr. W. H., or Shakespeare's feelings for Mr. W. H., or perhaps an amalgam of both meanings—has survived the "doome" prophesied for it. The second quatrain is concerned with the contemporary public world. Here too the prophecies of woe have proved groundless. The third quatrain establishes a connection between the public and the private worlds. The "balmie time" coincides with the revival of Shakespeare's "love," and instead of death threatening his private world (Mr. W. H. and Shakespeare's feelings for him) death now "subscribes" to Shakespeare, because he is a poet and poetry is immortal; that is, because of the *public status* of poetry. The final couplet then asserts the superiority of the private world to the public world. This sonnet, which is essentially a private statement of Shakespeare's feelings for Mr. W. H., will in fact prove a better memorial of him, when he does eventually die, than the "crests and tombs" provided by the public world.

The internal analogies and interconnections are so close throughout the sonnet that it can be taken for granted that the parallelism between the private situation described in the first quatrain and its public equivalent in the second extends beyond the general notion of unfulfilled prophecy. To deny this is to deny the sonnet's poetic coherence. Now it is to be noted that in the first quatrain, though the *object* threatened— "my true love"—is specified, the *source* of the threat is left undefined.

Something disastrous was about to bring the love-affair to an end, but the quarter from which the disaster was to come is left obscure. There is, however, a hint as to the *nature* of the disaster. The references to death later in the sonnet suggest that what Shakespeare's "owne feares" and the professional soothsayers—presumably this or something like it, is what "the prophetick soule Of the wide world" means in prose terms— had both expected was Mr. W. H.'s death. But the kind of death that had been feared—in battle, from the plague or some other disease, or on the block—is as indefinite as the source from which it might have emanated.

On the assumption, then, that the second quatrain reproduces the general situation described in the first quatrain in terms of a public world, we may expect to find in it a national object of Shakespeare's affections whose destruction had been feared. In addition, the beloved object will be specified, the source and nature of the threat to it being left undefined. Finally, if the parallelism is complete, the nature of the danger that had threatened the object of Shakespeare's public affections will be at least hinted. (As in the first quatrain, the danger may prove to be that of death.) These presumptions derive their strength from the logic of the sonnet's poetic evolution. Clearly the structural pattern of the poem as a whole demands at any rate the appearance of parallelism between the first two quatrains. Unless the reader can be made to recognize that the second quatrain does in fact reproduce the basic elements—the plot-formula, as it were—of the first quatrain, though of course in a very different social context, the sonnet's last six lines lose all their force. The whole point of the sestet is the concurrence of Shakespeare's private and public worlds. There can be the same happy ending at each level of experience *because* the crisis he had undergone as a lover had been similar to the national crisis. The individual and the citizen have coalesced.

It follows that whatever Shakespeare did or did not mean by the words "mortall Moone," he cannot conceivably have intended the phrase to refer to the Spanish Armada. The second quatrain *must* introduce, in fairly specific terms, an object of Shakespeare's public affections that his reader can mentally set by the side of Mr. W. H. As the "mortall Moone" is the only phrase in the quatrain that can possibly bear this sense, there must be a metaphoric reference here to some national institution that Shakespeare loved and revered *qua* citizen. The allusion might be to England or to the Church, but the traditional identification of the "Moone" as Queen Elizabeth is clearly the most plausible one. Elizabeth was often compared by her subjects to Diana, the virgin goddess of the moon, and she was a *mortal* moon, unlike either Diana or the physical moon, because she was a human being who must sooner or later die. I imagine the sonnet was written on the Queen's recovery from a serious illness. The metaphor of a lunar eclipse had been used by Thomas Cecil, in a letter to Robert Cecil, written July 9th, 1595, which appears to refer to Elizabeth's illnesses that year: "I left the moon in the wane at my last being at the Court; I hear now it is a half moon again, yet I think it will never be at the full, though I hope it will never be eclipsed."[4] It is just possible that Shakespeare's sonnet may have been written in the winter of 1595–96, when the Queen's health had been completely restored. Or the reference may be to the rumour of a similar crisis in 1599.[5]

The object, however, of this note is not to date this particular historical allusion, but to exemplify the literary conditions that any allusion imbedded in a poem or play must satisfy. The real objection to the Hotson interpretation of sonnet cvii is that it turns a good poem into a less good poem. It *must* be wrong, because it denies by implication the structural parallel on which the poem hinges. On his view not only is there no *object threatened* in the second quatrain to provide the parallel to Mr. W. H., but the *source of the threat,* to which the first quatrain offers nothing comparable, is described with all the emphasis of Shakespearian metaphor at its most magnificent. In other words, even if the sonnet is concerned, as Hotson suggests, with the position in England in 1588, the Armada is still a poetic irrelevance in line 5. It might have been implied—Samuel Butler, who also dated the sonnet 1588, thought that it was; it could not have been stated. Are there *any* valid reasons for positing a breach in the parallelism of the first two quatrains? If there are I am not aware of them. They have certainly not been propounded by Hotson. But until they can be produced the verdict of literary criticism must be that his interpretation is improbable *a priori,* because it is poetically indefensible.

A not less serious objection is Hotson's assumption that the "mortall Moone" was necessarily a crescent moon. If Shakespeare had wanted the word to bear this sense he would certainly have qualified it with some such epithet as *horned*. In the Elizabethan references to the Armada's moon-like formation cited by Hotson—"after the maner of a Moone cressant" (Petruccio Ubaldino), "horned Moone of huge and mighty shippes" (James Lea), "proportion of a half moone" (Sir William Winter), *"in forma Semilunij"* (Emanuel van Meteran)—a particular phase of the moon is always specified. Used without qualification the word, then as now, was as likely to imply a circle as a crescent. In Shakespeare's plays, indeed, in so far as any shape at all is implied, it is apparently *always* a circle, when the word is used without a qualifying

4 Salisbury Manuscripts, Historical Manuscripts Commission, 1894, pt. V, p. 273. The reference appears to be to Elizabeth, but it is not by any means certain that it is.
5 See "The 'Mortal Moon' Sonnet" in Sir E. K. Chambers's *Shakespearian Gleanings*, 1944, pp. 130–43.

epithet. In *Midsummer Night's Dream* III, ɪ, 203; *Othello*, IV, ɪɪ, 77;
and *Antony and Cleopatra*, V, ɪɪ, 80, the human *eye* is compared to the
moon (or *vice versa*). In *Richard II*, II, ɪv, 10 and *1 Henry IV*, I, ɪɪɪ,
202 it is the human *face*. Eyes and faces certainly suggest a full moon.
The one exception is *Macbeth*, III, v, 23–4, where Hecate speaks of "a
vap'rous drop" hanging on "the Corner of the Moone." This does no
doubt imply a crescent or half-moon shape. But the exception really
proves the rule—and disproves Hotson's assumption—because *Macbeth*
III, v is almost certainly an interpolated scene and not by Shakespeare.
In any case the metaphor of an eclipse rules out the possibility of a
crescent shape. A lunar eclipse can only occur when the moon is full.
It is just possible, of course, that Shakespeare may not have known this,
but the importance that was attached to eclipses at the Renaissance
makes it most unlikely. If this *is* Hotson's contention—he has not discussed the point, as far as I am aware—the *onus* of proof is surely on him.
Unless it can be shown that an Elizabethan dramatist would be unlikely
to know that a lunar eclipse necessarily involves a full moon, we are
entitled to assume that both in sonnet cvii and in the parallel passage in
Antony and Cleopatra ("Alacke! our terrene moone Is now eclips'd,"
III, xɪɪɪ, 153–4)[6] the metaphor is *not* that of a crescent.

On the internal literary evidence, then, the Hotson interpretation can
be safely dismissed. If Shakespeare had wished to introduce an allusion
to the Armada's crescent formation, he would certainly not have done it
in the particular context of sonnet cvii. Nor would he have called such
a formation *tout court* a *moon*. And if he had done so it is most improbable that he would have spoilt his metaphor by introducing the
notion of an *eclipse*.

The literary *consequences* of the Hotson interpretation are not less
fatal to it. The present tenses in lines 5–8 of the sonnet make it clear
that the public event referred to is contemporary or almost contemporary with its composition. If there is, as Hotson argues, an allusion to
the Armada, sonnet cvii *must* have been written in 1588 or 1589.[7] And
this is in fact the desperate conclusion that Hotson reaches. It *is* a desperate conclusion, because it assigns sonnet cvii—and by implication
most at any rate of the rest of Shakespeare's sonnets—to a period several

---

[6] Hotson's attempt to interpret the "moone" in this passage as Antony's crescent-shaped
fleet has been effectively disposed of by Arthur J. Perrett and G. Wilson Knight. (See *Times
Literary Supplement*, June 16th, July 14th, 1950.) The allusion is undoubtedly to Cleopatra—a fact that strengthens the case for identifying the "mortall Moone" of sonnet cvii
with Queen Elizabeth.

[7] I. A. Shapiro has argued for 1599–1600 as the date of composition on the ground that the
allusion to the Armada's crescent formation would have been more intelligible then than in
1588–89, because of its popularization in such works as Stow's *Annales* (1592). (See
Times Literary Supplement, April 21st, 1950.) But this suggestion betrays the same
inability to read the sonnet as a poem that Hotson displays. By "Now" (line 9) Shakespeare cannot possibly have meant "ten years ago."

years before either *Venus and Adonis,* which is usually dated 1592–93, or *Lucrece,* which cannot possibly have been written before 1593, since it is clearly the "graver labour" referred to in the dedication to Southampton prefixed to the first edition of *Venus and Adonis.* But the style of this sonnet is more mature, not less mature, than that of either *Venus and Adonis* or *Lucrece.* In other words, it is easy to see how the writer of the narrative poems will in process of time become the writer of the sonnet. But the reverse process posited by Hotson—from writing poetry like Donne, as it were, to writing like Spenser (that is what it amounts to)—is just incomprehensible. The point could be established in a dozen different ways. One argument that seems to me decisive is the absence from the sonnet of the rash of verbal antitheses that characterizes Shakespeare's early manner. I have not been able to find four consecutive lines in *Venus and Adonis* and *Lucrece* without one or more verbal antitheses. A passage of fourteen consecutive lines with only a single verbal antithesis (*Incertenties-assur'de*) can only be described as a stylistic impossibility for the Shakespeare of the early 1590s. Hotson is therefore committed to the hypothesis that the mastery of sentence-structure and verbal phrase evident in almost every line of sonnet cvii represents a style that Shakespeare had achieved in 1588–89 and then lost for a number of years, only to regain it about 1595 in such plays as *Midsummer Night's Dream. Quod est absurdum.*[8]

No, literary detection is a harmless avocation—"immeasurably more humane than cock-fighting," as E. E. Kellett once, not unreasonably, put it.[9] But the game has certain elementary rules. One of them is that in the assessment of clues the primacy must always be accorded to the literary fact.[10]

[8] It is perhaps worth noting that the form *incertainty* is only found in this sonnet, *Winter's Tale* and sonnet cxv, whereas *uncertainty* occurs in *Comedy of Errors* and *1 Henry IV,* two early plays, as well as in *Coriolanus.* In the same way *incertain* is only found in middle-period and later plays, whereas *uncertain* appears in *Richard III* and *Two Gentlemen of Verona* as well as in some of the later plays. It would be rash to press the point too far, as "incertenties" in line 7 may be a misprint, but its occurrence, if genuine, tends to confirm the pre-Hotson view that the sonnet is not earlier than 1596 or so.
[9] "The Literary Detective." In *Suggestions,* Cambridge, 1923.
[10] Hotson's handling of the literary facts—he does not disregard them altogether—borders on the disingenuous. Thus, in arguing against 1603 as the date of sonnet cvii's composition, he makes a great deal of the fact that by 1603 the sonneteering vogue was over, as no doubt it was. But when he comes to suggest his own date for the sonnet (1588–89), he conveniently overlooks the fact that the sonneteering vogue, which dates from the publication of Sidney's *Astrophel and Stella* (1591), had not started by then. *A priori* a sonnet was *less* likely to be written in 1588 than in 1603, when Drayton, Donne and Drummond among others were still writing, or about to write, sonnets.

EDWARD HUBLER

Shakespeare and the Unromantic Lady

In one of his plays Yeats asks, "If pleasure and remorse must both be there, which is the greater?" It is a question quite central to a consideration of Shakespeare's dark lady, for the sonnets devoted to her tell of an amour which began in pleasure and ended in moral loathing. Since remorse, for some time now, has been out of fashion in both literature and literary studies, the point of view expressed in these sonnets has not been taken very seriously. There has even been a tendency to deny its existence. It is true that the motivation of the remorse is complicated by the dark lady's liaison with Shakespeare's young friend, but that aspect of the matter can be reserved for other chapters without falsifying the central question. Besides, the pleasure and the remorse will provide more than enough material, for each is of a piece with the view of sex without romance disclosed throughout Shakespeare's works.

It should be stated in the beginning that this chapter assumes a certain order for the sonnets addressed to the poet's mistress. If the reader were to turn to an edition of the sonnets which reprints these poems, numbers 127 to 152, in their traditional order, he would be confronted with abrupt shifts from poem to poem. Invitations to love precede and follow rejections of it, and the anticipation of betrayal follows the betrayal itself. But if the sonnets are arranged in the order of the events of an ill-starred amour (compliments, invitations to love, consummation, joy, weariness, rejection) it will be found that the sonnets fall nicely into place and that no poem is left over. In Tucker Brooke's phrase, it is the order of their "psychological necessity."

There is nothing like the woman of Shakespeare's sonnets in all the sonnet literature of the Renaissance. The ladies of the sonnet tradition were idealizations; Shakespeare's heroine represents neither the traditional ideal nor his. The Elizabethan ideal of beauty was blonde; Shakespeare's heroine, if we may call her that, was dark, and the blackness of her hair and eyes and heart is so heavily stressed that she has come to be known as "the dark lady." He insists upon her darkness—first the darkness of her beauty, and later the darkness of her deeds. But from the beginning, even when his passion for her was untouched by regret, his praise of her beauty was marked by ambivalence. It was perhaps the dominance of the traditional and popular ideal which made him distrust the dictates of his senses. He opens the series with

> In the old age black was not counted fair,
> Or if it were, it bore not beauty's name.

But, he goes on to say, since nowadays the genuine beauty of former times is recreated by cosmetics, true beauty is living in disgrace, and your eyes have put on mourning for her; therefore your eyes, having a true relation to beauty, are beauty's legitimate successor. We notice that black is not the real thing, or can be thought so only after some rationalization. To modern tastes the sonnet is overingenious, and the compliment is oblique by any standards; yet the poem seems to have been offered to the lady as a tribute, and it appears that it could have been so received, for the woman is depicted as free from illusion. Though she deceived others, she seems not to have deceived herself. Sometimes the poet tells her that her eyes are black because they know of her disdain for him, that they have put on mourning in recognition of his bondage to her. Whatever their context, Shakespeare's compliments are always shadowed by his awareness of a discrepancy between the ideal and the fact, although there were times when the fact did not seem to matter:

> My mistress' eyes are nothing like the sun;
> Coral is far more red than her lips' red:
> If snow be white, why then her breasts are dun;
> If hairs be wires, black wires grow on her head.
> I have seen roses damask'd red and white,
> But no such roses see I in her cheeks;
> And in some perfumes is there more delight
> Than in the breath that from my mistress reeks.
> I love to hear her speak, yet well I know
> That music hath a far more pleasing sound:
> I grant I never saw a goddess go;
> My mistress, when she walks, treads on the ground:
>   And yet, by heaven, I think my love as rare
>   As any she belied with false compare.[1]

Aware of the ideal, he here declares himself in favor of alloyed reality. He does not say that he loves her in spite of her faults; he loves her faults and all.

[1] Sonnet 130.

Considered in itself, the sonnet is pure comedy, at least by Meredith's standard, which required that the possessor of the comic spirit see the ridiculous in those he loved without loving them less. The spirit of "My mistress' eyes" is the spirit in which Dogberry, Falstaff, and the whole world of lovable imperfections were created. In this sense the poem is the essence of comedy. But if the poem is read in the light of the sonnet tradition, it is also satire. If we would appreciate Shakespeare's complexity, we must realize that this is not an *either/or* matter. The sonnet is satire or comedy or both, depending on what the reader brings to it. The sonnet contains them both, the only variable being the reader's ability to see. In this respect the sonnet is like the greater part of Shakespeare's work—hardly ever simple, hardly ever exhausted at one level of meaning. The reader of Shakespeare's day who had the slightest acquaintance with modern poetry could not have missed the satire on the heroine of the sonnet tradition. She was the Renaissance descendant of chivalric love. Catullus and Ovid could not have imagined her, and Shakespeare could not take her seriously, though she was everywhere about him—in books, that is.

It is not necessary to consider the origins of the sonnet—Dante's use of it or its appearance in Provençal poetry. It is enough to say that Petrarch (1304–1374) fixed its form and content in the public mind and gave them currency. Petrarch's sonnets were written to Laura, who may or may not have been married when he first encountered her. Questions of her historic reality are not to the point, which is that during the greater part of his sonnets she appears as the loyal wife of another, and that the dominant characteristic of Petrarch's love is therefore its hopelessness. The hopelessness of Shakespeare's love is another matter. He despairs of his lady because there is no loyalty in her. She is, he remarks in nautical terms, "the bay where all men ride." But Petrarch's lady was unassailable, and his soul was overwhelmed with sadness. Loving her and knowing himself beneath her by virtue of her goodness, he idealized her and loved his idealization all the more. It was a situation which called forth the best uses of his poetic talents, creating for him an eminence from which he dominated the sonnet tradition for three centuries.

The kinds of experience to which Petrarch gave expression were those which Shakespeare also understood, but nowhere in his works does he regard them in isolation. Although an understanding of *Romeo and Juliet* assumes that under the depicted circumstances love is worth dying for, the love is not idealized to the point of irrelevance to actual life. It does not deny the body. Let Shakespeare's romance soar as high as it will, it is anchored in earth. The love always seems achievable, and partly because of the very human characteristics of his women in love. The qualities may be purer, more intense than in the work-a-day world, and sometimes, as in Cleopatra, they are innumerable. We might find a few of her qualities (less deeply felt, to be sure) anywhere, but she is the aggregate of infinite qualities of earth-dwelling womanhood.

The lady of the sonnet tradition may be a virgin, or she may be married, though not to the poet; but in either case her chief characteristic is her indomitable chastity. The lover professes his passion and devotion; she treats him with long disdain, and it is her fate to be taken at her word. She is "cruel" and "tyrannous" because she will not yield, a quality which drove Ronsard to the words "tigress" and "Medusa" and inspired a more homely epithet in the English Wyatt—"old mule." But these are passing irritations; the dominant tone is one of ardor and submission. The poet of the traditional sonnet often feels in his heart that his love is wrong, and he sometimes argues against himself on the side of morality—an understandable consequence of his towering idealization of the lady. One feels sometimes that nothing would disconcert him more than the sudden success of his suit, so dainty sweet is melancholy. There are, of course, exceptions: Spenser's *Amoretti* is the prologue to a marriage hymn. But the exceptions serve chiefly to emphasize the generality. The poet addresses the lady in terms of fire and ice (he is the fire, she the ice), of earth and air. He longs to touch her hand; he cherishes the glove that she has dropped. And so on! With Shakespeare, however, the essence of love is mutuality. With almost all the others the lover's condition is compared to a wrecked ship; with many the lady's hair is a golden net in which the lover is ensnared. He is desolate and sleepless, and his sighs trouble the heavens. The lady is described in terms of flowers, jewels, and all precious things. Her hair is threads of beaten gold, her forehead crystal, her eyes suns, her cheeks roses, her teeth pearls, her neck ivory or alabaster. Her features are detailed in what has come to be called the descending description. The poet begins with her hair and is restrained only by the limits of his ingenuity and the happy brevity of the sonnet form.

Sonnet number thirty-nine from the *Fidessa* of Bartholomew Griffin will provide an instance of the idle repetition of traditional formula. Griffin brings nothing to the tradition but the power to repeat, and the originality of his couplet, which is worse than nothing:

> My lady's hair is threads of beaten gold,
> Her front the purest crystal eye hath seen,
> Her eyes the brightest stars the heavens hold,
> Her cheeks red roses such as seld have been;
> Her pretty lips of red vermilion dye,
> Her hand of ivory the purest white,
> Her blush Aurora or the morning sky,
> Her breast displays two silver fountains bright,
> The spheres her voice, her grace the graces three;

> Her body is the saint that I adore;
> Her smiles and favors sweet as honey be;
> Her feet fair Thetis praiseth evermore.
>   But ah, the worst and last is yet behind,
>   For of a griffon doth she bear the mind.

It is not the failure of the sensibility which the couplet displays; it is the absence of it. Only when he is considered historically may Griffin be thought a part of the sonnet tradition. He repeats but he does not contribute. He is sub-literary. The weaknesses of Shakespeare's sonnets are often most striking in his couplets, but he has nothing like this. Nor is there anything in Shakespeare quite like the lapses of Sidney in, say, one of the four sonnets "made when his ladie had paine in her face." The basic conceit is that the poet had praised his lady's beauty so ardently that pain, enamored of her face, had gone to dwell there:

> Wo, wo, to me, on me return the smart:
> My burning tongue hath bred my mistress pain,
> For oft in pain to pain my painful heart
> With her due praise did of my state complain.
> I prais'd her eyes whom never chance doth move,
> Her breath which makes a sour answer sweet,
> Her milken breasts the nurse of child-like love,
> Her legs (O legs) her ay well stepping feet. . . .

From excesses like this, Shakespeare was saved by many things; for instance, his sense of comedy—the awareness of the ridiculous in those nearest him, and in himself. His failures were not, and could not have been, those which proceed from a solemn singleness of observation and intent.

In all truth there is very little in the dark lady sonnets which fails. The reader may dislike the punning "Will" sonnets, but once he sees through their complexity, it will be clear that they are brilliant examples of a departed fashion. Nor will he find that the virtuosity, once it is admitted, is unsuited to their subject—a laughing invitation to love. It turned out that Shakespeare's passion for the dark lady found its only joyous expression in comedy and word-play:

> When my love swears that she is made of truth,
> I do believe her though I know she lies,
> That she might think me some untutor'd youth,
> Unlearned in the world's false subtleties.
> Thus vainly thinking that she thinks me young,
> Although she knows my days are past the best,
> Simply I credit her false speaking tongue:
> On both sides thus is simple truth suppress'd.
> But wherefore says she not she is unjust?

> And wherefore say not I that I am old?
> O, love's best habit is in seeming trust,
> And age in love loves not to have years told:
>> Therefore I lie with her, and she with me,
>> And in our faults by lies we flatter'd be,[2]

Only a few of the twenty-six poems to the dark lady are in this mood of amused contentment.

Before long there were regrets, a deepening seriousness that made the lover think of his love as lust. When the seven deadly sins, recognized for what they are, have been given their proper names, the moral struggle has been defined, and everyone is on familiar ground; earlier, vision is not so clear. Of the time before realization the poet writes, "Love is too young to know what conscience is," using the word "conscience" in the double sense of "awareness" and "awareness of wrongdoing." Yet, he goes on to ask, who is there who does not know that conscience, in the second sense, is born of love? In this question, which the poet asks in passing, he glances at one of his most favored themes—the contribution of experience to moral knowledge. He was later to be more deeply concerned with the question, but in the sonnet under consideration[3] he goes on quickly to assert:

> My soul doth tell my body that he may
> Triumph in love; flesh stays no farther reason,
> But, rising at thy name, doth point out thee. . . .

At first glance the reader supposes that the lines of the sonnet which follow cannot be as frank as they seem to be; but they are, and the more one considers the lines, the more insistent their frankness becomes. The point is that the poet's relationship with the dark lady is neither dignified nor prettified; there is not a glimmer of romance. Later the relationship is considered and rejected, but for the time being it simply *is*. It is only one aspect of Shakespeare's view of love, but one that is characteristic of him, and quite uncharacteristic of literature in English as a whole, especially of the literature of our time. One thinks of Joyce's attitude toward Molly Bloom, and of very little else. In Steinbeck women of this sort are sentimentalized. In Hemingway love is essentially romantic, a fictional presentation of man's age-old dream of a fuller and more carefree realization of his desires. There is a suave defiance in Sadie Thompson, an unstated turning of the tables. Anna Christie is washed clean by the sea. With still other writers, women like the dark lady become symbols. But not with Shakespeare! With him they are women first. We think of them as human beings; afterwards we recall their attributes.

2 Sonnet 138.
3 Sonnet 151.

Doll Tearsheet, the girl on call at Mistress Quickly's tavern, is so minor a character that everything she says and everything which is said about her could be printed on a page or two. Commentators and actresses alike prefer to think of her as pure trollop, thus simplifying the act of comprehension and making the task of the actress easier than Shakespeare intended it to be. I hope that I do not seem to bestow on Doll Tearsheet any considerable dignity. She is, of course, the most common of mortals; but she is not simply a type. Shakespeare establishes her commonness in the beginning. "What pagan may that be?"[4] asks the Prince when she is first mentioned. And the Page replies, "A proper gentlewoman, sir; and a kinswoman of my master's." The Prince is not deceived: "Even such kin as the parish heifers are to the town bull." Nothing that follows belies the guess, and the estimate of her character is confirmed on her first entrance, made after having drunk too much canary, "a marvelous searching wine" which "perfumes the blood e're one can say, 'What's this?'" Her conversation demonstrates that in all truth she is as "common as the way between St. Alban's and London." Shakespeare never pampers her. When we last see her she is being dragged off to prison for being what she is. Nor does he patronize her. He allows her a kind of wit and abundant animal spirits (the whore in modern literature is generally anemic) and although her tact is not what it should be, she means well: "I'll be friends with thee, Jack: thou art going to the wars; and whether I shall ever see thee again or no, there is nobody cares."[5] It is comedy, but it is not farce. There is a humanity which the actress would do well to remember. Shakespeare's feeling for Doll is written in the lines. It cannot be abstracted, and it must not be ignored. She is the embodiment of warm and tawdry humanity, and she is *also* a trollop. If in our love of categories we think of her as only a trollop and fail to distinguish her from her sisters, we shall reduce Shakespeare's sketch to a stereotype.

There is no word for the point of view embodied here. "Rabelaisian" will not do, for the gusto it implies suggests a commitment absent from Shakespeare. "Elizabethan" and "Shakespearean" indicate but do not define the view so free from both bravado and apology. Sometimes we read that Shakespeare's view is naïve, but nothing could be further from the truth. Shakespeare is not naïve; it is simply that he is not sophisticated. He is not afraid of the commonplace, and he can accept the simple without condescension. In one of his sonnets[6] he lists the things which displease him most, and among them he places "simple truth miscall'd simplicity." He is not Olympian, though no writer ever had more

[4] *King Henry the Fourth,* part two, 2.2.168.
[5] *Ibid.,* 2.4.71.
[6] Sonnet 66.

reason to be. He is not neutral. One understands the temptation to find him so, but it will not do. No writer's view of life was ever less a priori than Shakespeare's. He came to conclusions about life, but first he saw it. And what is more remarkable is that there are so many areas of his observation which his point of view does little to color. His tenderness does not trap him into sentimentality; his wit never serves as protective coloring, sophisticating the trust of emotion to an easy obliquity. In the sonnets to the dark lady he accepts the passion, and, later, the remorse. "Everyone," wrote Aldous Huxley long ago when his wit was without solemnity, "feels a little Christian now and then, especially after an orgy." This is precisely the sort of awareness Shakespeare did *not* have; it diminishes both the Christianity and the orgy. One of the greatest aspects of Shakespeare's art (no other writer has it to a like degree) is his ability to give us contrasting things without the slightest diminution of either. It was a gift which found its fullest expression in *Antony and Cleopatra*.

Someone has suggested that Shakespeare's recollection of the dark lady served as a basis for his characterization of Cleopatra. Clearly we cannot know; yet we might look at the basic conception. "Would I had never known her," said Antony early in the play when the storms had begun to gather. And Enobarbus replied, "Then you had left unseen a wonderful piece of work, which, not to have been blessed withal, would have discredited your travel."[7] This is more than an expression of Enobarbus' wit; it is the witty expression of a basic attitude. Although the imprudence of knowing Cleopatra is not denied, it is recognized that prudence is not all. Nor, on the other hand, is love. Nor is the moral judgment either denied or depreciated. Nor is either the scene or the play amoral. What is being established in this scene is the nature of Antony's love, for which, eventually, he will lose the world. The world, on the other hand, is not well lost. In Shakespeare's view of Antony's love there is greatness *and* wrong.

Both Antony and Cleopatra are mature and experienced people who have passed beyond romance. Having much in common besides sex, they recognize the basically sexual nature of their attachment with the same clarity and in much the same spirit as that in which Shakespeare recognizes the nature of his attachment to the dark lady. Cleopatra envies the horse that bears Antony's weight and takes "no pleasure in aught an eunuch has." Shakespeare addressed the dark lady with the same cruel frankness Antony used toward Cleopatra: "I found you as a morsel cold upon dead Caesar's trencher." It seems to be difficult for the patterned mind to comprehend vulgarity in greatness, and the expression of it is a trying assignment for the actor. In her production of

7 *Antony and Cleopatra*, 1.2.161.

the play Miss Cornell, I thought, was magnificently regal, but at the cost of some of the coarseness. I am certain that if one is forced to a choice, Miss Cornell's choice was the right one, for I had seen the recent productions at Stratford and Paris which abandoned the queenliness altogether. As Maecenas (or was it Agrippa?) remarked in the barge scene at Paris, "Quel type!" The phrase did not matter; what mattered was the cliché of the mind to which Shakespeare's character had been reduced long before the phrase was spoken. This reduction of Shakespeare to a simplicity with which, because it is our simplicity, we can live in comfort, is the easy and common way of understanding him.

That Shakespeare should represent either Antony or himself as enslaved by sex is unpalatable to the Anglo-American tradition, which likes to have a good share of romance in the mythology by which it lives. Perhaps "Anglo-American" is not the phrase, but it will serve for something that is both English and American. Our spokesman is Hamlet in his antic disposition ". . . all which, sir, though I most powerfully and potently believe, yet I hold it not honesty to have it thus set down." Shakespeare's honesty allowed him to set down most unflattering views of mankind. On the night of the fulfillment of his love, young Troilus, fearful of going further, stands at his lady's door and engages her in forty lines of conversation. "This is the monstrosity in love, lady, that the will is infinite, and the execution confined; that the desire is boundless, and the act a slave to limit."[8] It is not an aspect of love which men often talk about together when talking about themselves. The lover may doubt, but it is not cricket to doubt himself. It is the kind of scene one might find in a French movie, but nothing like it has ever come out of Hollywood, where they know what the English-speaking public thinks it wants. Shakespeare gave his public both what they wanted and what he found true. Often they were the same thing, but what if they were not? Could there be more reason for sparing them than himself? His portrait as he has drawn it in the sonnets is not flattering. He presents himself as enslaved, and at times he is both witty and vulgar about it.

Away from his lady he imagines her faithless with his friend. Perhaps she is "wooing" the friend's "purity with her foul pride,"

> And whether that my angel be turned fiend,
> Suspect I may, yet not directly tell;
> But being both from me, both to each friend,
> I guess one angel in another's hell. . . .[9]

The reference is to that story in *The Decameron* usually left in Italian. In the edition before me it is printed in archaic French. Both Shake-

---

[8] *Troilus and Cressida*, 3.2.87.
[9] Sonnet 144.

speare's public and printers were more hearty and could face such matters. Indeed the heartiness of his public is so insisted upon nowadays that one is free to gather that Shakespeare indulged in vulgarity solely to please his public. This tactfully suggests that Shakespeare and his readers are above vulgarity, and thus everyone is left on the side of the angels except the people for whom he wrote. The truth is that Shakespeare had as fine a taste for the off-color remarks as Queen Elizabeth and that between them they shared as much sensibility and Norman blood as a whole theaterful of others. If the reader approaches Shakespeare with the courage of his own vulgarity, he need not be troubled; and if he cannot bring himself to do so, he had better stick to Trollope. Shakespeare's vulgarity is a part of his view of life, and almost always it is an integral part of the work in which it appears.

Shakespeare's sketch of the dark lady is of a piece with the view of sex without romance revealed throughout his works. He regards it in turn with humor, contentment, rebellion, and revulsion—but never simply or falsely. His view here is no less manifold than his view of life as a whole. The woman is depicted as younger than he—how much younger we cannot know. He seems to have been about thirty when the sonnets were written, and he no doubt felt older. Perhaps there is no age except the last when one feels older than at thirty. When a man is in his twenties he can think of himself as a promising young man, but if he has any sense at all he cannot persuade himself that young manhood extends to the thirties. Our knowledge of Shakespeare indicates that he matured early. Such friends of his youth as we know anything about were older than he. He married at eighteen and was soon a father. By his thirtieth year he had been working in London for some time, and without the success that had come to Marlowe. His oldest child was nearing womanhood. He was old enough to feel older than he was, but not too old to pretend to be an "untutored youth." With his gift of comic self-awareness he magnified his age.

We may guess that the young woman was in her early twenties. She was married, faithless to her husband in her liaison with the poet, and faithless to them both in her affairs with others. She had "robb'd others' beds' revenues of their rents."[10] And he cannot understand why he thinks her a "several [that is, private] plot" while his heart knows her to be the "wide world's common place."[11] She is the "usurer that put'st forth all to use."[12] In varying moods of reproach he refers to her "unworthiness"[13] and calls her a "cheater,"[14] "covetous,"[15] and "unjust."[16] The ladies of the sonnet tradition were cruel in their chaste denials; the dark lady is cruel because she is gaily promiscuous while enforcing his

[10] Sonnet 142.   [12] Sonnet 134.   [14] Sonnet 151.   [16] Sonnet 138.
[11] Sonnet 137.   [13] Sonnet 150.   [15] Sonnet 134.

bondage to her. To this attitude (enslavement to a woman one recognizes as unworthy) the old conceit of the conflict between the eye and
the heart is appropriate. Shakespeare might have found a fresher one,
but it was his habit to use what was at hand when it would do.

The sonnets ask why the heart should be bound by what the eye can
see is worthless. The question repeats, and the answer, when it comes,
is as familiar as the question: although everyone knows that lust is

> perjur'd, murderous, bloody, full of blame. . . .
> > none knows well
> To shun the heaven that leads men to this hell.[17]

Helpless in the grip of passion, he submits to her, forsaking his better
self, trying at times to persuade himself that she is better than he knows
her to be. He asks her to end the affair by saying that she does not love
him, or, in his company, to let it appear that she does. And when it is
clear that she will not be true, he begs her in a sonnet of extraordinary
plainness to go her way and come back to him later. At first sight
"feather'd creatures" for "chickens" looks like eighteenth-century poetic
diction, but it is not an elegant evasion of the commonplace. It is
intended to suggest a specious modishness in the successful rival:

> Lo, as a careful housewife runs to catch
> One of her feather'd creatures broke away,
> Sets down her babe, and makes all swift dispatch
> In pursuit of the thing she would have stay;
> Whilst her neglected child holds her in chase,
> Cries to catch her whose busy care is bent
> To follow that which flies before her face,
> Not prizing her poor infant's discontent:
> So run'st thou after that which flies from thee,
> Whilst I thy babe chase thee afar behind;
> But if thou catch thy hope, turn back to me,
> And play the mother's part, kiss me, be kind. . . .[18]

If in our admiration for Shakespeare we do not like to think of his playing this role, we should remember that this is his own sketch. If we
gloss over the matter, preferring to understand it in another sense, we
shall only contribute to the current puzzlement at his reputed rejection
of love in favor of friendship; but if we take Shakespeare at his word,
seeing the love as he asks us to see it, his ultimate choice is not only
clear, it is inevitable.

Although the view of love depicted in the sonnets is a partial one, it
accords with the larger view disclosed in his works as a whole. It will

[17] Sonnet 129.
[18] Sonnet 143.

do no harm to say that the concept is romantic if we will remember that it is also classical, that it is, in fact, as old as literature. It regards love as a wild plant which may very well flourish in ordered gardens, but whose nature urges it always to its original state. In Shakespeare's most charming and lighthearted love story, Cupid once shot a shaft that, missing its mark, fell by chance upon a little flower, "before milk-white, now purple with love's wound. . . ."

> The juice of it on sleeping eyelids laid
> Will make or man or woman madly dote. . . .[19]

The juice is applied by Puck at the behest of Oberon upon the eyelids of sleeping mortals who have no choice in the matter, and "Lord, what fools these mortals be!" Throughout his works Shakespeare expresses this view of love in different moods and terms and to different ends, but it is the same concept. Though the concept increased in content with his maturity, it was his from the beginning. It is basic to the love of Romeo, the passion of Antony, and that of the poet for the dark lady. The same concept centuries ago created Aphrodite to symbolize the willful and irrational dominance of passion.

In the sonnets Shakespeare writes that his eyes do not find the lady beautiful, that his ears are not delighted with her voice, and that

> Nor taste nor smell desire to be invited
> To any sensual feast with thee alone;
> But my five wits nor my five senses can
> Dissuade one foolish heart from serving thee. . . .[20]

It is the same simultaneousness of attraction and revulsion which was to become so characteristic of his dramatic treatment of sex in later years.

This is a complexity which has often been misconstrued, especially in our own age; for although modern writers are often unsentimental and antiromantic, they have accustomed us to a treatment of sex essentially different from Shakespeare's. Generally the reader views the antieroticism of, say, Eliot's poetry abstractly. It is not presented in a context of well-rounded characters and it remains to an extent disassociated from the life we live. Although the context of Eugene O'Neill's treatment of sex gives it immediacy, we accept it in spite of its unattractiveness because the temper of the time has prepared us for it. In none of O'Neill's major plays is an important sexual relationship viewed as satisfactory. Passion dominates and tortures, but it brings neither contentment nor release. This is acceptable to our time because the populariza-

---

[19] *A Midsummer Night's Dream*, 2.1.167.
[20] Sonnet 141.

tions of modern psychology have provided patterns by which it can be interpreted. In O'Neill's major plays, except *The Iceman Cometh*, passion deviates from the normal. The strongest sexual drives are diverted by mother-son, father-daughter, or brother-sister attractions. Thus the unhappiness of passion is both presented and accepted as the manifestation of neurosis. With Shakespeare this is not the case. The unhappiness is presented in itself as a commonly observed aspect of life. The passion which dominates and tortures is thought of as a manifestation of man's natural self. The view of human nature is not optimistic; there are *at once* incalculable potentials for both good and evil. This was and is the orthodox Christian view (it is also, among other things, Platonic), but there seems to be no great popular awareness of it; and it is clearly not the assumption on which the average English-speaking spectator responds to a dramatic situation. Nor has it been for some time! "It is now quite unfashionable," wrote John Wesley,[21] "to say anything to the disparagement of human nature; which is generally allowed, notwithstanding a few infirmities, to be very innocent, and wise, and virtuous." In the popular view what is evil in man is thought of as a deviation from a goodness he once possessed. Generally, even in our most robust fiction, the evil in man is in a sense man-made. Its social and neurotic origins are commonly explained, and the most terrifying aspect of evil is thus explained away. This is what the average reader has come to expect of literature, and not finding it in Shakespeare, he often reads it into the text. Shakespeare's works assume the reality of both good and evil, and while it is once or twice suggested that a certain trait of character is the result of training (the only notable instance is Coriolanus) sexual evil is never presented as the manifestation of a neurosis.

I do not of course mean to suggest that tragic suffering in both literature and life does not often have social or psychiatric origins. I simply remark that Shakespeare's assumptions in this respect are not ours and that we both obscure and diminish his work in trying to make his assumptions conform to our own. It is no objection to Freud to observe that in almost all instances the Freudian interpretations of Shakespeare have done him an injustice; but in order to have written more wisely the Freudian critics would have needed little but a more complete knowledge of Freud, who knew quite well that Shakespeare had preceded him in observing certain phenomena. Both of them knew that a sense of revulsion in erotic life is not necessarily either neurotic or puritanical. There is at least one passage in which Freud out-Shakespeares Shakespeare[22]: "So perhaps we must make up our minds to the idea

[21] Quoted by Louis A. Landa, *English Institute Essays, 1946*, Columbia University Press, New York, 1947, p. 34.
[22] *Freud: On War, Sex and Neurosis*, Arts & Science Press, New York, 1947, pp. 216–217.

that altogether it is not possible for the claims of the sexual instinct to be reconciled with the demands of culture. . . . This very incapacity in the sexual instinct to yield full satisfaction as soon as it submits to the first demands of culture becomes the source, however, of the grandest cultural achievements, which are brought to birth by ever greater sublimation of the components of the sexual instinct. For what motive would induce man to put his sexual energy to other uses if by any disposal of it he could obtain fully satisfying pleasure? . . . It seems, therefore, that the irreconcilable antagonism between the demands of the two instincts—the sexual and the egoistic—have made man capable of ever greater achievements, though, it is true, under the continual menace of danger, such as that of the neuroses to which at the present time the weaker are succumbing." We may believe that Shakespeare was not one of "the weaker" who succumbed, but that, since he was a man of strong passion and fine sensibility, the conflict between the claims of sex and his integrity as a civilized man were most apparent to him. It was inevitable that as a man of his time he should express the conflict in terms of body and soul, and that, when the expression pierces to ultimates, the point of view should be Christian.

This conflict is the essence of the later sonnets to the dark lady, and it is, of course, central to *Hamlet,* where it is nowhere better set forth than in Hamlet's excoriation of his mother. We should notice in passing that here again there is the opposition of the eyes and the heart:

> Have you eyes?
> Could you on this fair mountain leave to feed,
> And batten on this moor? Ha! Have you eyes?

On the basis of his own experience Hamlet understands the power of passion, but as a young man he cannot believe that it can so operate in his mother without infernal aid. There is, of course, a double value here: the revelation of particular character and the suggestion to the spectator of motives arising in realms beyond human control.

> . . . at your age
> The hey-day in the blood is tame, it's humble,
> And waits upon the judgment; and what judgment
> Would step from this to this. . . . What devil was't
> That thus hath cozen'd you. . . .

The dramatic fact is that the judgment had not functioned. The queen is not presented as a villainess for our scorn and hatred. The more fortunate of us may say of her, "There but for the grace of God go I." Up to this point in the play she had not recognized the enormity of her actions; she had never had the courage to look into her soul. Hamlet now forces self-knowledge upon her, and in her soul she sees

> such black and grained spots
> As will not leave their tinct.

Terrified at the realization of what she is, she tries to escape it. If, after all, her son should be mad, his revelation of her nature would be without reality. She prefers his madness, but it will not serve:

> Mother, for love of grace,
> Lay not that flattering unction to your soul,
> That not your trespass but my madness speaks;
> It will but skin and film the ulcerous place
> While rank corruption, mining all within,
> Infects unseen. Confess yourself to Heaven;
> Repent what's past, avoid what is to come,
> And do not spread the compost on the weeds
> To make them ranker.

No scene in dramatic literature is more deeply revealing or more theatrically varied. The recognition of lust moves with a speed it could not have in the sonnets—yet it is the same recognition, moving to the same conclusion with the same tearing back of surfaces.

For the moment we should note that in representing his uneasiness in the adulterous relationship, Shakespeare refers repeatedly to his being forsworn; that is, to the breaking of his vows, to the denial of his integrity. And if we glance again at the list of wrongs which, in sonnet sixty-six, made him in his weariness cry for "restful death," we shall find among them "purest faith unhappily forsworn." We should notice, too, that the sonnets depict a progress on the poet's part which is parallel to the spiritual progress of Lear. Lear's journey from arrogance to a knowledge of his own unworthiness shows, near the beginning, an attempt to lighten the growing burden by the assertion that although he has erred, the wrongs of others are greater: "I am a man more sinned against than sinning." In the sonnets the poet repeats that although he is forsworn, the lady is twice forsworn. Can she condemn him when her errors are more than his? This is a familiar attempt at the maintenance of illusion, but in Shakespeare it does not work. Their rationalizations failing, both Lear and Gertrude move on to self-knowledge. The poet of the sonnets comes to think of his love as a thing without health, as a fever always longing "for that which longer nurseth the disease." He comes to loathe his passion, and his loathing swells until it includes both himself and the dark lady:

> For I have sworn thee fair and thought thee bright,
> Who art as black as hell, as dark as night.[23]

The sonnets of deepest revulsion present an agony which cannot contain itself. One thinks of the writers of our own day—the desolation of *The Wasteland,* of the earlier novels by Huxley and their searing wit without the release of indignation. It is an awareness which must change because it cannot bear to be itself. With Shakespeare it moved to a magnification of the spirit and a renunciation of the flesh, set forth in a sonnet[24] of admirable compactness and, once the precision of its grammatical references are noticed, of perfect clarity:

> Poor soul, the center of my sinful earth,
> Thrall to[25] these rebel powers that thee array,
> Why dost thou pine within and suffer dearth,
> Painting thy outward walls so costly gay?
> Why so large cost, having so short a lease,
> Dost thou upon thy fading mansion spend?
> Shall worms, inheritors of this excess,
> Eat up thy charge? is this thy body's end?
> Then soul, live thou upon thy servant's loss,
> And let that pine to aggravate thy store;
> Buy terms divine in selling hours of dross;
> Within be fed, without be rich no more:
>   So shalt thou feed on death, that feeds on men,
>   And death once dead, there's no more dying then.

There is nothing with which the sonnets are more insistently concerned than with the aspiration to triumph over death. In the early sonnets immortality is to be won through propagation and poetry. At the close it is to be found in the salvation of the soul. Throughout there is a progressive growth in moral emphasis. I do not suggest, of course, that the sonnets are primarily a sequence of moral poems; and it should be pointed out that although the recognition of lust extends over many poems, there is only one poem which renounces the flesh. Still, the poem exists and seems to be the culmination of the sonnets to the dark lady. I can see no possible basis of agreement with the critic who does not believe that in this sonnet "Shakespeare is making out a case for immortality except as a formal device." What is there in all of Shakespeare's works, or in his background, which would lead us to suppose that when he speaks of the immortality of the soul he is "making out a case" for it?

Although the dominant mode of criticism in our time insists on the necessity of viewing a work of literature in relation to its historical background, certain predispositions of our own century have prevented modern criticism from recognizing so patent a matter as the essential nature of this poem. One may read all the commentaries on this sonnet

---

[24] Sonnet 146.
[25] "Thrall to" is a widely accepted conjectural emendation. In the original text the line begins with a manifest error.

in the New Variorum and hardly discover a centrally relevant remark. One summer evening not so many years ago, five critics gathered in a kind of symposium at The Bread Loaf School of English to discuss this poem. The meeting was without wine or auditors, although, in deference to one of their number, there were cigars. The conversation, as reported in *The American Scholar*,[26] was wonderfully sober in spite of a vein of fantasy arising, doubtless, from the privacy of the meeting. The remarkable thing about what was said is not that it was wrong-headed and learnedly foolish, for to be wrong and foolish a good part of the time is the normal state of mankind. The disturbing thing is that critics of distinction should have shown such fear of being plain. One of the critics, finding in himself a "tendency to take the images literally and seriously," saw " 'center' as perhaps the capital city of England and the 'rebel powers' as English Barons at the beginning of the 15th century." This is in spite of Shakespeare's warning that "they that dally nicely with words may quickly make them wanton." He continued, "Or I pause on the word 'array' to think of its connections with decoration and painting. 'Array' is a transitive verb and its use here is ambiguous. The rebel powers can array, or marshall, only their own troops—not the troops of the opposing soul."

Surely the less complicated reader will not be troubled in this way. He will notice that *thee* is the object of *array* and refers to the *poor soul* which is incarnated in the poet's flesh, his *sinful earth*. He will notice, too, that *excess* refers to the body, and he will not find that it "unescapably" suggests Aristotle's doctrine of the mean. It is the clear and completely appropriate word because, as the poem insists, the soul is immortal, and the flesh, being transient, has no essential value. It is excess impedimenta which we can carry only to the grave, where it will be consumed by worms. The notion of dissolution, as familiar in Shakespeare as it is in life, struck one of the Bread Loaf critics as "cannibalistic," the "imagery of the eating worms" being "so excessive as to destroy any calm ethical judgments in the argument." "Taken literally, the notions of these lines are horrid and to me very painful." These remarks are the expression of a sensibility so intent upon itself that it disregards the poem, except to distort it. Animals that prey upon each other, or upon carrion, do not suggest cannibalism to a more disengaged intelligence.

The ordinary reader reflecting on these remarks can only be shocked at the critic's refusal to turn his eyes from himself toward the object of criticism, and he could only be more deeply shocked at the degree to which contemporary criticism is compounded of such proud and private pedantry. Willfully private, in this instance, for the critic finds "few words in the poem that would directly indicate conventional religious dogma . . . the sonnet seems in spirit to be Platonic." Another member of the Bread Loaf symposium whose criticism is seldom far from center, finds that "the movement of the poem is ascetic." "Superficially, I suppose, we could call the doctrine Christian; it is conventional in its argument; it is almost sentimental in its doing away with the painful and the transient and the worthless, in its centering of man's hope upon immortality and a system of future rewards and punishments." This is better. Yet there is the horrid condescension to the subject matter of the poem, the feeling that there is something about Christianity a little unworthy of us, and certainly of Shakespeare. The feeling is strong enough to equate renunciation with asceticism and relegate it to the "movement" of the poem, allowing the critic to view it with the detachment one rightly accords to technical matters. And all this is representative of the greater part of the criticism of this sonnet. There is a reluctance to admit that Shakespeare means something; or, if a meaning is admitted, there is a refusal to view it simply. The criticism of this sonnet is on the whole a dismal record of the triumph of sophistication over sense.

"What strikes me particularly about this poem," said still another Bread Loaf critic, "is its tone. I find it jaunty, full of a kind of super-wit . . . in spite of this central mood of jauntiness, the opponents are the worms, the flesh, and the grave; therefore a certain grimness and irony are present." Surely it should be apparent to all men in their senses that although there is often wit in Shakespeare's seriousness, this is not a jaunty poem, that the poem is Christian, and that Shakespeare presents the Christianity without apology. The "opponents" are neither the worms nor the grave. The opponent is the inherent willfulness of the flesh, and the poem says that when sin is conquered death is conquered, for death has no power over the soul. There can be no error in seeing Platonic relationships in the poem, for they exist; but it is blindness not to see that the poem is first Christian. If we must have a written source for the poem, it can be found in the most obvious of places, the words of Saint Paul: "O death, where is thy sting? O grave, where is thy victory? The sting of death is sin. . . ." The triumph here is that of the spirit over sin, and in the light of this triumph death takes on insignificance. No one supposes that all readers of Shakespeare will share this belief, but it is a little late to deny the use of it to Shakespeare. The exhortation to his soul to find eternal life in shattering his sexual enslavement is an understandable consequence of the passion he describes. It is a sequence noted in Huxley's epigram, and, much more wisely, by Saint Paul. "Howbeit that was not first which is spiritual, but that which is natural; and afterwards that which is spiritual."

PATRICK CRUTTWELL

Shakespeare's Sonnets and the 1590's

THE 1590's are the crucial years. In the Elizabethan *fin-de-siècle* there occurred a change, a shift of thought and feeling, which led directly to the greatest moment in English poetry: the "Shakespearean moment," the opening years of the seventeenth century, in which were written all the supreme Shakespearean dramas. The 1590's brought about that deep change of sensibility which marks off the later from the earlier Elizabethans, which alters the climate from that of *Arcadia* and *The Faerie Queene* to that which welcomed *Hamlet*, which probably demanded the Shakespearean rewriting of that drama from its crude original blood-and-thunder Kyd, and which found its other great poet in the person of Donne. To think of the Elizabethan age as a solid, unchanging unity is utterly misleading. Within it there were two generations and (roughly corresponding to those generations) two mentalities. In the 1590's the one "handed over" to the other. Such a statement is, of course, the grossest simplification; in the realms of the mind and the imagination things do not happen as neatly as that. And in fact, the 1590's are intensely confused, precisely because the "handing over" was then taking place; new and old were deeply entangled, and all generalizations must be loaded with exceptions. But there *was* an old, and there *was* a new, and the task of criticism is to analyse and distinguish.

Of all the poetry then written, none shows better what was really happening than the Sonnets of Shakespeare. They deal with far more than the personal events which make up their outward material; they show an intensely sensitive awareness of the currents and cross-currents of the age. They have hardly received the properly critical attention that they deserve; real criticism, it may be, has fought shy of them because of the fatal and futile attraction they have exercised on the noble army of cranks, who are far too busy identifying the young man, the dark lady, the rival poet, and William Shakespeare, to bother about

From Patrick Cruttwell, *The Shakespearean Moment: and its Place in the Poetry of the 17th Century*, New York, Columbia University Press, 1955; pp. 1–2 and 6–16. Reprinted by permission of Columbia University Press and Chatto & Windus, Ltd.

the quality of the poetry. But the Sonnets are, in their own right, and quite apart from external "problems," poems of great and intriguing interest, as well as of beauty; they are much more subtle and varied than a casual reading reveals. The sweet and unchanging smoothness of their form is extremely deceptive; and it is partly this—the contrast between spirit and form—which makes them, of all the works of the 1590's, the best adapted to help us to a comprehension of the age's development in poetry. For what they show is a blending of new and old, the new in the old, and the new growing through the old; they use a form (the sonnet-sequence) which was above all the chosen form of the old, and in that form they say something completely at odds with the old, and destined to conquer it. On the surface they are fashionable and conventional, for the 1590's was the great age of the sonnet-sequence; below the surface, they are radically original. . . .

If, then, the Sonnets derive from an episode in Shakespeare's life in which he made some sort of contact with the world of elegance and aristocracy, the next problem is to find the nature of that experience. The Sonnets, as we said, are not a unity; the experience they present was neither simple nor single, but complex and changing. Although there is no evidence at all that the printed arrangement of the poems was Shakespeare's—no evidence, indeed, that there ever *was* an arrangement—still, one can trace a certain logical development, and the development is from simplicity to complexity.

The early sonnets—that is, to speak more exactly, those which come first in the printed text, though it seems very likely that they were also the earliest—show the simple sensibility of the early Renaissance. There is a vast deal of words to very little matter; the method is that of constant variations on the same theme. The language is smooth and mellifluous,[1] the imagery clear and unsurprising. Ideas are few, simple, and in a sense artificial: marry and beget children so that your beauty may outlive you, your beauty will survive your death in my verse. There is no need to think that these ideas were held insincerely, but they do come from the common stock of Renaissance poetry; they lack the force of a theme which has a particular value. Of these poems one may sometimes feel, what one could never feel of the later ones, that some other writer could have produced them.

The love that these early sonnets celebrates is a simple unqualified

---

[1] "Smooth," "mellifluous," "honey-tongued," etc., seem to have been the stock-epithets for the contemporary praise of Shakespeare's early writings: for examples—
   "Honie-tong'd Shakespeare" (John Weever: *Epigrammes,* 1599).
   "Mellifluous & hony-tongued S." (Meres: *Palladis Tamia,* 1598).
   "And S. thou, whose hony-flowing Vaine" (Richard Barnfield: *Poems in Divers Humors,* 1598).
   "O sweet Mr. S." (Anon.: *Return from Parnassus, c.* 1600).
It is not irrelevant to remember that when Ophelia recalls the unspoiled love of Hamlet, his romantic and chivalrous courtship, she remembers how she "suck'd the Honie of his Musicke Vowes."

adoration; neither it nor its object is questioned, criticized, or analysed. The object is a young man who is in no way characterized, or rendered with a sense of individual reality; he seems to be rather the ideal youth of the Renaissance, beautiful, highborn, wilful, and irresistible. He is regarded with a curious sexual ambiguity, as in the 53rd:

> *Describe Adonis and the counterfet,*
> *Is poorely immitated after you,*
> *On Hellens cheeke all art of beautie set,*
> *And you in Grecian tires are painted new.*

The symbols of male and female beauty are taken as interchangeable. The 20th sonnet makes that ambiguity more apparent:

> *A Womans face with natures owne hand painted,*
> *Hast thou the Master Mistris of my passion . . .*
> *And for a woman wert thou first created,*
> *Till nature as she wrought thee fell a dotinge,*
> *And by addition me of thee defeated,*
> *By adding one thing to my purpose nothing.*
> > *But since she prickt thee out for womens pleasure,*
> > *Mine be thy love and thy loves use their treasure.*

There is there, perhaps, a slight feeling of frustration, a sense that this sort of love is hardly satisfying, which comes to the surface in the wry punning jest of "prickt." Primarily, it means "marked thee in the list of males"—as Falstaff tells Shallow ("prick him") to mark down his recruits. But it also had a very current sexual meaning: as a verb, "to copulate," and as a noun, "the male sexual organ"—as in Mercutio's "the bawdy hand of the Dyall is now upon the pricke of Noone." This obscene jest in the 20th sonnet seems the first appearance in the sequence of a feeling and meaning not altogether simple; but in general, these first sonnets are quite at home in the climate of Renaissance "homosexual"[2] feeling, which was in part an æsthetic affectation, based perhaps on Hellenism, imitation of the Greeks, in part a quite genuine emotion, compounded from love of beauty, worship of noble birth, and an elegiac tenderness for youth. The 37th sonnet sums up the nature of the young man's attractiveness; it opens with a simile which likens Shakespeare to a "decrepit Father" who "takes delight To see his active childe doe deedes of youth," and then lists the qualities of his charm: "beautie, birth, or wealth, or wit." The homosexual feeling that undoubtedly exists in the Sonnets has a certain un-physical remoteness; it is never explicit and aggressive, as it is in Marlowe. But then Marlowe was a tough individual and a *mauvais sujet,* while Shakespeare appears to have been a respectable gentleman. There is, of course, no need to evoke the climate

---

[2] The word is to be taken with no implications of abnormality.

of the Renaissance in order to explain how a middle-aged, middle-class, provincial poet, sensuous and sensitive to his fingertips, conceived a passionate adoration for a young, highborn and courtly Adonis; there is no need, in fact, to go further back than Oscar Wilde and Lord Alfred Douglas. (No *literary* comparison intended.) The insistence that the loved one should get married is certainly curious; one can only explain it on the usual terms, that these first seventeen sonnets were "commissioned." But it does at least demonstrate that the quality of this love was neither physical nor possessive.

As the sequence proceeds, the texture of the poems, though the subject remains the young man, shows a slow thickening, an increasing complexity. They become much more introspective; the interest is often far more on the writer's general state of mind than on the object of his love or even the love itself. In the 29th, for instance ("When in disgrace with Fortune and mens eyes"), the real concentration of intensity falls on the sense of utter failure that fills the writer's being; the conclusion, which affirms that this failure is redeemed by his love, is weak and unconvincing by comparison. This pattern is followed in many sonnets; often, the real weight of the poem, which is thoroughly pessimistic, introspective, and not concerned at all with love, is feebly opposed by the final couplet alone. Of these the most striking is the 66th ("Tir'd with all these, for restfull death I cry"), in which the long piling Hamlet-like list of the world's iniquities utterly overwhelms the protesting little line at the end—"save that to dye, I leave my Love alone." In these poems and many more, an all-inclusive self-examination replaces or reinforces the narrow theme of love; self-disgust, self-contempt, self-reproach are the usual tones of this introspection, and even the rare moments of satisfaction are qualified and brushed aside at once:

> Sinne of selfe-love possesseth al mine eie,
> And all my soule, and al my every part;
> And for this sinne there is no remedie,
> It is so grounded inward in my heart.
> Me thinkes no face so gracious is as mine,
> No shape so true, no truth of such account,
> And for my selfe mine owne worth do define,
> As I all other in all worths surmount.
> But when my glasse shewes me my selfe indeed
> Beated and chopt with tand antiquitie,
> Mine owne selfe love quite contrary I read;
> Selfe, so selfe loving were iniquity . . .
>
> (62)

Bitterness at the thought of age, as here, is one of the points on which this self-hatred is focussed; but another, more particular, and also, it would seem, more deeply felt, is the conviction of failure as a poet. This is hinted at in some of the early sonnets, as for example in the 32nd:

> *If thou survive my well contented daie,*
> *When that churle death my bones with dust shall cover*
> *And shalt by fortune once more re-survay*
> *These poore rude lines of thy deceased Lover;*
> *Compare them with the bett'ring of the time,*
> *And though they be out-stript by every pen,*
> *Reserve them for my love, not for their rime,*
> *Exceeded by the hight of happier men . . .*

—but there seems no great bitterness there: it sounds like polite and conventional modesty, and just where the failure lies is not yet defined. It is defined later, with great and bitter precision, stimulated, it seems, by the coming of the more successful rival. His own verse has got into a rut; it is now old-fashioned and monotonous:

> *Why write I still all one, ever the same,*
> *And keepe invention in a noted weed,*
> *That every word doth almost tel my name,*
> *Shewing their birth, and where they did proceed?*
> (76)

The 78th particularizes further; the failure is seen as a lack of artistic grace and a deficiency in learning:

> *In others workes thou doost but mend the stile,*
> *And Arts with thy sweete graces graced be.*
> *But thou art all my art, and doost advance*
> *As high as learning, my rude ignorance.*[3]

What this sense of poetic failure means in Shakespeare's literary career, and in relation to the time when the Sonnets were written, will be looked into later.

The poems, as they proceed, then, move away from a simple and single contemplation and adoration of the young Adonis. They widen in scope, till every interest of the writer's life is brought within their reach: his dreams of social success and bitterness at social failure, the problems and rivalries of his career as an author, his perceptions of the evils and injustices in society, his private anguish at growing old and his private fear of death. The young man is still the centre, but he too is involved in the growing complexity. For now he is looked on with a critical eye, as a fallible individual and not as a symbol that cannot be questioned. The obsequious adoration which some of the sonnets award him—"my soverayne," "your servant," "your slave," "your vassal" —is qualified by hints of rebuke:

---

[3] It is interesting to see, so early and in Shakespeare himself, a recognition of what was to become the critical commonplace: that he "wanted art" (as Jonson put it) and was unlearned.

> No more bee greev'd at that which thou hast done,
> Roses have thornes, and silver fountaines mud,
> Cloudes and eclipses staine both Moone and Sunne,
> And loathsome canker lives in sweetest bud.
>
> (35)

A contrast is felt between his outward beauty and inward corruption:

> O what a Mansion have those vices got
> Which for their habitation chose out thee.
>
> (95)

And now he is looked at through the eyes of others:

> That tongue that tells the story of thy daies,
> (Making lascivious comments on thy sport)
> Cannot dispraise, but in a kinde of praise,
> Naming thy name, blesses an ill report.
>
> (95)

He is, as it were, becoming dramatized: seen in the round, seen and felt as a real human being, in the context of society and under the scrutiny of an observant though still loving mind.

When the dark lady makes her delayed but most effective entry (she does not effectively appear till the 127th sonnet[4]—one would almost think that Shakespeare's theatrical cunning had something to do with it), the process we have already traced continues, at a faster tempo and with ever-increasing intensity. These sonnets which deal with the lady (127 to 152) contain most of the greatness and most of the maturity in the whole sequence; they can be taken as a single poem, in the way in which (for instance) Donne's nineteen *Holy Sonnets* are a single poem. The lady is depicted with a familiar equality, a bitter and bawdy ferocity, such as are never accorded to the young man even at his naughtiest. His goings-on are excused and even admired; hers are neither. Her promiscuity is described in language of tough and "unpoetic" realism; and this too the young man never receives:

> If eyes corrupt by over-partiall lookes,
> Be anchord in the baye where all men ride,
> Why of eyes falsehood hast thou forged hookes,
> Whereto the judgement of my heart is tide?
> Why should my heart thinke that a severall plot,
> Which my heart knowes the wide worlds common place?
>
> (137)

The first of these images has an indecent pun on "ride," one of the commonest of Elizabethan verbs for describing male sexual activity (the

---

4 Sonnets 40–42 hint at her.

jestings of the Frenchmen, before Agincourt, about the Dauphin's horse, for example); the last is derived from the contemporary enclosures of common land ("severall plot" meaning "privately-owned piece of land"), and its play with the sexual meaning of the word ("promiscuous") was also a favourite Elizabethan jest. The language, when the lady is the subject, comes much nearer to that of common speech—and of the drama —and much farther from the lyrically "poetical," than when the young man is dealt with.

From this perception that the lady is a whore, come a moral tone far fiercer and deeper, and a self-examination more searching, than anything before. There is not only the famous 129th sonnet on lust, there is also the 146th, which is one of the very few passages in Shakespeare explicitly and traditionally theological, in its conflict between body and soul ("poore soul the centre of my sinfull earth"), its advice to the soul to thrive by denying the body, and its Donne-like ending:

> *So shalt thou feede on death, that feedes on men,*
> *And death once dead, there's no more dying then*

—which is very close to the last line of Donne's tenth Holy Sonnet:

> *And death shall be noe more; death, thou shalt dye.*

Of these sonnets' introspection, the dominant theme is that of a self-divided personality, of a love which exists in spite of the judgment of reason, in spite of a moral perception of its wrongness and of its object's worthlessness, even in spite of the senses' recognition that she is not particularly beautiful. Others do not find her so, and the others are probably right:

> *If that be faire whereon my false eyes dote,*
> *What meanes the world to say it is not so?*
> *If it be not, then love doth well denote,*
> *Loves eye is not so true as all mens . . .*
>
> (148)

There is an utter disintegration of the personality: senses, wits, and heart are at strife ("but my five wits, nor my five senses can Diswade one foolish heart from serving thee"[5]); the whole self is at odds with the love which it cannot resist ("when I against my selfe with thee per-take")[6]. It is not only self-division; it is also a perverted craving for self-deception, a deception that does not deceive. He asks to be cheated; but of course the mere asking implies that the cheat is already detected:

[5] 141.
[6] 149.

> *If I might teach thee witte better it were,*
> *Though not to love, yet love to tell me so,*
> *As testie sick-men when their deaths be neere,*
> *No newes but health from their Phisitions know.*
>   (140)

Behind this is a conviction that the whole relationship is wrong, is false in itself and founded on falsehood—in the sonnets devoted to the lady, the words "false" and "falsehood" occur nine times, "lie" or "belied" six times—and if all is false, then why should the parts be true? This comes to a climax in what is perhaps the most terrible poem of the whole sequence, the 138th: the most terrible, and also the nakedest, since it confesses things that are not easily confessed:

> *When my love sweares that she is made of truth,*
> *I do beleeve her though I know she lyes,*
> *That she might thinke me some untuterd youth,*
> *Unlearned in the worlds false subtilties.*
> *Thus vainely thinking that she thinkes me young,*
> *Although she knowes my dayes are past the best,*
> *Simply I credit her false speaking tongue,*
> *On both sides thus is simple truth supprest:*
> *But wherefore sayes she not she is unjust?*
> *And wherefore say not I that I am old?*
> *O loves best habit is in seeming trust,*
> *And age in love, loves not t' have yeares told.*
> > *Therefore I lye with her, and she with me,*
> > *And in our faults by lyes we flattered be.*

Of this climactic poem the last couplet, with its pun on "lye," is the very apex. The pun's grim seriousness is quite in the mature Shakespearean manner, like the remarkable triple pun in *The Winter's Tale*—Leontes raving with jealousy to his son:

> *Goe play (Boy) play: thy Mother playes, and I*
> *Play too; but so disgrac'd a part, whose issue*
> *Will hisse me to my Grave . . .*

—in which *play* means, first, the innocent childish play of the boy; next, the adulterous sexual sport of the wife; finally, the playing of an actor, in the shameful role of the cuckold. The pun in the sonnet forces together the physical union and its context, as it were, its whole surrounding universe, of moral defilement and falsehood. It says, in fact, what the opening of the 129th sonnet says:

> *The expence of Spirit in a waste of shame*
> *Is lust in action . . .*

and it says it with the same union of moral power and physical precision. "The expence of spirit," for the modern reader, has only emotional force;

it is in fact a piece of contemporary sexual physiology. From the heart to the sexual organs, was believed to go a vein, bearing in it the "spirit generative." "Expence" means "expenditure": what the phrase refers to is the loss of the "spirit generative" in the act of sex.

This love that is known to be wrong, and is yet persisted in, leads at last to a total reversal of the moral order. Good becomes bad in this love, and bad becomes good: "When all my *best* doth worship thy *defect*"—"that in my minde thy *worst* all *best* exceeds." "Fair" is equivocated against "foul," "bright" against "black":

> *Or mine eyes seeing this, say this is not,*
> *To put faire truth upon so foule a face*
> (137)

—which reminds one of the way in which the witches of *Macbeth* juggle and equivocate "fair" against "foul"; and there too the meaning is that the moral order is reversed. Clearest of all is the final couplet of 150:

> *If thy unworthinesse raisd love in me,*
> *More worthy I to be belov'd of thee*

—he has loved her for her unworthiness, this in turn has infected him, has made him unworthy, and hence his unworthiness makes him "worthy" of her. This hell is the exact antithesis of the Baudelairian heaven in *Moesta et Errabunda*—"où tout ce que l'on aime est digne d'être aimé." Substitute *indigne* for *digne*, and Baudelaire's meaning would be identical with Shakespeare's.

The sonnet which follows this (151) shows a slight change of tone, a relaxing of the moral struggle; it reads like a resigned sardonic acceptance of the utter wrongness of the whole business. It admits, in terms unusually religious for Shakespeare, that his love is betraying his soul:

> *For thou betraying me, I doe betray*
> *My nobler part to my gross bodies treason*

but the phrases addressed to her—"gentle cheater," "sweet selfe"—have an air of tired and tolerant affection. Two rogues together, might as well have some fun—the spirit is not unlike that of Villon in the *Ballade de la Grosse Margot*:

> *Ie suis paillard, la paillarde me suit.*
> *Lequel vault mieux? chascun bien s'entresuit.*
> *L'ung l'aultre vault; c'est a mau chat mau rat.*

And the rest of the sonnet carries on in that spirit with an almost cheerful obscenity, with an elaborate and thoroughly Donne-like conceit on male sexuality; the final couplet:

> *No want of conscience hold it that I call*
> *Her love, for whose deare love I rise and fall*

is exactly in the manner of the lines in Donne's nineteenth *Elegie:*

> *We easly know*
> *By this these Angels from an evil sprite,*
> *Those set our hairs, but these our flesh upright.*

We have come a long way from the lyrical idealism of the opening sonnet—

> *From fayrest creatures we desire increase,*
> *That thereby beautie's Rose might never dye*

—to reach a poem as complex as this, which in fourteen lines can range from religious solemnity to bawdy mockery. We have come, in fact, from Spenser to Donne.

G. WILSON KNIGHT

Time and Eternity

Oh! how should I not burn for Eternity, and for the marriage ring of rings—the Ring of Recurrence?

Never yet found I the woman by whom I would have children, save it be by this Woman that I love: for I love thee, O Eternity!

Thus Spake Zarathustra

. . . . The Sonnets offer no easy assurances. They never forget that

> Golden lads and girls all must,
> As chimney sweepers, come to dust.
> (*Cymbeline*, IV, ii, 262)

Their drama is set within contexts of diurnal and seasonal change. We see the Sun in glory of his rise and splendid in mid-career, but also reeling to his end so tragically that eyes are averted (7). Seasonal change is continually before us. We are not allowed to forget how

> never-resting Time leads summer on
> To hideous winter, and confounds him there.
> (5)

We watch "summer's green all girded up in sheaves," borne on the bier "with white and bristly beard" (12). The future promises "winter" storms, and the "barren rage of death's eternal cold" (13). Such is our setting.

Summer is wholly desirable, but winter is "full of care" (56). The loved youth is like "the spring and foison of the year" (53), sweet and perfect as "a summer's day" (18). But, in his absence, "teeming autumn," with all its "increase," is a mockery:

> For summer and his pleasures wait on thee,
> And, thou away, the very birds are mute.
> (97)

From Part I, Chapter IV, of *The Mutual Flame* by G. Wilson Knight (London, 1955). Reprinted by permission of Methuen & Company, Ltd. Several portions have been regretfully omitted, owing to considerations of space.

Either that, or their songs forebode "winter." Indeed, his absence makes it all a period of "freezings" and "December's bareness" (97). The thought is next elaborated: even "proud-pied April," who injects youth into all nature, is now no better than winter (98). Thinking of their three years' acquaintance, the poet writes:

> Three winters cold
> Have from the forests shook three summers' pride,
> Three beauteous springs to yellow autumn turn'd
> In process of the seasons have I seen,
> Three April perfumes in three hot Junes burn'd,
> Since first I saw you fresh, which yet are green.
> Ah, yet doth beauty, like a dial-hand,
> Steal from his figure and no pace perceiv'd . . .
> (104)

There is a contrast between "fresh" and "green." The sonnet started with, "To me, fair friend, you never can be old," but the doubt is clearly underlined. However miraculous his youth, the boy is part of nature and subject to her laws. . . .

Time's action is subtle and silent:

> Ah, yet doth beauty, like a dial-hand,
> Steal from his figure and no pace perceiv'd.

"Figure" is precisely used for both the youth and the dial's numberings. So the dial shows "how thy precious minutes waste" (77). The poet is said to "count the clock that tells the time" (12), ruminating on time like Henry VI and Richard II (3 *Henry VI*, II, v, 21–40; *Richard II*, v, v, 42–60). Time is a mysterious continuum within which all nature is contained and limited:

> Like as the waves make towards the pebbled shore,
> So do our minutes hasten to their end;
> Each changing place with that which goes before,
> In sequent toil all forwards do contend.
> (60)

In these passages time's paradox has been conveyed by suggestions of both slowness, as in "steal," "no pace," and "toil"; and speed, as in "hasten"; and elsewhere we find such phrases as "swift-footed Time" (19), "his swift foot" (65), Time's "continual haste" (123). Slow or fast, one thing is certain: Time is "never-resting" (5).

It also appears to be all-embracing. Significant passages emphasise how it brings to birth as well as destroys. The word "time" may accordingly be used for the immediate, and in one sense timeless, excellence whose transience raises all our problems. So the youth is said to be at "this thy golden time" (3), and standing "on the top of happy hours" (16). But this glory, so vividly "crowning the present," leaves one "doubting of the rest" (115). The contrast is between the "now"—Shakespeare's thought does not call it, though it may suggest, an "eternal now"—and the temporal sequence. He is concerned with the simple actuality of "all those beauties whereof *now* he's king" (63), as against the inevitable future; with time as now, and time as sequence. Normally "time" means "sequential time."[1]

Sequential time is destructive. The poet will not easily submit. Fearing "Time's furrows" in his love (22), he takes up the challenge and is "all at war with Time for love of you" (15). The words are apt. The Sonnets are exactly this: a poetic war with Time. Time, with its "wrackful siege of battering days" (65), is a besieging force, and would pierce, as with a weapon, beauty's heraldic crest: "Time doth transfix the flourish set on youth" (60). It is a powerful foe, since "nothing 'gainst Time's scythe can make defence" (12); "Time's fell hand," which can "deface" the proudest monuments, is out for the "spoil" of "beauty," and nothing of nature or human fabrication appears able to withstand the onset (64, 65). But it is scarcely an honourable foe. The youth is urged to "make war upon this bloody tyrant, Time" (16); its very hours are "tyrants" (5); "Time's tyranny" has no more respect for "sacred beauty" than—we may suggest—a ruthless conqueror desecrating the holy places of religion (115). It engages in a haphazard and general laying waste, indicated by the phrases "wastes of Time" (12) and "wasteful Time" (15); "Time's injurious hand" and "age's cruel knife" suggest the degree of its stony-hearted ruthlessness (63); "devouring Time" is as a beast with insatiable hunger, or, if at all human, is just criminal, and in destroying the loved one's beauty will be guilty of a "most heinous crime" (19). More, there is something intrinsically wrong, perverted, twisted, about Time's behaviour, as it "wastes" life with its "crooked knife" (100). As in *Troilus and Cressida*, Time is essentially underhand, mean, like a thief by night, the dial's "shady stealth" always witnessing his "thievish progress to eternity" (77). To sum up, Time is just "sluttish" (55); worse, he fools you (124, 116). It is a thoroughly degrading business.[2]

And it makes nonsense of our existence. It cannot be right. Time and Death are brutal allies. "Mortality" acts as in a "rage" (64, 65); it is both brutal and stupid, and its easy conquest of fine things appalling.

[1] For time in relation to birth see also *The Wheel of Fire*, XIII, 265, note. Time can also mean, as so often in the plays, what Tucker [*The Sonnets of Shakespeare*, ed. T. G. Tucker (Cambridge, 1924)] (202) calls "the vogue of the contemporary world." Such a use he notes in Sonnets 70, 76, 123, and 124. [*The Wheel of Fire* and other books unidentified by author in the text or footnotes are works written by G. Wilson Knight.—Ed.]

[2] These aspersions should be carefully compared with the long passage on Time as "Eater of youth" and spoiler of "antiquities" in *The Rape of Lucrece* (925–94).

The thought is an extension of Romeo's on his lady's conquest by "the lean, abhorred monster," Death:

> Thou art not conquer'd; beauty's ensign yet
> Is crimson in thy lips and in thy cheeks,
> And Death's pale flag is not advanced there.
> (*Romeo and Juliet,* v, iii, 94)

So in the Sonnets, the poet's love is called "much too fair" to be "Death's conquest" (6). Somehow he must be preserved

> Against the stormy gusts of winter's day
> And barren rage of Death's eternal cold.
> (13)

"That churl, Death," like Time, is a despicable thing (32). He must not be allowed to "brag" of this conquest (18). When the poet shall have fallen under his "fell arrest" (cp. *Hamlet,* "as this fell sergeant, Death, is strict in his arrest"; v, ii, 350), his love, which is his "spirit" and "better part," now housed in poetry, shall not remain "the coward conquest of a wretch's knife" (74).

It is all-important that the poet should somehow be able to say, "Death to me subscribes" (107). Somehow he must find a way and a reason to say it, since Time and Death are clearly usurpers. In contrast to our Rose, King, Crown, Sun and Gold impressions, these are ragamuffins, churls, deformed things, nonentities, usurping power—like Richard III, only worse—to which they have no proper right. This is the poet's insistence. He *wills* to conquer Time, insisting: "No, Time, thou shalt not boast that I do change." One suspects that, as the youth grows up, he *is* changing. Nevertheless, he continues, "Thy registers and thee I both defy," and concludes:

> This I do vow, and this shall ever be,
> I will be true, despite thy scythe and thee.
> (123)

That is, "I *will* be true despite Time's action on my love's appearance." The asseveration marks both a failing in love and a will towards an attainment greater than his failure. He can even assume authority greater than death's:

> But I forbid thee one most heinous crime:
> O carve not with thy hours my love's fair brow.
> (19)

Is this just rant? Or do we respond to anything deeper? Is there any point at all in talking like this? That is our problem. . . .

. . . [W]e shall now proceed to analyse the poet's various attempts to master the problem of time. Some of these we shall, whilst remaining conscious of the risks involved by the use of such terms, conclude to be "conventional," specious, and finally unsatisfying; some as adumbrating certain mysterious, poetic, powers which leave us in a state of half-satisfied expectation; and some, through their rhapsodic, dithyrambic, virtue, their inspirational quality, as all but directly stating a solution for which Shakespeare's own conceptual logic is inadequate. We shall study his apparent solutions under three main headings: (i) biological; (ii) artistic; and (iii) religious.

In the early sonnets the poet urges the young man to perpetuate his beauty by the begetting of a son in marriage. This is one very obvious answer to death on the biological plane, which we can all recognise. All Shakespeare's thought is rooted deep in nature, in the biological order, the thought-world of "common-sense," and from this he will not depart except under poetic pressure. It is accordingly right that his sequence should start with this solution, stated and reiterated from Sonnets 1 to 17.

But it is somehow unsatisfying. For one thing, we gather from the later sonnets that when the originally chaste youth is found mixing in what appears to be a gay society, the poet grows very angry. True, this is not marriage, but it might well lead to marriage, and certainly might produce a son. That may seem an irrelevant criticism, but the poet's affection was clearly both idealistic and possessive, and it is likely enough that he would have set so high a standard for the young man that any one individual applicant would be almost certain to fall below it. This is merest speculation, but, in terms of the account as we have it, it appears to be justified.

Poetically, the thought never really carries conviction. Continually the final couplet drives home the one point in such a way that we feel it to be a weak conclusion to a good poem. Here is an example:

> This were to be new made when thou art old,
> And see thy blood warm when thou feel'st it cold.
>
> (2)

And here another:

> Thy unus'd beauty must be tomb'd with thee,
> Which, used, lives th' executor to be.
>
> (4)

And a third:

> So thou, thyself outgoing in thy noon,
> Unlook'd on diest unless thou get a son.
>
> (7)

These, and there is one worse, are not good enough for their contexts, the last coming as an unworthy conclusion to the noble sonnet about the Sun on his "golden pilgrimage" from east to west.

But why, we may ask, does Shakespeare do this? The answer is: first, that it was a convention, to hand, and second, that it served his purpose. That it was a convention does not, by itself, detract one *iota* from its meaning or value; conventions exist to express meaning and value. Besides, when we hear that "breed" alone withstands "time" (12), we recognize that this is, as we have just seen, one, and the most obvious, answer to death, and, since answers to death are not so easy to come by, should certainly be surveyed. Nevertheless, it falls poetically flat, with a flatness witnessing the poet's instinct for a better answer, and we are forced to conclude that its primary office is to serve as an excuse for the main body of a poem *whose significance is not to be limited by its conclusion.* The poet uses it as a thought-mould into which to pour his exquisite apprehensions of the boy's loveliness, his horror at thought of its passing, and his *will* to save him from the worst "death" can "do"; to save him from "death's conquest" (6). The very form of the sonnet, with its final relaxation of tension, enables him to end with a glib couplet; the reader accepts the weakness as organic to the form, though it is far more than that, being really a fault intrinsic to the triviality of the thought. But the thoughts that build up to it are not trivial: here the building is nothing, the scaffolding everything.

Our next proposed solution, corresponding to Socrates' contrast of ideal as opposed to biological propagation in *The Symposium,* though it has much in common with the first, lands us in greater complexities. The last marriage sonnet concludes:

> But were some child of yours alive that time,
> You should live twice—in it, and in my rhyme.
>
> (17)

From then on, the thought of a literary immortality is reiterated. As before, we can hint an insincerity. When the prospects of successful immortalisation are improved by the praises of another poet of greater learning and repute, Shakespeare does not welcome him, any more than he welcomed the youth's first sexual engagements. Moreover, it is often supposed, as Butler supposes, that the publication of even his own sonnets would have caused Shakespeare suffering and it has generally been supposed that he had nothing to do with it. But we forget to ask: what, then, did he mean by all this emphasis on the immortalisation of the loved youth? If he sincerely desired that, you would expect him to have done his part to assure it. All that we know of Shakespeare suggests that he took little enough interest in literary immortality, for himself or anyone else.

As before, the poetic statements lack cogency. There is, indeed, an attraction about literary survival, and most writers know it; it is an extension of the parental instinct already discussed. But neither instinct enjoys more than a chance expectation of some moderately long period of time, and there is something poetically unsatisfactory about any too-great an emphasis on such speculations. True, when Pope in *The Rape of the Lock* promises a poetic immortality to Belinda's lock, we feel an engaging pleasure in recognising how the crippled poet, who must have felt deeply his severance from society, has indeed, up to our time, made Miss Fermor's lock a thing of splendour, though she is long forgotten. But is this of much use to her? Besides, Pope at least did his best to secure his work for posterity.

With Shakespeare, you certainly again feel like using the dangerous word "convention" in its more derogatory sense of a, to him, *dead* convention, though this will not cover the whole field of our enquiry. We find sonnets building up to a strong third quatrain with a drop, not only in tension, since this is expected, but in quality of thought too, in the last couplet. Examples are thickly sprinkled, occurring among many of the later pieces. This is typical:

> Yet do thy worst, old Time: despite thy wrong
> My love shall in my verse ever live young.
>
> (19)

The splendid sonnet containing

> Time doth transfix the flourish set on youth,
> And delves the parallels in beauty's brow

concludes:

> And yet to times in hope my verse shall stand
> Praising thy worth, despite his cruel hand.
>
> (60)

This is at once slack poetry and cold comfort. The even greater Sonnet 65 ends with a couplet only slightly more convincing.[3]

But there is more to say. When we are told that the poetry will make the youth "to be praised of ages yet to be" (101) so that his worth stands "even in the eyes of all posterity" (55), the conception of futurity as an infinite extension holds, in itself, a certain grandeur despite the dubious quality of the underlying thought. When the underlying thought itself is weighty, as with the "olives of endless age" of the na-

---

[3] In discussion of these weak couplets, Edward Hubler [*The Sense of Shakespeare's Sonnets* (Princeton, 1952)] (25–6) concludes that they are "poetically, but not intellectually, false"; that the weakness has nothing to do with what the couplet "says." My own finding is different, but I hope that the two arguments will be compared. Mark van Doren (*Shakespeare*, 7–10) finds a similar weakness in the couplets of *Venus and Adonis* and *The Rape of Lucrece*.

tional Sonnet (107), there is no doubt of it, though even here the logic may have to be forgotten. But, though the poet had no good reason to expect an everlasting peace, the phrase reverberates; and in the reverberation, the echoing response in our minds, lies its real meaning. . . .

Within "poetic time" the youth is felt to be immortal, present equally in antiquity and for posterity. But much depends on the poetry. What is its relation to the real thing? The poet knows well that getting a son is a more effective way of self-perpetuation than "barren rhyme" (16); that the youth's "eyes" hold more life than "both" his admiring poets can possibly devise (83); and that in the last resort he can only himself avoid falsification by repeating "you alone are you" and "you are you" (84), like Antony in his cups describing the crocodile (*Antony and Cleopatra,* II, vii, 47–57; *The Imperial Theme,* VII, 232). Poetry appears to be the only means of possessing the reality in temporal terms and yet written poetry is surely inadequate, and the inadequacy is driven home in two final literary-immortality couplets promising in one that the boy will remain "green" in these "black lines" (63), and in the other showing a specific doubt:

> O none, unless this miracle have might,
> That in black ink my love may still shine bright.
>
> (65)

In both the word "black" deliberately underlines an important contrast. It is a term natural to a poet who was careless of, and perhaps scorned, publication. And yet he is certainly aware of some *miraculous* possibility. The truth is, that there is indeed a poetic "miracle," but it is not just a matter of publication and perpetuity. Rather the poet knows that through his poetry, or the poetic consciousness, he establishes, or focusses, a supernal reality, or truth, what we may call a "poetic dimension," that cannot otherwise be attained; and of this the written poetry ("black ink"), though it be indeed necessary, is subsidiary, the carrot to the donkey, but not the journey's purpose. . . .

Shakespeare's meaning outdistances his concepts. He keeps close to actual experience and normal, even platitudinous, thought-moulds. He relies comparatively little on metaphysical paradox, and not at all on any esoteric symbolism. In so far as an explicit transcendence is spoken of, it is done through the orthodox religious conception of "doom," or Doomsday. The term held a precision and detonation far in excess of our abstract term "eternity"; it was known as a conclusion to time, as in *Macbeth* (IV, i, 117); but, though closely related to arithmetical time, it had, as may be seen from its use in a certain fine passage of *2 Henry VI* (V, ii, 40–5), the strongest emotional overtones. People believed in it, or thought that they did, without question, but it was also as mysterious as could be.

It appears in the Sonnets. The youth, through poetry, shall be known to "all posterity, that wear this world out to the ending Doom" (55). Comparing love's steadfastness with Time, the poet assures himself that:

> Love alters not with his brief hours and weeks
> But bears it out even to the edge of Doom.
>   (116)

A more than personal life-span is included: love lasts till Doomsday. Notice, too, how time itself ("hours and weeks") is, as a numerical sequence, trivial ("brief")—a thought found elsewhere in contrast of love's strength with "short-number'd hours" (124)—in comparison with the greater reality, or dimension, shadowed by "doom," or, as we should say, though with less impact, "eternity." It is, of course, difficult to respond simultaneously to such a long-time passage as "olives of endless age" in Sonnet 107, where the word "doom" is actually used as a *confining* term, and to the time-annihilating Doomsday. But, though rationally incompatible, they are both used as adversaries to time as we know it: a greater reality is adumbrated in contrast to time's triviality.

The poet plays every variation known to him on time and its antagonists. Time may be ruthless and villainous, but it may also hold an aura of almost religious grandeur and mystery, as aeons, past or future, swing into our view, with thoughts of "antiquity," "posterity" (55), and "the prophetic soul of the wide world dreaming on things to come" (107). The use of "soul" brings in religious associations; and such associations are even stronger in "doom," the great act of God annihilating Time. Rival and incompatible conceptions jostle each other, but that matters little, since the reality is behind, and indefinable.

The exact interrelation of our various attempts may be best seen from noticing the recurring and highly significant thought of loss and gain as mutually dependent on each other, as when we are told that "Time that gave doth now his gift confound" (60). The boy's beauty, destroyed, or hidden, by Time, is itself "Time's best jewel" (65). The gain and loss may be conceived as all but simultaneous, as aspects of a single activity. As we have seen, the same hours which "did frame" the boy work to "unfair" that "which fairly doth excell" (5). These paradoxes suggest a universal law. There is gain as well as loss. That the sun should be daily "new and old" (76) is obvious enough, but we have a more interesting thought concerning the continual contests of ocean and land, "increasing store with loss and loss with store" (64). Not only is all life "consum'd with that which it was nourish'd by" (73): we are almost tempted to put it the other way round, and the poet sometimes does so. This is done in terms of both (i) marriage-advice and (ii) literary-immortality. In the first, we have, "As fast as thou shalt wane, so fast thou grow'st" (11); that is, by getting a son. In the second we find, "As he takes from you, I engraft you new" (15); that is, in verse. Observe the nature-metaphors; a natural process is hinted; and that each mechanism should use this same thought suggests an underlying universal below the semi-conventional and often trite statements. We are accordingly not surprised to find the paradox once firmly stated in religious terms in a famous and valuable sonnet. The poet contrasts his "soul" with his "sinful earth" (cp. the elemental sonnets, 44, 45, and 74), and the one is said to grow as the other wanes:

> Then, soul, live thou upon thy servant's loss,
> And let that pine to aggravate thy store:
> Buy terms divine in selling hours of dross;
> Within be fed, without be rich no more:
>> So shalt thou feed on Death, that feeds on men,
>> And Death once dead, there's no more dying then.
>> (146)

Time ("hours") is sold in exchange for the "terms divine," but "fed" preserves contact with the natural order; it is a natural law.

Here we have a clear statement of what is elsewhere shadowy. It repeats, and interprets for us, our other thoughts on the universal principle of interaction and balance, loss and gain. These, and we shall later on observe yet another example, we have listed in relation to the temporal process, as a natural phenomenon; in terms of the marriage, biological, process; and in the literary-immortality thought-pattern. Clearly, we are to feel it as a universal principle of which all these are aspects, and it is the principle that matters. Here, in our religious sonnet, the great thing is firmly said, because an adequate thought-mould, in terms of a religious tradition, is being used.

But the precision is only got by once again relying on a "convention," or "tradition," and by the use of such, in our present context, question-begging terms as "soul," "divine," "within." On these the poet normally refuses, as Donne does not, to place any final emphasis. He prefers to use more human implements. The marriage-mechanism is, it is true, soon thrown over, and never re-introduced. But it is not so with the poetic-immortality thought-pattern: this he will not let rest. He keeps worrying at it. Our religious pieces at least show that the truth at which he is driving has strong religious affinities; it is a truth most easily, if not quite satisfactorily, expressed in terms of religious phraseology.

Such terms, for Shakespeare, had lost authority. They were somehow believed in, and yet not all-sufficient. To his more humanistic imagination, romantic love and beauty were not honoured, as he wished to honour them, by the orthodox tradition. Failing a complete submission to a religious dogmatism as precise and as firmly accepted by the whole community as that of the medieval church, this was bound to happen;

and not only with themes of love and beauty. The poet's instinct tells him that the wanted key is somehow in his own poetry: so poetic thought-patterns, images, symbols, must be found. . . .

We should explain it all—and yet how can a word be an explanation? —by use of the word "eternal." Shakespeare uses the word too, with various shades of meaning, sad and happy. We have the "barren rage of Death's eternal cold" (13); "thy eternal summer shall not fade" and the "eternal lines" of poetry's perpetuating (18); "eternal numbers" (38); "brass eternal" (64); "Time's thievish progress to eternity" (77); "eternal love" (108), and the "great bases" laid "for eternity" recently quoted (125). There is, too, a strange sonnet in which the poet apologises for having given away a gift, urging that a keepsake is unneeded since his friend's memory is already graven on his mind "beyond all date, even to eternity"; or at least, he adds, with a typical return to realism, so long as "brain" and "heart" last in "nature" (122). Here eternity probably means "Doomsday," so that the line means "beyond time up to the day of judgment," when "time" will be destroyed. However, most of our eternity-references appear to mean roughly what they would mean today. They suggest a state-of-being, or dimension, which can be thought of variously as infinite time or as timelessness. We may think of vertical time in the eternal dimension, or of time circling back on itself, recalling our antiquity passages. Anything will do, provided that it is not subject to ending. Once, after apologising for a temporary disloyalty, the poet reasserts his love with: "Now all is done, have what shall have no end" (110). The sonnets are indeed so thickly impregnated with this battering insistence that the insistence alone goes far towards establishing a generalised statement.

The last sonnet of the main series to the Fair Youth is a farewell in twelve lines, in which many past themes are interwoven. It runs:

> O thou, my lovely boy, who in thy power
> Dost hold Time's fickle glass his fickle hour;
> Who has by waning grown, and therein show'st
> Thy lovers withering as thy sweet self grow'st;
> If Nature, sovereign mistress over wrack,
> As thou goest onwards, still will pluck thee back,
> She keeps thee to this purpose, that her skill
> May Time disgrace, and wretched minutes kill.
> Yet fear her, O thou minion of her pleasure!
> She may detain, but not still keep, her treasure:
> Her audit, though delay'd, answered must be,
> And her quietus is to render thee.
>
> (126)

The poet writes without bitterness, admitting that the boy must grow up, whatever the loss ("waning"). There is the give-and-take process at work which we have already met in various forms, and somehow the "sweet self," the eternal self or soul as we may call it, is *within the growing*. Nature, always at work recreating what is dissolving, is herself in sovereign control over any destruction within her own domain. We have already found nature and time responsible for the making of the thing which they appear to kill. Here elucidation is gained by contrasting nature as responsible for the whole with time as destroyer. The youth must go onward in time, but nature continually ("still") preserves him, holding him "back," as in "Or what strong hand can hold his swift foot back" (65). Nature's hand, the "great creating Nature" of *The Winter's Tale* (iv, iii, 88), *is* strong enough, up to a point. But she cannot do it for ever. She must finally "render" him up, to death.

The sonnet comes near to establishing nature as itself a safeguard controlling destruction. We are near to reading into it the significance we have a right to find in the Witch's

> Though his bark cannot be lost
> Yet it shall be tempest-toss'd

in *Macbeth* (i, iii, 24). We cannot quite do so. But the words "sovereign mistress over wrack" and "may time disgrace," which are true enough of nature if a wide view be taken, remain too powerful for our paraphrase; "quietus," though a legal term, also suggests peace; and "render" surely indicates "render up safe." If nature be greater and more good than time, may there not also be some power greater and more good than nature? If so, and perhaps only if so, the use of "render" is felicitous.

In reading the Sonnets we are continually treading the brink of Abt Vogler's "There shall never be one lost good" in Browning's remarkable poem. Shakespeare does not quite say that, either because the thought was in his day impossible, or because he considered that it was not worth saying. But it must be remembered that for these shattering assurances Browning chose a musician improvising on the organ. They are *what the musician knew whilst living in the music*. Such was the Dinoysian experience celebrated by Nietzsche throughout *The Birth of Tragedy*, whereby, through music, your inmost self, to be distinguished from the superficial "ego," your deepest *I am*, sounds from "the abyss of being" and becomes one with the "Primordial Being" in wisdom and power (*The Birth of Tragedy*; v; xvii). You then *know*, subjectively, what cannot be proved, or known, or even thought, through the objective intelligence. Such a subjective wisdom is accorded by Nietzsche to the impassioned lyrist, the dithyrambist; and to reach any final judgment as to what the Sonnets, as poetry, mean, we must give exact attention to their more impassioned, emotionally authoritative, dithyrambic, moments; when, to borrow a metaphor from Shelley's *Defence of Poetry*,

the poetry becomes "a sword of lightning" which "consumes the scab-
bard that would contain it."

We must therefore not remain content with Apollonian logic, or even
with the Apollonian image; we must feel the kinetic, energic, Dionysian
movement; the heave of its ocean, its swell and crests. In many of the
Sonnets the power tends to rise at the second or third quatrain, and falls
at the conclusion. In this they point directly to his dramatic technique,
where every long speech advances in waves, two or three; flowers,
burgeons out, from within, like a fountain. Power increases; but the
conclusion is quiet. It is the same with his wider structures: his plays
gather momentum and power, taking a new lease of life in the third act,
as though a surface was burst open to reveal imaginative splendour; and
here, too, there is a quiet conclusion, a fall to commentary and ritual.
The same is true of Shakespeare's work as a whole, from the Histories
and the Romantic Comedies, to the violence of the Tragedies, the wonder of the Final Plays, and the ritualistic conclusion in *Henry VIII*. In
matters small and vast alike, this is the typifying Shakespearian form;
and we have it already within the Sonnets.

The third quatrain of the sonnet "Shall I compare thee to a summer's
day?" rises to:

> But thy eternal summer shall not fade,
> Nor lose possession of that fair thou ow'st,
> Nor shall Death brag thou wander'st in his shade . . .
>
> (18)

This crests and breaks as a wave of assurance, with a sense of victory
for which the opening lines had scarcely prepared us. Next we have:

> When in eternal lines to time thou grow'st.
>
> (18)

Starting by saying something large, the poet ends by saying something
small: the great claim "eternal" is subdued beneath "time," the thought
directly contradicting the definition of Time in *The Rape of Lucrece*
(967) as "thou ceaseless lackey to eternity." The poetry promises, in a
way *is*, eternity, as again in the line "eternal numbers to outlive long
date" (38), since it is the language of the eternal dimension; but the
poet has only actually said that it offers a considerable time-period
of memory. The conclusion

> So long as men can breathe or eyes can see,
> So long lives this, and this gives life to thee
>
> (18)

is only worthy of the earlier assurance in so far as we allow "breathe,"
"eyes," "lives" and "life" to carry such meanings that we are left with

the thought that poetry actually gives, and not merely records, life; and it needs more than *written* poetry to do that.

The crest may come in the second quatrain, as with the daring alliteration and conquering impact of:

> Then, in the blazon of sweet beauty's best,
> Of hand, of foot, of lip, of eye, of brow,
> I see their antique pen would have express'd
> Even such a beauty as you master now.
>
> (106)

Here the conquest is of past time; the excellence is so great that all past excellences are offered in vassalage to it; it is lord of antiquity as well as of the future. This is a fine example of the strong physical adoration lying at the heart of the poet's meanings. It is also a fine example of cresting, rising, movement. It is only in so far as we respond to these victorious, compelling, dithyrambic, assurances, or rather to the victori-ous*ness* and rhetorical compulsions *of* these assurances, that the greater meanings break through, the meaning I will not say *of*, but resounding *within*, such pieces as:

> Love's not Time's fool, though rosy lips and cheeks
> Within his bending sickle's compass come;
> Love alters not with his brief hours and weeks
> But bears it out even to the edge of Doom.
>
> (116)

Beauty fades; love, and he *wants* to say beauty too, does not. As we have observed, time here is "brief," a nothing, to the conjured vastness of "doom."

Sometimes a single word assumes a largeness of thought that is not otherwise explicit, as when, in one of our marriage-advice pieces, we start:

> But wherefore do not you a mightier way
> Make war upon this bloody tyrant, Time?
>
> (16)

"Mightier" is too strong for its context. The same is true of "pace" in this, one of the greatest sonnets of all, powerful though the context itself be:

> Not marble, nor the gilded monuments
> Of princes, shall outlive this powerful rhyme;
> But you shall shine more bright in these contents
> Than unswept stone, besmear'd with sluttish time.
> When wasteful war shall statues overturn,
> And broils root out the work of masonry,
> Nor Mars his sword nor war's quick fire shall burn

> The living record of your memory.
> 'Gainst death and all-oblivious enmity
> Shall you pace forth; your praise shall still find room
> Even in the eyes of all posterity
> That wear this world out to the ending doom.
> So, till the judgment that yourself arise,
> You live in this, and dwell in lovers' eyes.
>
> (55)

See how clear is the thought in the final couplet: the young man's immortality is not questioned. He will rise, presumably in good repair, at the day of judgment. But if so, what is all the fuss about? What does it matter whether he be known to readers of poetry during the few intervening centuries?

Clearly, there is more in the sonnet than this. It is throughout filled to overflowing with the elixir, the ecstasy, the dithyrambic certainties. Observe that the main emphasis is on, not love, but the powers of poetry. We have already seen how poetry is in the Sonnets felt as a medium for supernal intuitions. Here every image piles up to suggest that the poetry enjoys an authority, or exists from a dimension, to which all temporal fabrications and engagements are as nothing; and the weightiest and most serious are chosen for the purpose. This poetic authority creates a "living record." The phrase recalls "the living God" of the Gospels and St. Paul; like that god, it is conqueror over death. Read so, there need be no worry about the incompatibility introduced by "doom" and "judgment" day, since a context has been generated of sufficient power to absorb them, with all their awful associations, into the main assertion. The two ways of eternal understanding, poetry and religion, are happily balanced in our final juxtaposition of "judgment" and "lovers' eyes."

The truth present within the noble music of this sonnet is underlined by the simple word "pace":

> 'Gainst death and all-oblivious enmity
> Shall you *pace* forth . . .

Tucker's comment is: "Keep steadily on; but 'forth' implies conspicuousness before the world's eyes." But it also, I think, means, "Come forward," "come out of obscurity to be seen" as in the Friar's

> Romeo, come forth! Come forth, thou fearful man!

in *Romeo and Juliet* (III, iii, 1). "Pace" suggests a great numinous presence, recalling, once again, Donne's "great Prince," or Wordsworth's

> . . . huge and mighty forms, that do not live
> Like living men

in *The Prelude* (i, 398). Such was the presence hinted by our conception of the youth as an eternal archetype; it is both ghostly and royal, like the Ghost in *Hamlet*, but without his sepulchral and purgatorial connotations. It moves with authority. It is something, or somebody, to which "death" clearly "subscribes" (107).

This is, indeed, an intuition which Shakespeare laboured to possess or define in drama after drama. It is in the great speeches of eternal recognition in *Hamlet, Macbeth, King Lear, Timon of Athens,* and *The Tempest* (v, ii, 232–8; v, v, 19–28; v, iii, 8–19; v, i, 191–3, 219–24; iv, i, 151–8). It is in Romeo's dream of love beyond death:

> I dreamt my lady came and found me dead—
> Strange dream, that gives a dead man leave to think—
> And breath'd such life with kisses in my lips,
> That I reviv'd, and was an emperor.
> > (*Romeo and Juliet*, v, i, 6)

It is in Cleopatra's "I dream'd there was an Emperor Antony . . ." (*Antony and Cleopatra*, v, ii, 76); in Pericles' vision of Marina as "a palace for the crown'd Truth to dwell in" (v, i, 123), and

> Like Patience gazing on kings' graves and smiling
> Extremity out of act.
> > (*Pericles*, v, i, 140)

It is finally dramatised in the awakening of Hermione's statue in *The Winter's Tale*.

We cannot argue that Shakespeare ought to have expressed it more clearly, more rationally. What rationality is there in the dogma of the resurrection of the body? Or in Nietzsche's doctrine of eternal recurrence? What religion, what philosophy, what poetic symbols, ever have made immortality a simple thing? But again, what religion of highest worth, what philosophy of weight, what poet of calibre, have not levelled all their powers against Death? To take an example from an at-first-sight very different poet, Dante:

> The celestial love, that spurns
> All envying in its bounty, in itself
> With such effulgence blazeth, as sends forth
> All beauteous things eternal. What distils
> Immediate thence, no end of being knows;
> Bearing its seal immutably impressed.
> Whatever thence immediate falls, is free,
> Free wholly, uncontrollable by power
> Of each thing new . . .
> > (*Paradiso*, trans. Cary, vii, 60)

This is, too, what Shakespeare is saying. But the saying of it is, of course, in itself of slight value. What is wanted is its realisation. At the greatest moments of the Sonnets the realisation, both emotional and perceptual, is superb. Shakespeare's peculiar importance lies in his reluctance to part with flesh and blood, with actual dramatic experience, with the thing seen and known. He keeps as close as he can to nature, and to common-sense, though he does not stop there. We may even hazard the thought that his very reliance on conventional thought-moulds is an aspect of his strength: you cannot easily separate the one from the other.

J. W. LEVER

The Poet in Absence

THE SONNETS taken into this group comprise a number of variations on the theme of the Poet's absence from his Friend. The subject-matter is traditional—conceits on the eyes and heart, laments at separation, accounts of the sleeplessness or troubled dreams of the beloved. Shakespeare leaned far more heavily on contemporary models than in the Marriage group and signs of the "pupil pen" are to be seen in overlaboured conceits, over-rigid rhetorical patterns, and an uneven style. But although some of these poems have a conventional base, it would be wrong to dismiss them summarily. Imitation soon paves the way to self-expression and a discovery of new potentialities; well-worn conceits on absence become instruments for investigating the workings of poetic thought, its power to transcend space, its visionary quality; so that in relation to the Poet's part in the sequence the function of this group is comparable with that of the marriage sonnets on the Friend, and almost as serious a work of exploration.

XXIV, XLVI, and XLVII form a trio of sonnets based on aspects of the eyes–heart conceit. The first of these, "Mine eyes hath played the painter," is perhaps the most pointlessly elaborated sonnet that Shakespeare wrote. It was a commonplace of romance that Love entered through the eyes and penetrated to the heart. Renaissance fancy, probably expressed most gracefully by Ronsard,[1] developed the conceit, with love engraving upon the heart the lady's image. The engraving became for Constable a portrait, with the eyes as windows through which it could be seen:

From *The Elizabethan Love Sonnet* by J. W. Lever (London, 1956). Reprinted by permission of Methuen & Company, Ltd.

[1]   *Il ne falloit, Maistresse, autres tablettes*
            Pour vous graver, que celles de mon cœur,
            Où de sa main Amour nostre vainqueur
            Vous a gravée, et vos graces parfaites. (*Amours Diverses*, IV)
The analogue was first pointed out by David Klein, *Sewanee Review* (1905), XIII, p. 460f.

Thine eye, the glass where I behold my heart;
Mine eye, the window through the which thine eye
May see my heart, and there thyself espy
In bloody colours, how thou painted art.[2]

Shakespeare, while leaving out the personification of Love, produced a complete painter's shop, with the Friend's portrait hanging in the Poet's bosom, his body as the frame, and the Friend's eyes for shop-windows "where-through the sun Delights to peep." For a special touch of modernist complexity, the portrait was "perspective"—a fashionable device of sixteenth-century painting, whereby the likeness could only be discerned when the picture was viewed from a particular angle.[3] For this painting, however, "through the painter must you see his skill"; the image of the Friend in the Poet's heart could only be viewed by the Friend himself, looking into and through the Poet's eyes. In this sense, the Friend's eyes became the windows to the Poet's bosom; and the portrait enjoyed a privacy unfortunately denied to that of Giles Fletcher's Licia.[4] Ingenious enough to make Berowne's coach conceit pedestrian, the sonnet's one hint of seriousness lay in the final couplet:

Yet eyes this cunning want to grace their art,
They draw but what they see, know not the heart.

XLVI ("Mine eye and heart are at a mortal war") takes up an equally time-honoured subject, the dispute of eyes and heart; but the treatment already begins to show signs of independence. Following up the last lines of XXIV, the sonnet is concerned with the difference between outer form and inner reality. To whom does the "portrait" of the Friend truly belong—eyes or heart? There is litigation to decide the title; but the

---

2 *Diana* (1592), i. 9.
3 See Kathleen Tillotson's note to Drayton's *Mortimeriados,* 2332–8 (*The Works of Michael Drayton,* ed. Hebel, 1941, v, p. 43), which cites another reference to the "perspective" picture in *Twelfth Night,* v. i. 227–8:

One face, one voice, one habit, and two persons
A natural perspective, that is, and is not.

Mrs. Tillotson also refers to "the well-known portrait of Edward VI in the National Portrait Gallery . . . where the picture seems distorted until looked at from one particular point."
4

My love amaz'd did blush her selfe to see,
Pictur'd by arte, all naked as she was:
How could the Painter knowe so much by me,
Or Art effect, what he hath brought to passe?
It is not like, he naked me hath seene,
Or stoode so nigh, for to observe so much,
No, sweete, his eyes so nere have never bene,
Nor could his handes, by art have cunning such:
I showed my heart, wherein you printed were,
You, naked you, as here you painted are,
In that (My Love) your picture I must weare,
And show't to all, unlesse you have more care:
Then take my heart, and place it with your owne,
So shall you naked never more be knowne. (*Licia,* VI)

jury is packed with thoughts, all "tenants to the heart," and the court's decision is biased:

> As thus, mine eye's due is thine outward part,
> And my heart's right, thine inward love of heart.

This law-suit conceit was probably based upon *Astrophel and Stella* LII, where the poet acting as judge awarded Stella's soul to Virtue and her body to himself and Love. Shakespeare avoided abstract categories, and substituted appearance, seen by the "clear" eyes, and reality, known by the "dear" heart, for Sidney's body-soul antithesis.[5] The conceit was equally witty, and served similarly to advance the poet's understanding of himself, derived not from ideal principles but from observation and intuition. XLVII ("Betwixt mine eye and heart a league is took") adds a sequel, with eyes and heart now reconciled and doing good turns to each other. Sometimes the eye feasts upon the Friend's picture and invites the heart as his guest; sometimes the heart calls the eye to share his thoughts of love. Instead of the fierce inner conflicts of both faculties described in the Mistress series, here there is co-operation and goodwill. This is simpler and more pleasing than the previous conceits, and it will be noticed that instead of the fanciful picture on the heart's "table," a real portrait is indicated. Serious investigation of the Poet's thoughts may now develop unhindered by the need for mere cleverness, and the gain is to be seen in the last six lines of the sonnet, with their quiet beauty of diction and their flexible verse structure:

> So either by thy picture or my love,
> Thyself away art present still with me;
> For thou no further than my thoughts canst move,
> And I am still with them, and they with thee;
> > Or if they sleep, thy picture in my sight
> > Awakes my heart to heart's and eye's delight.

Here the true subject of the group is for the first time enunciated: the power of poetic thought to overcome space, and its visionary character. The sonnets that follow present these questions in terms of particular situations.

L ("How heavy do I journey on the way") opens with a description of the Poet on horseback riding away from the Friend. He plays with the notion that his heavy heart weighs upon the beast, which "plods dully on" and merely groans in response to the spur. The precedent for this conceit was in *Astrophel and Stella* XLIX:

---

[5] The subtle shift of emphasis indicates clearly an absence of physical homosexuality in the friendship. This is confirmed rather than contradicted by sonnet XX, which declares that nature has "defeated" the Poet in making the Friend a man—i.e. *had* the Friend been a woman, the Poet's love would have been sexual.

> I on my horse, and Love on me, doth trie
> Our horsmanships . . .

Sidney's comparison was elaborated on symbolical lines, with his thoughts as the reins, reverence as the bit, will as the whip, and so on. The method was a survival of the image-forming process in allegory, which expands a simile in all directions to accord with a preconceived pattern of experience. Shakespeare's treatment correspondingly typified the experiential mode of thought that results in metaphor. He sought to avoid personified abstractions; instead, a couple of actualities were noted: slow horse and sad rider. The beast's sympathetic "instinct," and its groan that seemed to utter the Poet's own grief, suggested an underlying resemblance, but so far the two figures remained distinct. Then in LI ("Thus can my love excuse the slow offence") they suddenly fused to precipitate a new image. Anticipating a joyous return the Poet saw his desire as a Pegasus whose spirited neighing contrasted with the dull groan of the actual horse on the outward journey:

> Then can no horse with my desire keep pace,
> Therefore desire, of perfect'st love being made,
> Shall neigh, no dull flesh, in his fiery race;

This winged steed of desire was a veritable child of the imagination, neither horse nor thought, but an originally created compound of the two.

The process of self-examination continues without interruption in XLIV–XLV. Here the relationship between horse and man is located within the Poet's own being. It is his own "dull flesh," his own "fiery race" of desire, that these sonnets now contemplate. If the dull substance of his flesh were thought, then space would no longer exist—

> For nimble thought can jump both sea and land
> As soon as think the place where he would be.

Both thought and desire now correspond to the magic horse traversing sea and land with instantaneous leaps, while flesh remains earth-bound. The terms "dull" for flesh and "fiery" for desire, with air-borne thought, suggest the elements, while the Poet's tears complete the scheme, with the fourth or watery element. While desire and thought, composed of fire and air, surmount physical distance and rejoin the Friend, the Poet remains with his flesh and tears, the heavy elements of earth and water, which weigh him down with sadness and bring him almost to death. To modern readers this may seem like a return to mere ingenuity; we forget that the correspondences of humours and elements were considered authentic science, so that the train of thought in XLIV–XLV was clearly distinguished from the pure exercise of fancy that produced Love the horseman or the portrait painted on the heart.

But orthodox science, however reputable, was still not as convincing as personal discovery, and self-examination only came to a satisfactory end in the four sonnets xxvii, xxviii, xliii, and lxi, on the Poet's thoughts at night. What they reveal had already been foreshadowed in the couplet of xlvii:

> Or if they sleep, thy picture in my sight
> Awakes my heart to heart's and eye's delight.

Now the original concept is modified—it is thoughts that portray the Friend when the picture, through darkness, is no longer visible to the eye. In xxvii ("Weary with toil") the Poet, fatigued after his travels, hastens to bed. But instead of true rest, a journey of the mind begins. His thoughts make "a zealous pilgrimage" to the Friend, and he lies awake, staring into the dark. In this condition, his "soul's imaginary sight"

> Presents thy shadow to my sightless view,
> Which, like a jewel hung in ghastly night,
> Makes black night beauteous and her old face new.

There is a suggestion, as Malone noticed, of Romeo's first glimpse of Juliet at the ball of the Capulets—

> It seems she hangs upon the cheek of night
> Like a rich jewel in an Ethiop's ear.
> (*Romeo and Juliet*, i. v. 49–50)

But the fanciful details, with their "fixities and definites," have fallen away before "imaginary sight," which is not governed by simple association or unconscious memory. What distinguishes this vision from a hundred others in romance literature is that it is the projection of an alert mind and heightened sensibility. Sidney's dream of Stella had been the effect of sleep and subconscious desire;[6] Spenser's description of his lady's bosom had been given the properties of a dream;[7] as far back as the Troubadours the nocturnal vision had served to express the poignancy of desire uninhibited by waking thoughts.[8] Shakespeare's Poet alone is concerned with the workings of the imagination, its transcending of sense-perception, its power to generate an inner light.

---

[6] Cf.   This night, while sleepe begins with heavy wings
To hatch mine eyes, and that unbitted thought
Doth fall to stray . . . (*Astrophel and Stella*, xxxviii)

[7] *Amoretti*, lxxvi–lxxvii.

[8] Compare in this respect the verse epistle of Folquet de Romans to his lady—a typical expression of Troubadour sentiment—*Que la nueit, quan soi endurmiz*. H. J. Chaytor translated the passage: "For at night when I am asleep, my spirit goes forth to you, lady; then such happiness is mine that when I wake and memory returns, I scarce believe my eyes . . . for I would like to sleep ever so that I might hold you in my dreams" (*The Troubadours and England*, 1923).

In comparison with this crucial sonnet, xxviii and xliii show a slackening of tension. "How can I then return in happy plight" continues the lament on absence along conventional lines, with Day and Night personified as rival tyrants "shaking hands" to afflict the Poet, and some decorative panegyrics comparing the Friend with sun and stars, which fall far below the metaphorical seriousness of the Marriage group. "When most I wink" likewise adds nothing to the inner development of the series, with its Arcadian play on the simple juxtapositions day–night, bright–dark, light–shade. The compelling vision of xxvii has degenerated into a dream, as it was for other poets, and one so indistinct that no genuine image arises. But lxi ("Is it thy will thy image should keep open") returns to the original experience. Here the Friend's "shadow" takes on a volition of its own, less agreeable for the beholder: it seems to gaze back at the Poet; regarding him with mockery; prying into his idle hours and secret shames. For eight lines the sonnet conjectures that the Friend's will, impelled by jealousy, has overcome the barriers of space by a mental telepathy analogous to the Pegasus leaps of the Poet's thoughts. Then, in the third quatrain, the possibility is dismissed.

> Oh no! thy love, though much, is not so great:
> It is my love that keeps mine eye awake;
> Mine own true love that doth my rest defeat,
> To play the watchman ever for thy sake.

This rational interpretation, which replaces the former Chapman-like toyings with the occult, is strikingly bold. The Poet's own sense of guilt, his personality divided between an everyday self and a sublimated lover's self, have projected the menacing quality of the vision. And a further consideration enters into the couplet:

> For thee watch I whilst thou dost wake elsewhere,
> From me far off, with others all too near.

The Poet's higher self must watch, not only over his own baser nature, but also over the Friend, who may at that moment be "waking" in a double sense: keeping wakes with rival companions, or perhaps waking in his bed "all too near" to "others" not specifically named. If there is a quality of guilt in the Poet, there is also a quality of corruptibility in the Friend.

Other sonnets may well belong to the group, but I have preferred to mention only those most closely linked. There is a clear unity of development from the first heart-and-eyes conceit of xxiv, with its superfluous cleverness, to the psychological penetration of this last sonnet. The fanciful picture on the heart becomes first a real portrait, then a vision of the inner eye. The debate between eyes and heart becomes a study of the processes of thought, formulated in terms of contemporary science, and followed by an intuitive revelation of the soul's imaginary sight. In effect, this group complements the previous one[9]: what time signifies to the beauty and truth of the Friend, space signifies to the eyes and heart of the Poet, and both antinomies await their resolution through the functioning of the Poet's imagination, inspired by his love. But in the last sonnet there are suggestions of latent guilt and corruptibility which, though partly accounted for by the Mistress series, will call for full investigation in the coming groups before this resolution can be brought about.

The Poet and His Rivals

Gaunt.	Though Richard my life's counsel would not hear,
	My death's sad tale may yet undeaf his ear.
York.	No; it is stopp'd with other flattering sounds,
	As praises of his state: then there are fond
	Lascivious metres, to whose venom sound
	The open ear of youth doth always listen:
	Report of fashions in proud Italy,
	Whose manners still our tardy apish nation
	Limps after in base imitation.

(Richard II, II. i. 15–23)

Richard's character vividly calls to mind the fashionable young nobleman of Shakespeare's time, with his Italianate manners and his taste in verse for Ovidian erotics. The theme of ornament which underlay *The Merchant of Venice* is transposed in *Richard II* from romance of politics and social conduct, with disastrous results for the brilliant *roi fainéant*. A similar transposition of theme from sexual to social faults takes place in the sonnets of the present group, whose core is LXXVIII–LXXX and LXXXII–LXXXVI, according to the reasonably coherent Quarto numbering. Already in the previous group[10] casual mention had been made of

> That tongue that tells the story of thy days,
> Making lascivious comments on thy sport . . . (XCV)

[9] [I.e., the first nineteen sonnets, discussed by Lever in the preceding section of his book.—Ed.]

[10] [I.e., the sonnets discussed by Lever in the preceding section of his book under the heading "The Friend's Fault." He writes, "The sonnets in which the Friend's sensuality is suspected but denied, admitted but excused, and finally accepted as one more contradiction in a bewildering universe, are spread through the main body of the collection from XXXIII to XCVI" (p. 209).—Ed.]

Now this is expanded into a full consideration of the writers whose poems or dedications flatter the Friend. A literary parallel may be drawn between the situation in *Richard II* where Gaunt, representing the old order, is supplanted by modish young courtiers, and the situation in this group of sonnets where the Poet is displaced by the modernists of the fifteen-nineties.

The form of these sonnets is essentially rhetorical, and the dominant technique is irony. While the ostensible tone remains courtly and deferential throughout, again and again the imagery and diction carry double meanings or have ambiguous implications. These are part of the conscious intention, and the reader may legitimately set out to detect their presence without much fear of importing irrelevancies.

In LXXVIII ("So oft have I invoked thee for my Muse") the Poet, while identifying his Muse with the Friend, points out that now every "alien pen" has got his "use," and "disperses" poetry under this inspiration. The term *alien* suggests not merely another writer, but an outsider who has no birth-right to such aid; while the Poet's "use," besides the use of his pen, carries an implication of interest or gain. Other writers, that is, have both stolen the Poet's occupation and appropriated the Poet's share of reward; while in *dispersing* their poetry they are not only publishing it but at the same time dissipating its value. They are, in fact, squandering the benefit accruing to them from their intimacy with the Friend—an intimacy which by right belongs to the Poet. The mention of "alien pens" leads by a common Shakespearean association to the image of a bird in flight:[11]

> Thine eyes, that taught the dumb on high to sing,
> And heavy ignorance aloft to fly,
> Have added feathers to the learned's wing,
> And given grace a double majesty.

Now in XXIX ("When in disgrace with fortune"), the Poet's own powers had been described by a different bird image. While "desiring this man's art and that man's scope," recollection of the Friend had sent his imagination soaring like a lark away from sullen earth. For the rival poet, in contrast, the Friend has performed a different kind of service. He has added feathers to the rival's wings—the reference being to a practice of hawking, whereby "feathers missing or broken were replaced by sound ones or spliced."[12] The rival is thus associated with a hawk, belonging to a predatory species, alien to the Friend's congenital disposition; an incapacitated hawk, moreover, aided by the imping out of his wing with borrowed plumes. The Poet's verse, on the other hand, owes

---

11 See Edward A. Armstrong's discussion of image clusters in chapter II of *Shakespeare's Imagination* (1946).
12 C. Knox Pooler, *The Sonnets* (Arden edition, 1918), p. 79.

its very life to the Friend; it is conceived under his influence, "thine and born of thee"; created therefore *ab ovo* a veritable lark; while in the works of others the Friend can but "mend the style," patching up by his presence the deficiencies of a foreign genius.

This sonnet is a fine example of Shakespearean irony, with every significant word and image chosen for its undertones of meaning. Two concepts emerge from it, which are already familiar, in a different guise, from previous groups. One is the contrast in poetry between natural breeding—the process of authentic inspiration—and usurious gain—the "use" or exploitation of a theme by a writer of a different bent. The other is the contrast between truth in poetry—the natural flight of the lark—and ornament—the hawk's flight assisted by extraneous trappings. LXXIX ("Whilst I alone did call upon thine aid") continues the ironical method and extends the scope of these concepts. Here the Friend ceases to be identified with the "Muse," which term instead becomes a synonym for the Poet's own genius; the reason being that the sonnet is primarily concerned with stressing, not so much the alien qualities of the rivals, as their imitativeness. The Poet's Muse is said to be "sick"; she has given place to another. He grants that the theme of the Friend deserves the "travail" of a worthier pen—"travail" signifying a true state of poetic gestation, as when Astrophel was "great with child to speak";[13] but instead there is only a kind of shabby commercial trick, the rival poet first robbing the Friend of his attributes, and then returning them to him as a gift:

> He lends thee virtue, and he stole that word
> From thy behaviour; beauty doth he give
> And found it in thy cheek; he can afford
> No praise to thee but what in thee doth live.

Not only does no natural increase ensue from this mode of writing; the rival even expects to take a breed of thanks for his barren metal:

> Then thank him not for that which he doth say,
> Since what he owes thee thou thyself dost pay.

The payment may indeed be actual as well as figurative: a cashing in of the Friend's excellence which is met out of the Friend's own pocket. We are reminded of the Poet's claim in XXI: "I will not praise that purpose not to sell."

On the other hand, the lavish praise of the rival in LXXX ("O! how I faint when I of you do write") serves to destroy this writer's reputation by its very hyperbole. A "better spirit" makes the Poet tongue-tied—not by the quality of his verse, we note, but by merely speaking of the Friend. The two writers are next represented as ships sailing the ocean

[13] *Astrophel and Stella*, I.

of the Friend's worth; the Poet a "saucy bark," the Rival a man-of-war "of tall building and of goodly pride." Superficially the comparison is to the Poet's detriment; but to the Elizabethan reader the image immediately suggested the little English ships that fought the Armada. Nashe compared himself with Gabriel Harvey in a similar conceit; and Fuller, describing the wit-combats of Shakespeare and Jonson, would again employ the figure.[14] The proud Spanish galleon was a fit transposition from the "alien pen," as predatory as the hawk (and as liable, it might be inferred, to be incapacitated). But there was yet a lower level of meaning. In sonnet convention the ship represented the lover, with the beloved as the harbour to which it sailed. Here the Friend was the ocean itself, with the Rival "riding" on its "soundless deep." For all the apparent dignity of the metaphor, it was basically the same as that applied to the Mistress, "the bay where all men ride." If she was physically accessible to all, the Friend by his acceptance of flattery was spiritually just as promiscuous. The innuendo is, of course, private, perhaps not wholly conscious, and certainly not discernible to the Friend as a reader of the sonnet; but it points to a new element in the Poet's irony which will become gradually more apparent in other sonnets of this group.

The contrast of use and natural increase shades off in LXXXII to the second antithesis of ornament and truth. This sonnet opens with an apparently humorous concession to the Friend's point of view: "I grant thou were not married to my Muse." The Poet's Muse, we remember, is sick: indeed she is not, at any point in this group, a very robust figure to choose as a life-companion. But the comment is also a reminder of the Friend's own plight. Who then is he to marry? He has rejected a union of kind that would perpetuate him in the flesh; his one hope of immortality lies in marriage to a "Muse." But if indeed he is resolved to stay fancy-free, then he extends his sterile dalliance from body to spirit. Like Richard II once again, he is in love only with novelty—

> Where doth the world thrust forth a vanity—
> So it be new there's no respect how vile—
> That is not quickly buzzed into his ears? (II. i. 24–6)

but he will find that "rhetoric" is no substitute for being "sympathized" in "true plain words." Finally rhetoric, as the meretricious opposite to

---

14 Nashe wrote: "As much to say as why may not my Muse bee as great an Appollo or God of Poetrie as the proudest of them? but it comes as farre short as . . . a Cocke-boat of a Carricke" (McKerrow, III, p. 104). The conceit is used, as in Shakespeare, for sarcastic effect. It was expanded by Fuller as a description of Shakespeare himself: "Many were the *wit-combates* betwixt him and Ben Johnson, which two I behold like a *Spanish great Gallion* and an English *man of War;* Master Johnson (like the former) was built far higher in Learning; *Solid,* but *Slow* in his performances. *Shake-spear,* with the *English-man of War,* lesser in *bulk,* but lighter in *sailing,* could turn with all tides, tack about and take advantage of all winds, by the quickness of his Wit and Invention." (*Worthies of England* (1622), Warwickshire.)

true poetry, is identified with ornament, the painting that imitates beauty's cheek—

> And their gross painting might be better used
> Where cheeks need blood: in thee it is abus'd.

The conclusion is amplified in LXXXIII ("I never saw that you did painting need") and coupled with an attempted defence of the Poet's own silence:

> I found, or thought I found, you did exceed
> The barren tender of a poet's debt.

Painting and barren payment are now brought together as substitutes, in the false world of ornament, for the sympathetic insight and creative travail of true poetry. Hence the declaration:

> For I impair not beauty, being mute,
> When others would give life and bring a tomb.

The central symbol for ornament in *The Merchant of Venice*, the golden casket enclosing a skull, is latent in these lines. But this negative stance does not fully explain the Poet's own failure to engage in creative writing. It is better, no doubt, to say nothing than to offer the golden casket: but why does he refuse a more positive rôle? The answer is insinuated, seemingly by accident, in the quiet parenthesis of line 3: "I found, *or thought I found* . . .". Perhaps, after all, the Friend is intrinsically worth no more than the barren offerings he welcomes. If so, to be dumb must be the only response of a poet concerned with the truth.

It becomes increasingly evident that the Poet's fight is on two fronts: against his rivals on the one side; on the other, against the Friend's own spiritual fault that brought the rivalry into being. Any show of passion in either instance would expose the Poet to the charge of vulgar jealousy; hence the subtleties of ambiguous praise or mock-deference in referring to the rivals. But in addressing the Friend such irony is barred. The only means of expression is a series of indirect hints that the Friend's acceptance of insincere eulogies undermines the whole relationship and deprives the Poet of his very theme. This is the true meaning of the Poet's silence, as well as of the notable omission of any pledge to immortalize the Friend. Even in LXXXIV ("Who is it that says most?") where the phrasing and imagery look back unmistakably to the issues of the Marriage group, the promise is withheld. The supreme praise, "that you alone are you," does not answer the warning of XIII:

> O that you were yourself; but love, you are
> No longer yours than you yourself here live.

And there is an ominous implication in the word "immured" as applied to the Friend's person—

> In whose confine immured is the store
> Which should example where your equal grew.

If the Friend's store is walled up in his own body, the prediction of sonnet IV will come true:

> Thy unus'd beauty must be tomb'd with thee,
> Which, used, lives th' executor to be.

Finally, instead of the necessary pledge of immortalization, the sonnet ends with a carefully planted ambiguity:

> You to your beauteous blessings add a curse,
> Being fond on praise, which makes your praises worse.

This can mean that the praise given by rival poets only derogates from the Friend's true fame; but the comma after "praise" carries the graver insinuation that it is the Friend's own "fondness," or folly, that lessens his repute.

LXXXV opens with further humorous deprecation of the Poet's own Muse. She is "tongue-tied" and "in manners holds her still," overawed by the whole troop of muses summoned by the Rival Poet. It is evident that besides the minor sycophants there is one rival with pretensions to learning, whose "precious phrase" is adorned by history, astrology, mathematics, and the other arts. In comparison, the Poet of the sonnets is reduced to the position of an "unlettered clerk" who can only add his "Amen" to another's hymns. Yet despite his ignorance and his Muse's bashfulness, the Poet's thought deserves priority over the Rival's words, as far as unspoken love is superior to glib erudition. The sonnet ends with a contrast between the "breath of words" and "dumb thoughts" in which the bubble of the Rival's self-importance is lightly but effectively pricked—learning without true sympathy being reduced to a mere wordy breath.

The more extreme the afflatus given to the Rival, the lower he is made to fall. But with him too falls the Friend. There is a return in LXXXVI to the metaphor of the tall ship, which is combined with the tomb association of "immured" in LXXXIV:

> Was it the proud full sail of his great verse
> Bound for the prize of all too precious you,
> That did my ripe thoughts in my brain inhearse,
> Making their tomb the womb wherein they grew?

The Friend is now the objective of the great galleon, not the ocean on which it sails; he is the precious silver of the new world in danger of being captured as prize. Not only is the Poet, his thoughts inhearsed in his brain, frustrated as a creative artist, but the Friend, with his store immured in his body, is correspondingly frustrated in his hope of increase. The expedition may be profitable for the Rival Poet; but the image reduces the Friend to the condition of barren metal, useless to itself, and merely passive to exploitation by another. Yet why has the Poet's verse been rendered still-born? He was not "struck dead" by the Rival's "spirit, by spirits taught to write"—a word-play linking spirit (which could mean personality) with the mention of all the muses as the Rival's aids. This play is presently reinforced by the ambiguity of "his compeers by night," who may be the muses of inspiration, but who are more likely to be the Rival's own clique of versifiers. Finally these mysterious visitors are particularized in one figure—

> that affable familiar ghost
> Which nightly gulls him with intelligence.

A "familiar" might be a spirit—or a boon companion. "Intelligence" signified both secret information and mental proficiency. And the word "gulls"—as the birds that in folklore incarnated the spirits of the dead, but also with the colloquial meaning of fraud—exploded the Rival's pretensions in one shattering monosyllable.[15] No flyting of a learned poet could be more destructive than to say that he was gulled with intelligence. Yet all this is only incidental to the sonnet's main argument. None of the Rival's humbug, the Poet continues, has caused his silence or given him any ground for fear:

> But when your countenance fill'd up his line,
> Then lack'd I matter; that enfeebled mine.

It is not merely that the Friend's beauty, his physical countenance, has gone to "fill up" the line, to complete a dunce's metre or provide a stock simile. But the Friend's *moral* countenance, his commendation and patronage, have swelled the Rival's exsufflicate verse. And this being so, the very theme of the sonnets, the truth of the Friend, has evaporated. He is lost to the Poet who could have immortalized him; he belongs to the Bushys and the Greens in their world of ornament.

The process of disillusionment that began with the revelation of the Friend's sensual fault is brought to a conclusion in these sonnets. They do not sound the emotional depths touched in the previous group, and

---

[15] It is interesting to compare Shakespeare's thought processes in this conceit with those described by a modern psychopathic patient, writing, as he declares, in a state of manic hyper-aesthesia. ". . . the gulls terrified me for two reasons: firstly because I thought of myself as a sort of super-gull who had been 'gulled' into selling his soul; and secondly because I thought I was responsible for all the death and evil in the world and that the spirits of all the lost seamen since the world began were in those gulls calling for vengeance on me." (John Custance, *Wisdom, Madness and Folly* (1951), pp. 33–4.)

only criticize the Friend by implication or oblique reference. But the rupture of the relationship is all the more evident for being expressed on an intellectual plane. Previously the Poet had flattered and reproved; he had oscillated between the parts of pander and father-confessor; he had torn up his Elizabethan world picture in the course of excusing sensual faults by sense. Nothing remained of the great hierarchy of perfections which the Friend had summed up in human form; instead there was the universal levelling of corruption, the stained sun of heaven equated with the stained son of the world. All this ensued from imaginative speculation on a cosmic plane; now, in terms of practical man-to-man relationships and problems of literary composition, the friendship is accurately weighed—and found wanting. The irony directed at the rivals may be crushing in its easy mastery; but it does not restore the creative power that has been baulked by the Friend's desertion. In consequence a parting is inevitable, and a long pause may be taken to follow the end of this group.

Yet even these sonnets, like those that treated the Friend's sensual fault, contribute a certain positive element to the sequence. The encounter with the rivals has crystallized the distinction in poetry between ornament and truth, "painted rhetoric" and true, plain words. Authentic poetry is seen as a creative function, operating from within through sympathy with its subject. The sham substitute is barren and commercial, exploiting the subject for the sake of fame and profit. Ultimately sympathy, not superimposed erudition, is the true mettle of the imagination, which begets children of the heart and brain. But for the present this necessary sympathy has been lost, and mere wishing will not restore it. Time must pass, until the Poet has himself undergone the same test as was applied to the Friend, and the process of self-knowledge has completed its course with the writer as well as his theme.

JOHN CROWE RANSOM

Shakespeare at Sonnets

ONE MAY be well disposed to the New Deal, and not relish the attitude of giving comfort to the enemy by criticizing Mr. Roosevelt publicly, yet in a qualified company do it freely. The same thing applies in the matter of the poet Shakespeare. It is out of respect to the intelligence of the editors and readers of a serious literary publication that I will not hold back from throwing a few stones at Shakespeare, aiming them as accurately as I can at the vulnerable parts. I have no fear that any group of intellectual critics may succeed beyond their intentions in demolishing Shakespeare, so that he will suffer extinction and be read no more, and I am well aware that if this should happen the public attendance upon poetry in our language would be reduced one-half. For Shakespeare is an institution as well established as the industrial revolution, or the Protestant churches. In the midst of the bombardment he will smile, and smile, and be a villain.

In this paper I must limit attention to the Sonnets, and within this field to a few features only. In a way the Sonnets should prove the most interesting of all this poet's works—unless the reader's interest in the poetry is tangled hopelessly with his interest in drama, the form which dominates most of Shakespeare's verse. For here I must propose a certain distinction, and it will be arbitrary in the sense that I will not argue it. Let us distinguish drama as one literary form, and lyric or pure poetry as another. In poetic drama, a hybrid, it is the dramatic form which rules. The poetry is the auxiliar. At any moment it is relative to the action, and to that extent determinate, not free. In the plays Shakespeare furnishes a multitude of characters with always-appropriate speeches—with speeches big and royal, tender and pitying, conspiratorial, even philosophizing speeches and soliloquies, indeed speeches of almost any sort, and thoroughly poeticized—but probably none of them will quite do as a round and separate poem. None is really so intended.

The standard of poetic range and complication which is practical for a successful producing playwright cannot be so high as that adhered to by some formal poet who cares nothing about the affections of the people, and knows that his art for a long time, certainly since Caxton set up for business, has been of a mental age far beyond its original oral condition. I will come to my point at once. It is not likely that John Donne could have written Shakespeare's plays, but on the other hand it seems impossible that Shakespeare could have got into the plays the equivalent of Donne's lyrics.

The virtue of formal lyrics, or "minor poems," is one that no other literary type can manifest: they are the only complete and self-determined poetry. There the poetic object is elected by a free choice from all objects in the world, and this object, deliberately elected and carefully worked up by the adult poet, becomes his microcosm. With a serious poet each minor poem may be the symbol of a major decision. It is as ranging and comprehensive an action as the mind has ever tried.

Shakespeare left monument enough behind him, but no face of it is of that precise significance which is attested by a large and assorted volume of minor poems. The truth is that Shakespeare, as compared with writers like Sidney and Spenser, had rare luck as a literary man, and I do not mean to say this out of any regard to whether he was or was not a superior man naturally. It would be impossible to tell how much our poet was determined by the fact that he was not an aristocrat, did not go to the university and develop this technical skill all at once, got into the rather low profession of acting, grew up with the drama, and never had to undergo the torment of that terrible problem: the problem of poetic strategy; or what to do with an intensive literary training. Yet Shakespeare did indulge in one diversion from his natural and happy career as a dramatist. He composed a laborious sonnet sequence. And in the degree that the sonnets are not tied down to "story," to the simple dramatizing of the stages in a human relation, they give us a Shakespeare on the same terms as those on which we are used to having our other poets.

2

I begin with a most obvious feature: generally they are ill constructed.

They use the common English metrical pattern, and the metrical work is always admirable, but the logical pattern more often than not fails to fit it. If it be said that you do not need to have a correspondence between a poet's metrical pattern and his logical one, I am forced to observe that Shakespeare thought there was a propriety in it; often he must have gone to the pains of securing it, since it is there and, considering the extreme difficulty of the logical structure in the English sonnet, could not have got in by a happy accident. The metrical pattern of any sonnet is directive. If the English sonnet exhibits the rhyme-scheme ABAB CDCD EFEF GG, it imposes upon the poet the following requirement: that he write three co-ordinate quatrains and then a couplet which will relate to the series collectively.

About a third of the sonnets of Shakespeare are fairly unexceptionable in having just such a logical structure. About half of them might be said to be tolerably workmanlike in this respect; and about half of them are seriously defective.

Already the poet Spenser had calculated very well what sort of thing could be done successfully in this logical pattern. It was something like the following (*Amoretti, LVI*):

> Fayre be ye sure, but cruell and unkind,
> As is a Tygre, that with greedinesse
> Hunts after bloud; when he by chance doth find
> A feeble beast, doth foully him oppresse.
>
> Fayre be ye sure, but proud and pitilesse,
> As is a storm, that all things doth prostrate;
> Finding a tree alone all comfortlesse,
> Beats on it strongly, it to ruinate.
>
> Fayre be ye sure, but hard and obstinate,
> As is a rocke amidst the raging floods;
> Gaynst which, a ship, of succour desolate,
> Doth suffer wreck both of her selfe and goods.
>
> That ship, that tree, and that same beast, am I,
> Whom ye do wreck, do ruine, and destroy.

Now Spenser's metrical scheme has a special and unnecessary complication, it exhibits rhyme-linkage; the second quatrain begins by echoing the last rhyme of the first quatrain, and the third by echoing the last rhyme of the second. It makes no difference logically. The three quatrains are equal yet sharply distinct. Possibly the linking was Spenser's way of showing off his virtuosity at rhyming, and possibly also he used it as a mnemonic device, to say, The new quatrain must be just like the old one, a logical co-ordinate, but wait till we come to the couplet, which will not be linked and must not be co-ordinate. At any rate, his quatrains nearly always are true co-ordinates. In his architectural design he is superior, I believe, to any other writer of the four-part or English sonnet.

And this means that he carefully attended to the sort of object which might permit this three-and-one division. In the given example each quatrain is a simile which he applies to the lady, and the couplet is a summary comment which is brief, but adequate because the similes are simple and of the same kind. It is not every matter, or logical object, which allows this; and, particularly, the couplet does not give enough room for the comment unless the burden of the quatrains has been severely restricted. If the poet is too full of urgent thoughts, he had better use the two-part or Italian form, which is very much more flexible. The English form, with the more elaborate and repetitive pattern, implies the simpler substance; in this it would be like other complicated forms, such as the ballade or sestina.

But structurally good also is the following Shakespearean sonnet, the one numbered LXXXVII:

> Farewell! thou art too dear for my possessing,
> And like enough thou know'st thy estimate;
> The charter of thy worth gives thee releasing;
> My bonds in thee are all determinate.
>
> For how do I hold thee but by thy granting?
> And for that riches where is my deserving?
> The cause of this fair gift in me is wanting,
> And so my patent back again is swerving.
>
> Thyself thou gav'st, thy own worth then not knowing,
> Or me, to whom thou gav'st it, else mistaking;
> So thy great gift, upon misprision growing,
> Comes home again, on better judgment making.
>
> Thus have I had thee, as a dream doth flatter,
> In sleep a king, but waking no such matter.

This sonnet is daring and clever. It is legalistic, therefore closely limited in its range, yet the three quatrains all manage to say the same thing differently, and the couplet translates the legal figure back into the terms of a lover's passion.

It is only a large minority of Shakespeare's sonnets in which we can find this perfect adaptation of the logic to the metre. In the others we can find the standard metrical organization, and then some arbitrary logical organization which clashes with it. At least twice we find only fourteen-line poems, with no logical organization at all except that they have little couplet conclusions: in LXVI, "Tir'd with all these, for restful death I cry," and in CXXIX, "The expense of spirit in a waste of shame." Occasionally, as in LXIII, "Against my love shall be, as I am now," the sonnet divides frankly into octave and sextet, so far as the logic goes, though it does not follow that an honest printer has set it up just so. Many modern sonnet-writers, such as my friend, Mr. David Morton, are careful to have their sonnets set up as two-part structures though their rhyme-scheme is four-part. I am afraid some critics will always be wondering whether the poets are unequal, or simply insensitive, to the logical demands made by the English form. I scarcely think that Shakespeare's practice sanctified a procedure.

Possibly the commonest irregularity of logical arrangement with Shakespeare is in sonnets of the following type (LXIV):

> When I have seen by Time's fell hand defac'd
> The rich proud cost of outworn buried age;
> When sometime lofty towers I see down-raz'd,
> And brass eternal slave to mortal rage;
>
> When I have seen the hungry ocean gain
> Advantage on the kingdom of the shore,
> And the firm soil win of the watery main,
> Increasing store with loss and loss with store;
>
> When I have seen such interchange of state,
> Or state itself confounded to decay,
> Ruin hath taught me thus to ruminate,
> That Time will come and take my love away.
>
> This thought is as a death, which cannot choose,
> But weep to have that which it fears to lose.

Here the three quatrains look co-ordinate, but only the first two really are so. The third begins with the same form as the others, but presently shows that it is only summary of their content, and then actually begins to introduce the matter which will be the concern of the couplet. We must believe that Shakespeare found the couplet too small to hold its matter, so that at about line ten he had to begin anticipating it. But, as I said, this sonnet represents a pattern fairly common with him, and it is possible to argue that he developed it consciously as a neat variant on the ordinary English structure; just as Milton developed a variant from the Italian structure, by concluding the logical octet a little before or a little after the rhyme-ending of the eighth line.

Probably Shakespeare's usual structural difficulty consists about equally in having to pad out his quatrains, if three good co-ordinates do not offer themselves, and in having to squeeze the couplet too flat, or else extend its argument upward into the proper territory of the quatrains. But when both these things happen at once, the obvious remark is that the poet should have reverted to the Italian sonnet.

Structurally, Shakespeare is a careless workman. But probably, with respect to our attention to structure, we are careless readers.

3

Poetry is an expressive art, we say, and perhaps presently we are explaining that what it expresses is its poet; a dangerous locution, because the public value of the poem would seem to lie theoretically in the competence with which it expresses its object. There is no reason why it should not offer an absolute knowledge of this object, so far as the adjective is ever applicable to a human knowledge, including a scientific knowledge, and a knowledge however "objective." Nevertheless one knowledge will differ from another knowledge in glory, that is, in the purity of intention, and sometimes it is scarcely a knowledge at all; it is rather a self-expression. There is probably a poetry of the feelings just as much as there is a poetry of knowledge; for we may hardly deny to a word its common usage, and poetry is an experience so various as to be entertained by everybody. But the poetry of the feelings is not the one that the critic is compelled to prefer, especially if he can say that it taints us with subjectivism, sentimentality, and self-indulgence. This is the poetry, I think, which we sometimes dispose of a little distastefully as "romantic." It does not pursue its object with much zeal, and it is so common that it involves in a general disrepute all poets, the innocent as well as the guilty, by comparison with those importunate pursuers, the scientists—who will not exactly be expected to fail to make the most of the comparison.

This sort of poetry, I am afraid, is as natural to Shakespeare as language is, and he is a great master in it. In XXXIII we read:

> Full many a glorious morning have I seen
> Flatter the mountain-tops with sovereign eye,
> Kissing with golden face the meadows green,
> Gilding pale streams with heavenly alchemy.

It is pure Shakespeare, it sounds like nobody else; and in it the failure of objectivity, or perhaps "realism" we might prefer to call it, is plain about as soon as we look closely. What the poet intends is simply to have something in the way of a fine-morning quatrain, with an all-ruling fair-weather sun to be the symbol of his false friend, as the sonnet goes on to disclose. But this sun is weakly imagined; rather, it may be said to be only felt, a loose cluster of images as obscure as they are pleasant, furnished by the half-conscious memories attending the pretty words. (In strict logic: I suppose this sun's eye flatters the mountain-tops in that his look makes them shine; but at once he is kissing the meadows, which is unseemly for a face that contains a sovereign eye; then in the character of an alchemist he is transmuting streams. A mixed and self-defeating figure, and a romantic effect unusually loose; but it does not seem to matter.)

So this is poetry; a poetry that has in mind the subjective satisfactions of the poet, and of reputed millions of readers after him. The cognitive impulse of the participating millions has to be of low grade, yet there is an object, and it is rich and suggestive even while it is vague and cloudy. This is what we might call an associationist poetry. The pretty words have pleasing if indefinite associations; and they are fairly harmonious, that is, the associations tend rather to cohere than to repel each other. And if they do not cohere into a logical or definitive object, at any rate—this is the subtlety of the romantic style—they are arranged externally with great care into a characteristic musical phrase, or at least a metrical one, which is really (by comparison) objective and absolute. Metric saves this kind of poetry, and its function could not be shown to better advantage than here; a meretricious function, as it lends its objectivity to an act in which the subject does not really propose to lose himself in the object. In other words, it persuades us, unless we are professionally critical, that this is a poetry of wonderful precision, when logically it is a poetry of wonderful imprecision, and the only precision it has is metrical, therefore adventitious. It is not without significance that the age gave to this poet his adjective: sweet. It would be hard to estimate the extent of the influence which Shakespeare's way of writing poetry has exerted upon subsequent English poetry. But Exhibit A would be the actual poems, and Exhibit B, scarcely less significant, would be the critical dictum upon which almost innumerable writers seem to be in perfect agreement, that science if it likes may try to know its object, but that the business of poetry is to express its author's feelings. The Restoration and Eighteenth Century in their poetry resisted Shakespeare's example of sweetness, but the Nineteenth Century did not, and when we are grieving because modern poetry has learned how to furnish such exquisite indulgences to the feelings and yet at the same time so little food for the intellect, there is no reason why we should not remember who is its most illustrious ancestor.

The image is often conventional, or "literary," which means that it is not really shaped by a genuine observation. In LIII:

> Describe Adonis, and the counterfeit
> Is poorly imitated after you;
> On Helen's cheek all art of beauty set,
> And you in Grecian tires are painted new.

Asseverations like this are the right of a literary lover, but they do more credit to his piety than to his wit. (The mediæval lover had a code which obliged him to say, My lady is more beautiful than yours, though I have not seen yours.) The urgency is that of a subject to express his own feelings, not that of an object so individual as to demand expression. But the phrasing is grave and musical; there is great care behind it to get words with the right general associations, and to make the melody; phrase, in this subjective sense, and regarded as the trick of the poet as workman, receives commonly the particularity that might have gone into the object.

Mr. Santayana says something like this when he remarks, with his usual wisdom, that Shakespeare's poetry is an art like landscaping; for it is pervasive, and tones down every object exposed to it, and is not like architecture, which articulates its objects right to the last constituent stone. Carrying out our figure, Shakespeare's poetry would not be so much the wall, or the temple, as the ivy that clings to it sentimentally, and sometimes may very well even obscure it.

Violence of syntax and of idiom is supposed to express strength of feeling. In the sonnets are many violences. For instance, in XXV,

> The painful warrior famoused for fight,

and in LXIV,

> The rich proud cost of outworn buried age.

In the first of these Shakespeare makes a verb of an adjective, but his coinage could not give it a currency, for it is not that kind of adjective. He also makes a qualitative noun of *fight*, which is less exceptionable, though its present currency seems to lie within the American sporting jargon. Both these forced meanings follow surprisingly upon *painful*, which is exact and even Miltonic. The other bristles with logical difficulties. They attach to the meaning of *cost*, and of the adjective series *rich* and *proud*, and of *outworn* and *buried*. Malone worried over the line and proposed *rich-proud*, but it still strongly resists paraphrase. These phrases will illustrate what is common in romantic poetry: a very great "obscurity," unknown to some "intellectualist" poetry which popularly rates as difficult.

I quote also, and I think not vindictively, from XII:

> When I do count the clock that tells the time,
> And see the brave day sunk in hideous night,
> When I behold the violet past prime,
> And sable curls, all silver'd o'er with white. . . .

The third line of this quatrain interests me as a critic. Shakespeare ordinarily plays safe by electing good substantial conventional objects to carry his feelings, but here his judgment should have come to his aid. The violet, in its exalted context, looks to me like a poet's *ridiculus mus*, for no instance of floral mortality could well be more insignificant. This little mouse had the merit of being named with three syllables, and a two-minute imaginary tour in the garden does not seem to disclose another one of like syllabic dimensions who would do any better. Shakespeare did not bother; he trusted in the music, and the power of the pleasant associations, to make the line impervious to logical criticism. He trusted also, and not without reason, for the point will generally be conceded by critics who are grateful for any excellence in their difficult art, in the comfortable faith that a poetical passage is unlike a chain in that its true strength is that of its strongest part.

On the other hand, there are certainly sonnets of Shakespeare's in this romantic vein which are without absurdities, structural defects, and great violences, and which are also compact, that is, without excessive dispersion in the matter of the figures; and they are doubtless the best sonnets of the kind there could possibly be. It would be presumptuous to deny this general type of poetry, or Shakespeare's occasional mastery of it.

Those perfect sonnets are not many. It is not a wild generalization, when we look at the sonnets, to say that Shakespeare was not habitually a perfectionist; he was not as Ben Jonson, or Marvell, or Milton, and he was not as Pope.

4

The sonnets are mixed in effect. Not only the sequence as a whole but the individual sonnet is uneven in execution. But what to the critic is still more interesting than the up and the down in one style is the alternation of two very different styles: the one we have been considering, and the one which we are accustomed to define (following Doctor Johnson) as metaphysical. What is the metaphysical poetry doing there? Apparently at about the time of *Hamlet,* and perhaps recognizably in the plays but much more deliberately and on a more extended scale in the sonnets, Shakespeare goes metaphysical. Not consistently, of course.

So far as I know, Shakespeare has not ordinarily been credited with being one of the metaphysicals, nor have specimen sonnets been included in lists or anthologies of metaphysical poems. But many sonnets certainly belong there; early examples of that style. If it was not then widely practised, had no name, and could hardly yet have been recognized as a distinct style, then I would suppose that the sonnets as a performance represent Shakespeare seeking such effects as John Donne, a public if still unpublished wonder, by some curious method was achieving. But there was also, on a smaller scale, the example of a genuine pioneer in this field in the person of Sidney, if Shakespeare cared to look there; see his *Astrophel and Stella,* XCIV, "Grief, find the words, for thou hast made my brain."

Certainly Shakespeare's LXXXVII, "Farewell! thou art too dear for my possessing," already quoted as an instance of good structure, is in the style. For its substance is furnished by developing the human relation (that of the renouncing lover) through a figure of speech; a legal one, in which an unequal bond is cancelled for cause. Three times, in as many quatrains, the lover makes an exploration within the field of the figure. The occasions are fairly distinct, though I should think their specifications are hardly respective enough to have satisfied Donne. But the thing which surprises us is to find no evidence anywhere that Shakespeare's imagination is equal to the peculiar and systematic exercises which Donne imposed habitually upon his. None, and it should not really surprise us, if we remember that Donne's skill is of the highest technical expertness in English poetry, and that Shakespeare had no university discipline, and developed poetically along lines of least resistance.

He is upon occasions metaphysical enough, but not so metaphysical as Donne; nor as later poets, Donne's followers, who were just as bold in intention as their master, though not usually so happy in act.

The impulse to metaphysical poetry, I shall assume, consists in committing the feelings in the case—those of unrequited love for example—to their determination within the elected figure. But Shakespeare was rarely willing to abandon his feelings to this fate, which is another way of saying that he would not quite risk the consequences of his own imagination. He censored these consequences, to give them sweetness, to give them even dignity; he would go a little way with one figure, usually a reputable one, then anticipate the consequences, or the best of them, and take up another figure.

The simplest way to define Shakespeare's metaphysical accomplishment would be by comparison with Donne's, which is standard. I have often tried to find the parallel cases where the two poets developed the same figure of speech. But I have always been forced to conclude that these poets do not even in outline or skeleton treat quite the same things; Shakespeare's things being professionally conventional, and Donne's being generally original. The nearest I can come to this sort of illustration is by comparing Sonnet LV with that Valediction of Donne's which has the subtitle: *of the booke.* It is a "strong" sonnet, not quite intelligent enough to be metaphysical. It begins,

> Not marble, nor the gilded monuments
> Of princes shall outlive this powerful rime,

yet what it develops is not the circumstantial immortality of the rime, and of the beloved inhabiting it, but the mortality of the common marbles and monuments, an old story with Shakespeare, and as to the immortality makes this single effort:

> 'Gainst death and all-oblivious enmity
> Shall you pace forth.

The only specific thing here is something about a gait.

The immortality of the rime, and of the beloved preserved in it (like a beautiful fly stuck in amber? let poets tell) is as classical, or typical, as anything in European sonnetry; but its specific development is not. It remained for Donne, and hardly anybody or nobody else, really on its own merits to develop it, or an easy variation from it, and that not in a sonnet. In the Valediction he bids his lady, when he is going on an absence from her, to study his manuscripts, "those Myriades of letters," and writes the annals of their love for the sake of posterity. I quote the third stanza, with a little editing of the punctuation:

> This Booke, as long-liv'd as the elements,
> Or as the world's forme, this all-graved tome
> In cypher writ, or new made Idiome
> (We for love's clergie only are instruments),—
> When this booke is made thus,
> Should again the ravenous
> Vandals and Gauls inundate us,
> Learning were safe; in this our universe
> Schooles might learn Sciences, Spheares Musick,
>   Angels Verse.

One understands that he really means what he says: a book. In the three stanzas following he shows respectively what the Divines, the Lawyers, and the Statesmen will learn from this book, and in a final stanza returns to relate to a lover's absence the labor of compiling it. Donne would have performed well with an English sonnet-structure, where he might have gone on three separate little adventures into his image; there are three here, though the stanza is bigger, and perhaps therefore easier, than quatrain. (Structurally, there is no firmer architect of lyric anywhere in English than Donne.) The trick consists, apparently, in guiding the imagination to the right places and then letting it go. To make this controlled yet exuberant use of the imagination is an intellectual feat; though it would not follow that there is no other recipe which will confer upon verse its intellectual distinction.

Metaphysical poetry has received in our time a new analytic attention, and for example from Professor Grierson. (Less formally if not less influentially from Mr. T. S. Eliot.) The revival of interest in this poetry evidently suits the taste of our post-romantic generation. And Professor Grierson says in many places that what Donne does is to combine intellect and passion. But no poet would find that a practicable formula; and we may well shiver with apprehension lest theory, or the æsthetic of poetry, waver and relax and perish under such a definition. The primary business of theorists is to direct their analyses of poetry to what is objective in it, or cognitive, and they will always be safe in assuming if they like that behind any external body of knowledge there will have been feeling enough, possibly amounting to passion, to have attended the subject through his whole exercise. Indeed, the feeling must have been entirely proportionate to the exercise. It is right to attribute the feelings to Donne's lover, in the poem, but our assurance is inferential; the intellectual effects appear as the fruits of the feelings. Ferdinand's feelings for Miranda, said Prospero to himself, are measurable better by the wood he will chop for her than by the passion, or even the iambic melody, of his protestations.

But may I talk a little about feelings? I have often wanted to. It is conceivable that Ferdinand might have expressed his in a garland of metaphysical poems, and that Prospero might have been fully competent to judge of the comparative values in this art, and therefore that the poems might have served alone as a sufficient index, obviating the wood-pile. They would have been just as objective an evidence. For what are feelings? I am sure I do not know, but I will suppose for the present they are calls to action, and always want to realize their destiny, which is to turn into actions and vanish. I will suppose also, and this is from experience, that we find ourselves sometimes possessed of powerful feelings and yet cannot quite tell what actions they want of us; or find ourselves even learning to enjoy the pangs of feelings, in the conceited consciousness they are our very own, and therefore reluctant to resolve them in action, and taking a perverse pleasure in stirring them up, like a harrowing of hell; for we are marvellously indeterminate in our inner economy. That is what comes fundamentally, I think, from our egoism, a strange and peculiarly human faculty. For I do not think animals distinguish their feelings at one end of a scale from their actions at the other end, since Nature as plain biologist would hardly seem to require it. But we distinguish; clearly we are able to stop at the feeling-end, or to perform half-way actions that will partly relieve the feelings and partly permit them still to luxuriate, but less painfully.

Lovers (and other persons too) often have feelings which cannot take, and do not seek, their natural outlet in physical actions. The feelings may be too complex anyhow, and too persistent, to be satisfied with simple actions, they overrun the mark; or perhaps the lovers have to go upon an absence, and the feelings get dammed up. Then they find appropriate actions through imagination, in intellectual constructions. These lovers at their best are poets. These poets at their best perform complete actions, very likely by means of metaphysical poems. So, on the one hand, there is an associationist poetry, a half-way action providing many charming resting-places for the feelings to agitate themselves; and, on the other hand, there is a metaphysical poetry, which elects its line of action and goes straight through to the completion of the cycle and extinction of the feelings.

This gives us associationist poetry *versus*, I think, behavioristic. For our discussion seems to have turned psychological. If romantic poets are not fully aware of what they are doing, metaphysical poets are self-conscious and deliberate, and in fact they are very like technical psychologists. They start with feelings, they objectify these imaginatively into external actions. They think that poetry, just as behavioristic psy-

chologists think that psychology, can make nothing out of feelings as
they stand.

5

And now a little moralization.

A metaphysical poem is an intellectual labor, and all the intellect may
be active in it, but it is under the presidency of imagination. And here
comes a difficulty. Feelings are not satisfied by a ridiculous and impossible action, for they themselves are painfully real. But what is imagination? A faculty of excessive versatility: equally ready to take the
photograph of objective reality, or to reproduce it from memory, or to
create it originally in a painting; and if the last, the detail is perceptual
but not actually perceived. This is the great trouble. The deterrent to
our reception of metaphysical effects is distrust; we do not believe in
the validity of the imaginative organ. It is for us a powerfully inherited
distrust, going back to the tyranny of that modernism, technically to be
defined as scientific positivism, which killed the religious credulity of
Europe, beginning in the Renaissance; it was going strongly by Shakespeare's time, and was quite sufficient to damn the foolish magic which
Spenser, by mistaken strategy, had lifted from mediæval poetry and
stuffed into his *Faerie Queene*. We cannot escape it. A nice exhibit of
our scruple is to be found later in Coleridge's rejection of fancy as the
irresponsible bastard variety of the image-forming faculty, though necessarily he discovered insuperable difficulties in drawing the exact line
round it. And altogether proper must we think anybody's insistence that
imagination must be representative, or realistic, in order that poetry may
speak the truth. It seems too early in our history, or else intelligence is
simply too weak, to arrive at any but dogmatic judgments respecting a
nest of exquisite problems with which sensitive moderns are too well
acquainted: how far a "metaphysical" particularity which goes beyond
actual observation is valid; how far the body of modern science, symbol
of what is valid and eternal, is itself built upon this sort of particularity;
whether any particularity is still eligible in religion, which deals with
supernaturals that always escape observation; and, at the same time,
whether natural bodies do not imply supernatural ones, and whether
there can be supernatural ones which propose to have no particularity
at all. We can only observe that the moment looks favorable to an
improvement in the public status of imaginative works.

But Professor Grierson makes an acute observation when he notes the
almost solid Catholic front (Anglo-Catholic and Roman) upon which
we are fairly astonished to find the seventeenth-century metaphysical
poets arrayed. (This test might eliminate Shakespeare, if we applied it

too strictly, for he does not group with them in a public or official sense.) It is hardly a mere coincidence. Catholicism is not afraid of particularizing the God, evidently believing that you cannot have "God in general," you must have Him in particular if at all. But Protestantism is afraid. It is subject to a fatal scruple of conscience. On its behalf it should be said that for modern men Protestantism is probably a necessity; it represents the scepticism which is incidental to sincere epistemological studies, and at a certain point of scientific advancement is inevitable. But this scepticism once started finds no end, and promises to conclude by destroying what is most peculiarly human in our habit of mind; indeed, it seems to proceed on a psychological assumption suitable to the animal societies, that superfluous feelings are not significant, and that it is simple, and desirable, to suppress them.

Doctor Johnson had a dry Protestant temper, and also something of the Catholic inheritance which he may have thought of as an old-fashioned decency. Oscillating fairly between these two prejudices, he was a just if never profound critic. He admired while he deprecated and repudiated the metaphysical poets. But in 1747 he prepared for Garrick's reading a Prologue upon the opening of Drury Lane Theatre, and began it as follows:

> When Learning's triumph o'er her barbarous foes
> First reared the stage, immortal Shakespeare rose;
> Each change of many-colored life he drew,
> Exhausted worlds, and then imagined new;
> Existence saw him spurn her bounded reign,
> And panting Time toiled after him in vain.
> His pow'rful strokes presiding Truth impressed,
> And unresisted Passion stormed the breast.

A defender of metaphysical poetry might suggest that in these eight lines the poet cites about that number of separate figures, and takes the profit of them, when there could be no profit to be taken except on the understanding that they were as mines, that might be or had been worked by real metaphysical imaginations. This poet offers no bodily manifestations of Learning triumphing o'er her foes, and then rearing the stage, which she could never have accomplished without being involved with shapes, agents, and events that were capable of images; or of Shakespeare rising, exhausting old worlds, imagining new ones, spurning the bounds of Existence; or of Time panting in his pursuit; or of Truth presiding over something, and impressing Shakespeare's strokes; or of Passion in some military manner storming the breast. It is necessary after all to raise the question of intellectual integrity against Doctor Johnson, as against many a Protestant at one time or another. If he rejects the metaphysicals he should reject also their fruits. These verses come out of the handsome enlightenment which lives substantially but without knowing on the scraps of a past from which it thinks it is emancipated.

6

But Shakespeare honestly realizes the metaphysical image, and I shall cite, with some remark, the sonnets in which he seems to me to have the most conspicuous success.

I begin with XXX, "When to the sessions of sweet silent thought"; it is smart work, but only half the sharpness belongs to the strict object; the rest is accidental or mechanical, because it is oral or verbal; it is word-play, and word-play, including punning, belongs to the loose poetry of association. Technically perfect and altogether admirable in its careful modulation is LVII, "Being your slave, what should I do but tend"; and so faithfully does it stick to the object, which is the behavior suitable to the slave kept waiting, that not till the couplet is there any direct expression of the feelings of the actual outraged lover.

Sonnet LX, "Like as the waves make toward the pebbled shore," is ambitious and imperfect. The first quatrain says that our minutes are always toiling forward, like waves. The second quatrain introduces a different and pretentious image of this tendency, and shows its fatal consequence:

> Nativity, once in the main of light,
> Crawls to maturity, wherewith being crown'd,
> Crooked eclipses 'gainst his glory fight,
> And Time that gave doth now his gift confound.

The lines will be impressive to that kind of receptivity whose critical defences are helpless against great words in musical phrases. Nativity means the new-born infant, but maturity seems only an object in his path, or at the goal of his path, evidently a crown which he puts on. Thereupon the astrological influences turn against nativity, and Time enters the story to destroy his own gift; this must be the crown that nativity has picked up. We are confused about all these entities. In the third quatrain Shakespeare declines to a trite topic, the destructiveness of Time, and represents him successively as transfixing the flourish set on youth (however he may do that), delving the parallels in beauty's brow (as a small demon with a digging instrument?), feeding on the rarities of nature's truth (as gluttonous monster), and mowing everything with his scythe (as grim reaper). A field of imagery in which the explorer has performed too prodigiously, and lost his chart.

And now LXXIII, with its opening quatrain:

> That time of year thou mayst in me behold
> When yellow leaves, or none, or few, do hang
> Upon those boughs which shake against the cold,
> Bare ruin'd choirs, where late the sweet birds sang.

The structure is good, the three quatrains offering distinct yet equivalent figures for the time of life of the unsuccessful and to-be-pitied lover. But the first quatrain is the boldest, and the effect of the whole is slightly anti-climactic. Within this quatrain I think I detect a thing which often characterizes Shakespeare's work within the metaphysical style: he is unwilling to renounce the benefit of his earlier style, which consisted in the breadth of the associations; that is, he will not quite risk the power of a single figure but compounds the figures. I refer to the two images about the boughs. It is one thing to have the boughs shaking against the cold, and in that capacity they carry very well the fact of the old rejected lover; it is another thing to represent them as ruined choirs where the birds no longer sing. The latter is a just representation of the lover too, and indeed a subtler and richer one, but the two images cannot, in logical rigor, co-exist. Therefore I deprecate *shake against the cold*. And I believe everybody will deprecate *sweet*. This term is not an objective image at all, but a term to be located at the subjective pole of the experience; it expects to satisfy a feeling by naming it (that is, by just having it) and is a pure sentimentalism.

No. LXXXVII, "Farewell! thou art too dear for my possessing," which we have already seen and remarked, needs only the further comment that it is rare and charming among sonnets for the almost complete prevalence of the feminine rhyme.

I cite XCIV, "They that have power to hurt and will do none"; it has proved obscure to commentators, but I think it is clear if taken in context, as an imaginary argument against the friend's relation with the woman, or with any woman, exactly opposite to the argument of the sonnets which open the sequence. And XCVII, "How like a winter hath my absence been," where the logical structure has some nicety though the detail is rather large of scale.

I am interested in CVII, which begins,

> Not mine own fears, nor the prophetic soul
> Of the wide world dreaming on things to come.

The argument is that the auguries of disaster and death to his love need not be trusted; it concludes disappointingly in an old vein, that at any rate this love will endure in the poet's rhyme. I am particularly bothered by the image of the world's prophetic soul; as who is not? The world-soul is a technical concept, I suppose, in the sense that it was of use to Paracelsus and to other theosophists, who knew what they wanted to make of it. It indicates a very fine image for some metaphysical poet who will handle it technically; for Donne or another university poet. It is not fit for amateurs. The question is whether Shakespeare's theological touch here is not amateurish; elsewhere it sometimes is, as in Hamlet's famous soliloquy beginning, "To be or not to be." It is my impression that our poet is faking, or shall we say improvising; the *wide,* denoting extension, seems to destroy the world's aspect as soul, the *dreaming* is too pretty a form for the prophetic action.

There is evenness in CIX, "O! never say that I was false of heart." In CXXI, " 'Tis better to be vile than vile esteem'd," the language of the opening quatrain sounds close and technical enough for a passage of Donne's, but the argument is rather obscure; the later quatrains seem to shift the argument. No. CXXV, "Were 't aught to me I bore the canopy," is admirable though not unitary enough to be very metaphysical. And finally there is CXLVI, "Poor Soul, the centre of my sinful earth," the most Platonic or "spiritual" sonnet in the entire sequence, a noble revulsion in the progress of the poet's feelings, and the poet might well have employed it to conclude the unhappy history, leaving quite off the eight miscellaneous and indeterminates ones that follow. Perhaps he would have done so if he and not the printer had directed the publication.

7

I conclude with a note, which is in answer to an editorial query, and may serve as anticipating what will probably be a dissatisfaction on the part of some readers over my estimate of Shakespeare as a metaphysical poet.

Is not Shakespeare a very bold and successful contriver of metaphysical effects in his later plays? For the sonnets come before the final period of playwrighting, and it is our common impression that this poet's powers developed steadily to their final climax.

It has been remarked above that drama is no place to look for complete little poems; that metaphyhical lyrics in particular, like Donne's, would be destructive of any drama into which they might be admitted. Shakespeare's characters have to speak to the point, that is, to an immediate situation within the action of the play. But sometimes a character will get into general difficulties, and have profound if not quite directed feelings of despair; or into a state of happiness, and feel a diffuse joy; and such a character may be allowed to soliloquize (a very suspicious action dramatically, which shows Shakespeare trying to burst the bonds of drama in favor of a freer poetry); and why should not the result be a sizable passage of true metaphysical poetry?

The odds on its being so are here at their greatest. But I should think the passage will be too intellectual to give the oral effect necessary for an audience; for that matter, cannot be spontaneous enough even to suit a reader's sense of dramatic propriety. I look through a few of the soliloquies and seem to find my point confirmed. Macbeth's speech upon hearing of the Queen's death (in V, v) is cited for my benefit, but here is the speech:

> To-morrow, and to-morrow, and to-morrow,
> Creeps in this petty pace from day to day,
> To the last syllable of recorded time;
> And all our yesterdays have lighted fools
> The way to dusty death. Out, out, brief candle!
> Life's but a walking shadow, a poor player
> That struts and frets his hour upon the stage,
> And then is heard no more; it is a tale
> Told by an idiot, full of sound and fury,
> Signifying nothing.

It is a very fine speech. But instead of presenting a figure systematically it presents a procession or flight of figures. The tomorrows creep along till they have crept far enough, and bring up against—what? A syllable; remarkable barrier. After the tomorrows, in the whirling sublogical mind of this harried speaker, the yesterdays, by the suggestion which prompts antithesis; and, at a venture, he remarks that what they did was to light fools to their death. (I do not know why dusty death; it is an odd but winning detail.) But speaking now of lights, out with this one, a mere candle! Lights also imply shadows, and suggest that life is a walking shadow. Then the lights lead to the torches of the theatre, and the walking shadow becomes a strutting player, who after an hour will be heard no more. Finally, since one thing leads to another, we may as well make life into the thing the player says, the story, whose sound and fury have no meaning. The connections between part and part in this speech are psychological, and looser than logical, though psychological will always include logical, and indeed act as their matrix. And the point is that mere psychological connections are very good for dramatic but not for metaphysical effects. Dramatically, this speech may be both natural and powerful; so I am told. Metaphysically, it is nothing.

Once more: Shakespeare could put a character into a situation that called for a desperate speech, and give him one. But he could not seat this character at the table to compose a finished poem, and then let him stand up and deliver it.

If this is the way of the drama at its most favorable moments, there is still less chance of its achieving metaphysical effects in the usual give and take of dialogue. I think of the brilliant figures crowding a late work like *Antony and Cleopatra*, and note, at random, the passage where Antony is having his account with Cleopatra after the defeat at Actium (III, ix):

Now I must
To the young man send humble treaties, dodge
And palter in the shifts of lowness. . . .

Antony is a figurative man, and full of feelings. The sending of humble treaties is not enough to express them, therefore he elects to dodge, and also to palter, and he will be in shifts of—of what? Lowness will do. And this vigorous jumping from one thing to another registers Antony very well, and may claim its theoretical justification under dramatic method. But in the coherent poetry of Donne and the metaphysicals there is nothing like it; no more than there is anything there like the peculiar jumpiness and straining of a modern such as, let us say, Mr. Joseph Auslander.

It is not likely that the plays of Shakespeare, even the later ones, can furnish better metaphysical effects than the sonnets do, which deliberately intend them, and in intending them do not have to worry about the peremptory and prior claims of drama.

YVOR WINTERS

Poetic Style in Shakespeare's Sonnets

THE SHORT POEM of the late middle ages, of the sixteenth century, and of the early seventeenth century was usually rational in structure, and in fact was very often logical. This structure began to break down toward the middle of the seventeenth century: the signs are most obvious in *Lycidas,* but one can find them in Marvell and Vaughan and elsewhere. The rational structure was often used for unreasonable ends, as in much of Sidney and Donne, but the structure is almost always there. These facts are well known to scholars by now, and they may seem unworthy of mention; but they appear to be unknown to many of our critics, and I need to call attention to them for the sake of what I shall say later. Within this rational frame, however, there were two main schools of poetry in the sixteenth century and earlier: on the one hand there were the poets of the plain style, and on the other hand the poets of the style which has been variously labeled courtly, ornate, sugared, or Petrarchan. Some poets employed both methods, but most poets worked mainly in one or the other, for the difference was a difference of principle, and the principles were commonly understood. Wyatt, Gascoigne, Raleigh, Greville, and Jonson wrote mainly in the plain style. Sidney and Spenser can serve as examples of the courtly.

Donne can hardly be described as courtly or sugared, but he is ornate, and to this extent Petrarchan. Donne is only superficially a rebel against the tradition of Sidney; essentially he is a continuator, at least in a large number of his poems. His mind is more complex than that of Sidney, and more profound; his temperament is more violent and more perverse; his virtues and his vices are more striking; but in most of his famous poems he is working in the same tradition. . . .

In Shakespeare's sonnets we find both plain and ornate styles, sometimes in the same poem, but both, more often than not, in a state of

Extracted, with the omission of two final sections, from "Poetic Styles, Old and New" by Yvor Winters, in *Four Poets on Poetry,* edited by Don Cameron Allen, The Johns Hopkins Press, 1959. Reprinted by permission of the publisher and of Professor Winters through his agent, Alan Swallow.

decay; and we find also the only decay of rational structure which I can recollect among the major poets of the time. . . .

II

There are few of Shakespeare's sonnets which do not show traces of genius, and genius of an unusually beguiling kind; and in a fair number we have more than traces. Yet in the past ten years or so I have found them more and more disappointing.[1]

In the first place there is in a large number of the poems an attitude of servile weakness on the part of the poet in the face of the person addressed; this attitude is commonly so marked as to render a sympathetic approach to the subject all but impossible, in spite of any fragmentary brilliance which may be exhibited. It will not do to reply that this is a convention of the courtly style and should not be taken seriously. If it is a convention of the courtly style, then it is a weakness in that style. But it is not an invariable quality of the courtly poets; it occurs very seldom in poets of the plain style; and Shakespeare seems to mean it seriously.

In the second place, Shakespeare seldom takes the sonnet form with any real seriousness. The sonnets are almost invariably conceived in very simple terms and are developed through simple repetition or antithesis, so that they never achieve the closely organized treatment of the subject which we find in the best of Jonson and Donne. This weakness is often aggravated by the fact that Shakespeare frequently poses his problem and then solves it by an evasion or an irrelevant cliché: this is more or less the method of the courtly style at its weakest, but the element of genius which goes into many of these sonnets raises one's expectations to the point that one cannot take this sort of triviality with good grace.

In the third place, Shakespeare often allows his sensitivity to the connotative power of language to blind him to the necessity for sharp denotation, with the result that a line or passage or even a whole poem may disappear behind a veil of uncertainty: in this last weakness he is even farther from his major contemporaries than in any of the others. I shall endeavor to illustrate these weaknesses as they occur in poems which I shall discuss.

I will begin with LXVI:

[1] John Crowe Ransome antedates me by quite a few years in this heresy. See his essay "Shakespeare at Sonnets" in *The World's Body* (1938). [Pages 87–105, above.—Ed.] Ransom's objections and my own are similar in some respects and different in others. My own tardiness in seeing Shakespeare's weaknesses is evidence (a) of the effect of established habit on critical judgment and (b) of the curious way in which a shifting mixture of the good and the bad can produce a result which it is difficult to judge objectively.

> Tir'd with all these, for restful death I cry
> As to behold desert a beggar born,
> And needy nothing trimm'd in jollity,
> And purest faith unhappily forsworn,
> And gilded honor shamefully misplac'd,
> And maiden virtue rudely strumpeted,
> And right perfection wrongfully disgrac'd,
> And strength by limping sway disabled,
> And art made tongue-tied by authority,
> And folly—doctor-like—controlling skill,
> And simple truth miscalled simplicity,
> And captive good attending captain ill:
> > Tir'd with all these, from these I would be gone,
> > Save that, to die, I leave my love alone.

This is one of a number of Elizabethan poems dealing with disillusionment with the world. Others are Gascoigne's "Woodmanship," "The Lie" by Raleigh, and "False world, goodnight," by Ben Jonson. But whereas Gascoigne, Raleigh, and Jonson offer the best solutions that they can, Raleigh with righteous defiance, Gascoigne and Jonson with a combination of scorn for corruption and Christian acceptance of the individual fate, Shakespeare (like Arnold after him, in "Dover Beach") turns aside from the issues he has raised to a kind of despairing sentimentality, and the effect is one of weakness, poetic and personal. The same thing occurs in many other sonnets: for examples XXIX ("When in disgrace with fortune and men's eyes") and XXX ("When to the sessions of sweet silent thought"). I do not wish to deny the many felicities in these poems, for they are real; but the poems do not rise to the occasions which they invoke. The poem which I have just quoted would be a fine example of the plain style, except for the couplet, which represents sentimental degeneration of the courtly rhetoric.

It would be easy to make a list of inept phrases from the sonnets. The clichés, for example, are numerous and well known, and so are the bad plays on words ("When first your eye I eyed"). But most poets sin in this fashion much of the time, or in some comparable fashion. There is another kind of weak phrasing in Shakespeare, however, which is prevalent in his work and more serious than the cliché or the bad pun; it is characteristic of later ages rather than his own, and it sets him apart from his great contemporaries. This is his use of words for some vague connotative value, with little regard for exact denotation. An interesting example occurs in CXVI:

> Let me not to the marriage of true minds
> Admit impediments. Love is not love
> Which alters when it alteration finds,
> Or bends with the remover to remove:

O no! it is an ever-fixed mark,
That looks on tempests and is never shaken;
It is the star to every wandering bark,
Whose worth's unknown, although his height be taken.
Love's not Time's fool, though rosy lips and cheeks
Within his bending sickle's compass come;
Love alters not with his brief hours and weeks,
But bears it out even to the edge of doom.
  If this be error and upon me proved,
  I never writ, nor no man ever loved.

The difficulty here resides in the word *worth.* The fixed star, which guides the mariner, is compared to true love, which guides the lover. The mariner, by taking the height of the star, can estimate his position at sea, despite the fact that he knows nothing of the star's "worth." *Worth,* with reference to the star, probably means astrological influence, though it might mean something else. The lover, by fixing his mind on the concept of true love, similarly can guide himself in his personal life. But what does *worth,* as distinct from height, mean in this second connection? For the lover can scarcely guide himself by a concept of true love, he can scarcely indeed have a concept of true love, unless he has some idea of the worth of true love. The comparison blurs at this point, and with it the meaning. One may perhaps push the astrological influence here and say that the lover, although he has a general knowledge of the nature and virtue (if virtue can be separated from worth) of true love, yet does not know precisely the effect upon him that true love will have. But this will not do: he obviously knows something to the effect, for the rest of the poem says that he does. There is simply no such separation between the two functions of true love as there is between the two functions of the star, yet the comparison is made in such a way as to indicate a separation.

This kind of thing does not occur in Greville or Donne or Jonson. Even in the more ornate Sidney—for example in the clumsy figurative language of "Leave me, O love"—it is usually possible to follow the thought even though the figure may be mishandled. But here one loses the thought. Greville, in "Down in the depth," employs the language of theology; Donne employs the language of astrology (and other technical language) in the "Valediction of my Name in a Window." Nothing is lost by this precision, but on the contrary there is a gain, for the emotion cannot have force when its nature and origin are obscure. Shakespeare contents himself here with a vague feeling of the mysterious and the supernatural, and the feeling is very vague indeed.

The sonnet is characteristic in other respects. The successive quatrains do not really develop the theme; each restates it. This makes, perhaps, for easy absorption on the part of the more or less quiescent reader, but it makes also for a somewhat simple and uninteresting poetry. The sonnet form is short, and the great poet should endeavor to use it more efficiently, to say as much as can be said of his subject within its limits; such efficiency is never characteristic of Shakespeare. Lines nine and ten are clichés, which are barely rescued by an habitual grace, and the concluding couplet is a mere tag, which has no dignity or purpose in relationship to the sonnet or within itself. Yet the first four lines have precision, dignity, and simplicity, which are moving, and the twelfth line has subdued grandeur, due in part to the heavy inversion of the third foot and to the heavy anapest and iamb following. The high reputation of the sonnet is due about equally, I suspect, to its virtues and its faults.

One of the most perplexing of the sonnets is CVII:

> Not mine own fears, nor the prophetic soul
> Of the wide world, dreaming on things to come,
> Can yet the lease of my true love control,
> Supposed as forfeit to a confin'd doom.
> The mortal moon hath her eclipse endured,
> And the sad augurs mock their own presage;
> Incertitudes now crown themselves assured,
> And peace proclaims olives of endless age.
> Now with the drops of this most balmy time
> My love looks fresh, and death to me subscribes,
> Since, spite of him, I'll live in this poor rime,
> While he insults o'er dull and speechless tribes:
>   And thou in this shalt find thy monument
>   When tyrants' crests and tombs of brass are spent.

The sonnet has given rise to a great deal of scholarly speculation, most of which the reader can find summarized in Rollins's variorum edition of the sonnets. One of the commonest interpretations is that which identifies the mortal moon with Elizabeth and the eclipse with her death. The friend, then, is Southampton, who was released from prison upon the accession of James, and lines six, seven, eight, nine, and ten refer to the general fears that there would be civil disorder upon the death of Elizabeth and to the fact that James was nevertheless crowned with no disorder. The interpretation is fairly plausible, though by no means certain; but it involves two difficulties which, I think, have never been met. The tone of the poem is scarcely explained by this interpretation: the tone is sombre and mysterious, as if supernatural forces were under consideration—this tone is most obvious in the first quatrain, but it persists throughout. Furthermore, in line eleven we have a monstrous non sequitur, for there is not the remotest connection between Southampton's release from prison or the events leading up to it and Shakespeare's making himself and Southampton immortal in verse. To this objection the reader may reply that the concluding lines are merely in a Petrarchan convention and should not be taken too seriously. They may represent such a convention, but they have to be taken seriously, for the tone of seriousness and mystery, the magnificence of the language, are such that we are not prepared for triviality at this point. If this interpretation (or I think any other in the variorum editions) is accepted, then the poem stands as one of the most striking examples of Shakespeare's inability to control his language, of his tendency to indulge vague emotion with no respect for meaning. And the poem may, in fact, be such an example.

Leslie Hotson, however, has come forward with another theory.[2] He believes that the mortal moon (mortal: deadly, death-dealing) is the Spanish Armada, of which the line of battle was moon shaped, and which attacked England and was defeated in 1588, a year of which there had been many dire predictions for generations, some of the prophets having thought it the year in which the world would end. Hotson is an irritating writer, as everyone who has read him carefully must know. But whatever objections one may have to Hotson's theory, there is no denying the fact that he documents it fully and impressively. Furthermore—and this is a point which Hotson fails to mention—this interpretation explains the mysterious tone of the poem (for in these terms we are dealing literally with supernatural forces, as well as with the most terrifying of natural forces), and it eliminates the non sequitur (for the lives of both the poet and the friend had been threatened, and both have survived.) Hotson's theory clarifies the poem at every point, in spite of the conventional elements in the poem and the obscurely allusive manner of writing.

One can make certain obvious objections to Hotson's theory. For example, Hotson claims that the entire sequence was done by the age of twenty-five: this in spite of the facts that Shakespeare repeatedly refers to himself as an aging man and that there are many parallels in phrasing between the sonnets and the later plays. Furthermore, Hotson bases this claim on the explication of only one sonnet other than the sonnet just discussed. The management of the iambic pentameter line would seem to be too sensitive and skillful for a young man in 1588, although anything, of course, is possible when we are dealing with a poet of genius. But in favor of Hotson's view would be the very weaknesses which I have been describing—weaknesses which might well be those of a young man—although Hotson appears to be unaware of them. However, these weaknesses might easily be those of an older man, more at home in the dramatic form, writing carelessly for a private audience, and working in a style which in the course of his mature life became obsolete. Even with Hotson's explanation, however, or with another as

2 *Shakespeare's Sonnets Dated, and other essays,* by Leslie Hotson (London, 1949). [See pages 8–21, above.—Ed.]

good, the poem is faulty. No poem is wholly self-contained, but most poems work within frames of reference which are widely understood. This poem appears to have a very particular frame of reference about which it will always be impossible to be sure. The poem is almost all connotation, with almost no denotation; it is almost purely vehicle, with almost no tenor; it is almost wholly ornament, with almost nothing to which the ornament can be attached. It would be easy to say that such a poem is a kind of forerunner of some of the deliberately obscure work of the past hundred years; but this work is all based on closely related theories—those of Mallarmé or of Pound, for examples—and Shakespeare had no such theories. Shakespeare's ideas about the nature of poetry were those of his age, but he was often unable to write in accordance with them. Such a poem as this must have been the result of inadvertence.

Whatever the faults of the sonnets as wholes, their incidental beauties are numerous. These beauties are often of the most elusive kind, and they are probably felt by many readers without ever being identified. Consider, for example, line six of Sonnet XIX:

> And do Whate'er thou wilt, swift-footed Time.

There is a plaintive desperation in the line which it is impossible to describe but which any sensitive reader can feel. In what is being said there is a stereotyped but real and timeless fear, and this is expressed in part by the helplessness of the imperative and in part by the archaic cliché *swift-footed*. It is expressed also in the emphases of the rhythmical pattern: the first three feet are all heavily accented, but each succeeding foot more heavily than the one preceding, so that we reach a climax on *wilt*, followed by the long pause of the comma, the pause in turn followed by a foot lighter and more evenly stressed, and this by a very heavily stressed foot. This is not an original line nor a great one; it is derivative and minor—but it is moving.

More obvious are the moral perceptions in the second quatrain of XXIX:

> When in disgrace with fortune and men's eyes
> I all alone beweep my outcast state,
> And trouble deaf heaven with my bootless cries,
> And look upon myself, and curse my fate,
> Wishing me like to one more rich in hope,
> Featur'd like him, like him with friends possessed,
> Desiring this man's art, and that man's scope,
> With what I most enjoy contented least;
> Yet in these thoughts myself almost despising,
> Haply I think on thee,—and then my state,
> Like to the lark at break of day arising
> From sullen earth, sings hymns at heaven's gate;

> For thy sweet love remember'd such wealth brings
> That then I scorn to change my state with kings.

The first quatrain of this sonnet is a passable example of what the French would call *la poésie larmoyante;* it is facile melancholy at its worst. And yet the next four lines are precise and admirable; they are a fine example of the plain style. In the third quatrain we have the lark which has made the sonnet famous. The lark is an ornament, in the same way as Donne's compasses. In the last six lines we are told, of course, that the poet's state of mind has changed; and we are told why—he has thought of the friend or lady, whichever it may be. But this is a sentimental, and almost automatic, change, and it is hard to understand after the four lines preceding. It is what I have previously called an evasion of the issue posed. And the lark is a sentimental lark: at the descriptive level, *sullen, sings hymns,* and *heaven's gate* are all inaccurate. The lark is burdened with the unexplained emotions of the poet. But the lark is not representative of any explanatory idea. The lark suffers in these ways from comparison with the pigeons of Wallace Stevens, of which I shall write briefly at the end of this essay.[3] We have more lark than understanding in these lines, and more easy sentiment than lark.

One of the most fascinating passages is the description of the imperceptible but continuous action of Time in CIV:

> Ah! yet doth beauty like a dial hand
> Steal from his figure, and no pace perceived;
> So your sweet hue, which methinks still doth stand,
> Hath motion, and mine eye may be deceived.

And yet even here we are in grammatical difficulty, for it is the dial hand (or its shadow) which should steal from the figure; it is not beauty. Or if we take *figure* to mean the human form or face, then the dial hand is left with no reference, and there is no basis for the second half of the comparison. We understand the passage, of course, but the statement is careless.

One can find good poems among the sonnets which do not achieve at any point the greatness of certain lines from sonnets which fail. Such, for examples, are XXIII, CXXIX, and CXLVI. The first of these is correct but minor; the second ("The expense of spirit") is powerful in phrasing, but repetitious in structure—as Douglas Peterson has shown (*Shakespeare Quarterly* V-4), it derives its structure and much of its matter from a passage in Wilson's *Art of Rhetorique*—and appears to be a forceful exercise on a limited topic; the third is somewhat commonplace when compared with the best of Donne's *Holy Sonnets*.

The most impressive sonnet of all, I suspect, is LXXVII, in which the

3 [This later section is here omitted.—Ed.]

peculiarly Shakespearian qualities are put to good use, in which the peculiar faults are somehow transformed into virtues. Jonson, Donne, and Greville—indeed most of the great poets of the Renaissance—tend to deal with the experiential import of explicit definitions and sometimes to offer explicit and figurative excursions from definitions. In the plain style at its plainest, the passion with which the human significance of the definitions is felt is communicated by the emotional content of the language in which they are stated: that is, we do not have definition here and emotion there, but meaning and emotion coexist at every moment; in the relatively ornate style, the excursions are controlled in a general but clear way by the definitions. But Shakespeare's approach to his subject is indirect and evasive. In LXXVII the explicit subject is not very important: it provides the occasion for the entry into the poem of certain perceptions which appear to be almost accidental but which are really Shakespeare's obsessive themes.

LXXVII appears to have been written to accompany the gift of a blank book:

> Thy glass will show thee how thy beauties wear;
> Thy dial how thy precious minutes waste;
> The vacant leaves thy mind's imprint will bear,
> And of this book this learning may'st thou taste.
> The wrinkles which thy glass will truly show
> Of mouthed graves will give thee memory;
> Thou by thy dial's shady stealth may know
> Time's thievish progress to eternity.
> Look! what thy memory cannot contain
> Commit to these waste blanks, and thou shalt find
> Those children nursed, delivered from thy brain
> To take a new acquaintance of thy mind.
>   These offices, so oft as thou wilt look,
>   Shall profit thee and much enrich thy book.

The first quatrain states the ostensible theme of the poem: time passes and we age, yet by writing down our thoughts, we take a new acquaintance of our mind, acquire a new learning. The second quatrain enlarges upon the passage of time; the last six lines revert to the moralizing.

But something very strange occurs. The imperceptible coming of wrinkles displays the physical invasion of the enemy, just as the imperceptible movement of the dial's shadow displays the constant movement of the enemy. In the ninth line, however, the enemy invades the mind, the center of being; it was the figure of the book which enabled the poet to extend the poem to this brilliant and terrifying suggestion, yet so far as the development of the theme is concerned, the extension occurs almost by the way, as if it were a casual and merely incidental feeling.

> Look! What thy memory cannot contain
> Commit to these waste blanks . . . .

This command, in isolation, is merely a command to make good use of the book, and the remainder of the passage deals wholly with the advantages of doing so; yet the command follows the lines in which we have observed the destruction of the physical being by time, and in this position it suggests the destruction of the mind itself. This terrifying subject, the loss of identity before the uncontrollable invasion of the impersonal, is no sooner suggested than it is dropped.

There is a related but more curious employment of pure suggestion in the word *waste* in the same passage. The word is obviously a pun, with the emphasis on the secondary meaning. It means not only *unused* or *blank* (this is the primary meaning, and it gives us a tautology), but it means *desert* or *uninhabited* or *uninhabitable,* a sense reinforced by the verb *waste* in the second line; but rationally considered, the pages are not waste in this second sense, but are instruments offered for actually checking the invasion of the waste. A feeling, in other words, is carried over from its proper motive to something irrelevant to it, and the dominant feeling is thus reinforced at the expense of the lesser; this dominant feeling, one should add, arises not from the ostensible theme of the poem—the book and its use—but from the incidental theme which has slipped into the poem. In order to express the invasion of confusion, the poem for a moment actually enters the realm of confusion instead of describing it. The poem, I think, succeeds; but after having examined the unsuccessful confusion of other sonnets, I cannot decide whether the success is due to skill or to accident. . . .

ROBERT GRAVES *and* LAURA RIDING

A Study in Original Punctuation and Spelling
SONNET 129

. . . [E. E. Cummings] has perhaps learned a lesson from the fate of Shakespeare's sonnets: not only have his editors changed the spelling and pronunciation, but certain very occasional and obvious printer's errors in the only edition printed in Shakespeare's life time have been made the excuse for hundreds of unjustifiable emendations and "modernizations." Mr. Cummings and Shakespeare have in common a deadly accuracy. It frightens Mr. Cummings' public and provoked Shakespeare's eighteenth-century editors to meddle with his texts as being too difficult to print as they were written. We shall find that though Shakespeare's poems have a more familiar look than Mr. Cummings' on the page, they are more difficult in thought: Mr. Cummings accurately expresses, in a form peculiar to himself, what is common to everyone; Shakespeare expressed, as accurately but in the common form of his time, what was peculiar to himself.

Here are two versions of a sonnet by Shakespeare: first, the version found in *The Oxford Book of English Verse* and other popular anthologies whose editors may be assumed to have chosen this sonnet from all the rest as being particularly easy to understand; next, the version printed in the 1609 edition of the *Sonnets* and apparently copied from Shakespeare's original manuscript, though Shakespeare is most unlikely to have seen the proofs. The alterations, it will be noticed in a comparison of the two versions, are with a few exceptions chiefly in the punctuation and spelling. By showing what a great difference to the sense the juggling of punctuation marks has made in the original sonnet, we shall perhaps be able to persuade the plain reader to sympathize with what seems typographical perversity in Mr. Cummings. The modernizing of the spelling is not quite so serious a matter, though we shall see

Reprinted from Robert Graves, *The Common Asphodel: Collected Essays on Poetry 1922–1949* (London, 1949), by permission of International Authors N. V. An earlier version of this essay appeared in *A Survey of Modernist Poetry* by Laura Riding and Robert Graves (London, 1927).

that to change a word like *blouddy* to *bloody* makes a difference not only in the atmosphere of the word but in its sound as well.

I

Th' expense of Spirit in a waste of shame
Is lust in action; and till action, lust
Is perjured, murderous, bloody, full of blame,
Savage, extreme, rude, cruel, not to trust;
Enjoy'd no sooner but despisèd straight;
Past reason hunted; and, no sooner had,
Past reason hated, as a swallow'd bait
On purpose laid to make the taker mad:
Mad in pursuit, and in possession so;
Had, having, and in quest to have, extreme;
A bliss in proof, and proved, a very woe;
Before, a joy proposed; behind, a dream.
   All this the world well knows; yet none knows well
   To shun the heaven that leads men to this hell.

II

Th' expence of Spirit in a waste of shame
Is lust in action, and till action, lust
Is periurd, murdrous, blouddy full of blame,
Sauage, extreame, rude, cruell, not to trust,
Inioyd no sooner but dispised straight,
Past reason hunted, and no sooner had
Past reason hated as a swollowed bayt,
On purpose layd to make the taker mad.
Made In pursut and in possession so,
Had, hauing, and in quest, to haue extreame,
A blisse in proofe and proud and very wo,
Before a ioy proposd behind a dreame,
   All this the world well knowes yet none knowes well,
   To shun the heauen that leads men to this hell.

First, to compare the spelling. As a matter of course the *u* in *proud* and *heauen* changes to *v*; the Elizabethans had no typographical *v*.[1] There are other words in which the change of spelling does not seem to matter. *Expence, cruell, bayt, layd, pursut, blisse, proofe, wo*—these words taken by themselves are not necessarily affected by modernization, though much of the original atmosphere of the poem is lost by changing them in the gross. Sheer facility in reading a poem is no gain when one tries to discover what the poem looked like to the poet who wrote it. But other changes designed to increase reading facility involve more than changes in spelling. *Periurd* to *perjured*, and *murdrous*

---

[1] [I.e., no medial *v*. Typographical *v* was used as an initial letter, however, for both *v* and *u* (e.g., *verse* and *vnless*).—Ed.]

to *murderous,* would have meant, to Shakespeare, the addition of another syllable. *Inioyd,* with the same number of syllables as *periurd,* is however printed *Enjoy'd;* while *swollowed,* which must have been meant as a three-syllabled word (Shakespeare used *ed* as a separate syllable very strictly and frequently allowed himself an extra syllable in his iambic foot) is printed *swallow'd.* When we come to *dispised,* we find in the modern version an accent over the last syllable. These liberties do not make the poem any easier; they only make it less accurate. The sound of the poem suffers through re-spelling as well as through alterations in the rhythm made by this use of apostrophes and accents. *Blouddy* was pronounced more like *blue-dy* than *bluddy;* the *ea* of *ex-treame* and *dreame* sounded like the *ea* in *great;* and *periurd* was probably pronounced more like *peryurd* than *pergeurd.*

But it is the changes in punctuation which do the most damage: not only to the atmosphere of the poem but to its meaning. In the second line a semicolon substituted for a comma after the first *action* gives a longer rest than Shakespeare gave; it also cuts the idea short at *action* instead of keeping *in action* and *till action* together as well as the two *lust's.* A comma after *blouddy* makes this a separate characterization and thus reduces the weight of the whole phrase as rhythmic relief to the string of adjectives; it probably had the adverbial form of *blouddily.* Next, several semicolons are substituted for commas; these introduce pauses which break up the continuous interpenetration of images. If Shakespeare had intended such pauses he would have used semicolons, as he does elsewhere. Particularly serious is the interpolation of a comma after *no sooner had,* which confines the phrase to the special meaning "lust no sooner had *past reason* is hated past reason." Shakespeare did not write in the syntax of prose but in a sensitive poetic flow. The comma might as well have been put between *reason* and *hated;* it would have limited the meaning, but no more than has been done here. On the other hand a comma is omitted where Shakespeare was careful to put one, after *bayt.* With the comma, *On purpose layd*—though it refers to *bayt*—also looks back to the original idea of *lust;* without the comma it merely continues the figure of *bayt.* In the original there is a full stop at *mad,* closing the octave; in the emended version a colon is used, making the next line run on and causing the unpardonable change from *Made* to *Mad.* The capital "I" of *In* shows how carefully the printer copied the manuscript. Evidently, Shakespeare first wrote the line without *Made,* and then, deciding that such an irregular line was too dramatic, added *Made* without troubling to change the capital "I" to a small one. In any case *Made* necessarily follows from *make* of the preceding line: "to make the taker mad, made (mad)"; but it also enlarges the mad-making bayt to the generally extreame-making lust. The change from *Made* to *Mad* limits the final *so* of this line to *Mad* and provokes a change from comma to semicolon—"Mad in pursuit and in possession so (mad)"—whereas *mad* is only vaguely echoed in this line from the preceding one. The meaning of the original line is: "Made In pursut and in possession as follows," and also: "Made In pursut and in possession as has been said."

The comma between *in quest* and *to have extreame* has been moved forward to separate *have* from *extreame*. This line originally stood for a number of interwoven meanings:

1. The taker of the bait, the man in pursuit and in possession of lust, is made mad: is so made that he experiences both extremes at once. (What these extremes are the lines following show.)

2. The *Had, having and in quest,* might well have been written in parentheses. They explain, by way of interjection, that lust comprises all the stages of lust: the after-lust period (*Had*), the actual experience of lust (*having*), and the anticipation of lust (*in quest*); and that the extremes of lust are felt in all these stages (*to have extreame*—i.e. to have in extreme degree).

3. Further, one stage in lust is like the others, is as extreme as the others. All the distinctions made in the poem between *lust in action* and *till action lust,* between lust *In pursut* and lust *in possession* are made to show that in the end there are no real distinctions. *Had, having and in quest* is the summing up of this fact.

4. *Had* and *having* double the sense of *possession* to match the double sense of *action* implied by *Th' expence of Spirit in a waste of shame;* and *in quest* naturally refers to *In pursut,* which in turn recalls *till action.*

5. Throughout the poem it must be kept in mind that words qualifying the lust-interest refer interchangeably to the man who lusts, the object of lust and lust in the abstract. This interchangeability accounts for the apparently ungrammatical effect of the line.

With the emended punctuation the line has only one narrow sense, and this not precisely Shakespeare's; the semicolon placed after *so* of the preceding line, cuts the close co-operation between them. The shifting of the comma not only removes a pause where Shakespeare put one, and thus changes the rhythm, but the line itself loses point and does not pull its weight. In this punctuation the *whole* line ought to be put into parentheses, as being a mere repetition. The *to have* linked with *in quest* is superfluous; *extreme* set off by itself is merely a descriptive adjective already used. Moreover, when the line is thus isolated between two semicolons, *Had, having,* etc., instead of effecting a harmony between the interchangeable senses, disjoints them and becomes ungrammatical. *Mad in pursuit, and in possession so* refers only to *the taker mad.* The next line, *A blisse in proofe and proud and very wo,* should explain *to have extreame;* it is not merely another parenthetical line as in the emended version. To fulfill the paradox implied in *extreame* it should mean that lust is a bliss during the proof and after the proof, and also *very wo* (truly woe) during and after the proof. The emended line, *A bliss in proof, and proved, a very woe,* which refers only to lust in the abstract, not equally to the man who lusts, means that lust is a bliss during the proof but a woe after the proof—and thus denies what Shakespeare has been at pains to show all along, that lust is all things at all times.

Once the editors began repunctuating the line they had to tamper with the words themselves. A comma after *proof* demanded a comma after *provd.* A comma after *provd* made it necessary to change *and very wo* so that it should apply to *provd* only. Another semicolon which they have put at the end of this line again breaks the continuity of the sense: the succeeding line becomes only another antithesis or rhetorical balance ("a joy in prospect, but a dream in retrospect," to repeat the sense of "a bliss during proof but woe after proof"), instead of carrying on the intricate and careful argument that runs without a stop through the whole sestet. The importance of the line is that it takes all the meanings in the poem one stage further. Lust in the extreme goes beyond both bliss and woe: it goes beyond reality. It is no longer lust *Had, having and in quest;* it is lust face to face with *love.* Even when consummated, lust still stands before an unconsummated joy, a proposed joy, and proposed not as a joy possible of consummation but as one only to be known through the dream by which lust leads itself on, the dream behind which this proposed joy, this love, seems to lie. This is the overriding meaning of the line. It has other meanings, but they all defer to this. For example, it may also be read: "Before a joy can be proposed, it must first be renounced as a real joy, it must be put behind as a dream"; or: "Before the man in lust is a prospect of joy, yet he knows by experience that this is only a dream"; or: "Beforehand he says that he proposed lust to be a joy, afterwards he says that it came as involuntarily as a dream"; or: "Before (in face of) a joy proposed only as a consequence of a dream, with a dream impelling him from behind." All these and even more readings of the line are possible and legitimate, and each reading could in turn be made to explain precisely why the taker is made mad, or how lust is *to have extreame,* or why it is both *a blisse* and *very wo.* The punctuated line in the emended version, cut off from what has gone before and from what follows, can mean only: "In prospect, lust is a joy; in retrospect, a dream." Though a possible contributory meaning, when made the *only* meaning it presents as the theme of the poem that lust is impossible of satisfaction, whereas the theme, as carried on by the next line, is that lust as lust *is* satisfiable but that satisfied lust is in conflict with itself.

The next line, if unpunctuated except for the comma Shakespeare put at the end, is a general statement of this conflict: the man in lust is torn between lust as he well knows it in common with the world and lust in his personal experience which crazes him to hope for more than lust from lust. The force of the second *well* is to deny the first *well:* no one really knows anything of lust except in personal experience, and only through personal experience can lust be known *well* rather than "well-known." But separate the second *well* from the first, as in the emended version, and the direct opposition between *world* and *none, well knowes* and *knowes well* is destroyed, as well as the word-play between *well knowes* and *knowes well;* for by the removal of the comma after the second *well,* this becomes an adverb modifying *To shun* in the following line—*well* now means merely "successfully" in association with *To shun,* instead of "well enough" in association with *knowes.* This re-punctuation also robs *All this* of its significance, since it refers not only to all that has gone before but to the last line too: "All this the world well knowes yet none knowes well" the moral to be drawn from the character of lust (i.e. to shun the heaven that leads men to this hell). The character and the moral of lust the whole world well knows, but no one knows the character and the moral really well unless he disregards the moral warning and engages in lust: no one knows lust well enough to shun it because, though he knows it is both heavenly and hellish, lust can never be recognized until it has proved itself lust by turning heaven into hell.

The effect of this emended punctuation has been to restrict meanings to special interpretations of special words. Shakespeare's punctuation allows the variety of meanings he actually intends; if we must choose any one meaning, then we owe it to Shakespeare to choose at least one he intended and one embracing as many meanings as possible, that is, the most difficult meaning. It is always the most difficult meaning which is the most nearly final. No prose interpretation of poetry can have complete finality, can be difficult enough. Shakespeare's editors, in trying to clarify him for the plain man, weakened and diluted his poetry and in effect deprived him of clarity. There is only one way to clarify Shakespeare: to print him as he wrote or as near as one can get to this. Making poetry easy for the reader should mean showing clearly how difficult it really is. . . .

Only a few points of the original sonnet have been left uncovered by our typographical survey, and these occur principally in the first few lines, which suffer from fewer emendations than the rest of the poem. The delicate inter-relation of the words of the two opening lines should not be overlooked: the strong parallelism between *expence* and *waste* and *Spirit* and *shame* expressing at once the terrible quick-change from lust as lust-enjoyed to lust as lust-despised; the double meaning of *waste* as "expense" and as "wilderness," the *waste* place in which the Spirit is *wasted;* the double meaning of *expence* as "pouring out" and as the "price paid"; the double meaning of *of shame* as "shameful," i.e. "deplorable" and as *ashamed,* i.e., "self-deploring"; the double meaning of *shame* itself as "modesty" and "disgrace"; and the double meaning of *lust in action* as "lust unsuspected by man in his actions because disguised as shame" (in either sense of the word), and as "lust in progress" as opposed to "lust contemplated." All these alternate meanings interacting on one another, and other possible interpretations of words and phrases besides, make as it were an oracle which can be read in many senses at once, none of the senses, however, being incompatible with any others. The intensified inbreeding of words continues through the rest of the poem. *Periurd* is another example, meaning both "falsely spoken of" and "false." Again, *heaven* and *hell* have the ordinary prose meaning of "pleasure" and "pain"; but "heaven," for Shakespeare, was the longing for a temperamental stability which at the same time he mistrusted; his "hell" was akin to Marlowe's hell, which

> . . . hath no limits nor is circumscribed
> In one selfe place, for where we are is hell.

The reader who complains of the obscurity of modernist poets must be reminded of the intimate Shakespearian background with which he needs to be familiar before he can understand Shakespeare. The failure of imagination and knowledge in Shakespeare's editors has reduced his sonnets to the indignity of being easy for everybody. Beddoes, an early nineteenth-century imitator of Shakespeare, said:

> About Shakespeare. You might just as well attempt to remodel the seasons and the laws of life and death as to alter one "jot or tittle" of his eternal thoughts. "A Star," you call him. If he was a star all the other stage-scribblers can hardly be considered a constellation of brass buttons.

Few of the modernist poets are Stars, but most of them are very highly polished brass buttons and entitled to protect themselves from the sort of tarnishing which Shakespeare, though a Star, has suffered.

Shakespeare's attitude towards the perversely stupid reorganizing of lines and regrouping of ideas is jocularly shown in the satire in repunctuation given in the prologue of *Piramus and Thisby* in *A Midsummer Night's Dream:*

> QUINCE: If we offend, it is with our good will.
> That you should thinke, we come not to offend,
> But with good will. To shew our simple skill,
> That is the true beginning of our end.
> Consider then, we come but in despight.
> We do not come, as minding to content you,
> Our true intent is. All for your delight,

We are not heere. That you should here repent you,
The Actors are at hand; and by their show,
You shall know all, that you are like to know.

THESEUS: This fellow doth not stand vpon points.

.   .   .   .   .

LYSANDER: His speech was like a tangled chaine: nothing
impaired, but all disordered . . .

WILLIAM EMPSON

Some Types of Ambiguity in Shakespeare's Sonnets

[*First-type ambiguities arise when a detail is effective in several ways at once, e.g. by comparisons with several points of likeness, antitheses with several points of difference, "comparative" adjectives, subdued metaphors, and extra meanings suggested by rhythm.*]

. . . The fundamental situation, whether it deserves to be called ambiguous or not, is that a word or a grammatical structure is effective in several ways at once. To take a famous example, there is no pun, double syntax, or dubiety of feeling, in

> *Bare ruined choirs, where late the sweet birds sang,*[1]

but the comparison holds for many reasons; because ruined monastery choirs are places in which to sing, because they involve sitting in a row, because they are made of wood, are carved into knots and so forth, because they used to be surrounded by a sheltering building crystallised out of the likeness of a forest, and coloured with stained glass and painting like flowers and leaves, because they are now abandoned by all but the grey walls coloured like the skies of winter, because the cold and Narcissistic charm suggested by choir-boys suits well with Shakespeare's feeling for the object of the Sonnets, and for various sociological and historical reasons (the protestant destruction of monasteries; fear of puritanism), which it would be hard now to trace out in their proportions; these reasons, and many more relating the simile to its place in the Sonnet, must all combine to give the line its beauty, and there is a sort of ambiguity in not knowing which of them to hold most clearly in mind. Clearly this is involved in all such richness and heightening of effect, and the machinations of ambiguity are among the very roots of poetry. . . .

[1] Sonnet lxxiii, line 4.

[*In second-type ambiguities two or more alternative meanings are fully resolved into one.*]

. . . It is clear that ambiguity, not of word, but of grammar, though common enough in poetry, cannot be brought to this pitch without chaos, and must in general be used to produce a different effect. Where there is a single main meaning (the case we are now considering) the device is used, as in the following examples from Shakespeare Sonnets, to give an interpenetrating and, as it were, fluid unity, in which phrases will go either with the sentence before or after and there is no break in the movement of the thought.

> *But heaven in thy creation did decree*
> *That in thy face sweet love should ever dwell,*
> *Whate'er thy thoughts or thy heart's workings be,*
> *Thy looks should nothing thence, but sweetness tell.*   xciii.

You may put a full stop either before or after the third line.

> *That tongue that tells the story of thy days*
> *(Making lascivious comments on thy sport)*
> *Cannot dispraise, but in a kind of praise,*
> *Naming thy name, blesses an ill report.*   xcv.

The subject of *blesses* is either *tongue* or *naming*, and *but in a kind of praise* qualifies either *blesses* or *dispraise*. These devices are particularly useful in managing the sonnet form because they help it to combine variety of argumentation and the close-knit rhythmical unity of a single thought.

There is in the following Sonnet one of those important and frequent subtleties of punctuation, which in general only convey rhythm, but here it amounts to a point of grammar.

> *If thou survive my well contented daye*
> *When that churle death my bones with dust shall cover*
> *And shalt by fortune once more re-survey:*
> *These poor rude lines of thy deceased Lover:*
> *Compare them with the bettering of the time, . . .*   xxxii.

Line 4 is isolated between colons, carries the whole weight of the pathos, and is a pivot round which the rest of the Sonnet turns. *Re-survey* might conceivably be thought of as intransitive, so that line 4 could go with line 5 in apposition to *them,* but the point is not that either line 3 or line 5 could stand without line 4, it is in fact next to both of them, and yet it stands out from either, as if the Sonnet had become more conscious of itself, or was making a quotation from a tombstone.

> *Thou doost love her, because thou knowest I love her,*
> *And for my sake even so doth she abuse me,*
> *Suffering my friend for my sake to approve her,*
> *If I loose thee, my loss is my love's gaine,*
> *And loosing her, my friend hath found that losse. . . .*   xlii.

According as line 3 goes backwards or forwards, the subject of *suffering* is either *she* or *I*. The device is not here merely a rhythmic one, but it carries no great depth of meaning; the Elizabethans were trained to use lines that went both ways, for example in those chains of Sonnets, such as the *Corona* of Donne, in which each began with the last line of the one before.

Donne, indeed, uses these methods with vehemence; I shall break this series from the Sonnets for a moment to quote an example from the *Epithalamion for Valentine's Day.*

> *Thou mak'st a Taper see*
> *What the sunne never saw, and what the Arke*
> *(Which was of Soules, and beasts, the cage, and park)*
> *Did not containe, one bed containes, through thee,*
> *Two Phoenixes, whose joyned breasts . . .*

"You make a taper see what the ark did not contain. Through you one bed contains two phoenixes." "You make a taper see what the sun never saw. Through you one bed contains what the ark did not contain, that is, two phoenixes." The renewal of energy gained from starting a new sentence is continually obtained here without the effect of repose given by letting a sentence stop.

> *Who lets so fair a house fall to decay,*
> *Which husbandry in honour might uphold*
> *Against the stormy gusts of winter's day*
> *And barren rage of death's eternal cold?*
> *O none but unthrifts,* dear my love you know,
> *You had a Father, let your Son say so.*   xiii.

The phrase in roman is equally suited to the sentences before and after it; taking it as the former, a third meaning shows itself faintly, that *you know unthrifts;* "the company you keep may be riotous or ascetic, but is not matrimonial." Having quoted this for a comparatively trivial point of grammar, it seems worth pointing out that its beauty depends first on the puns, *house* and *husbandry,* and secondly on the shift of feeling from *winter's day,* winter is short, like its days; "your child will grow up after you and your house will survive to see another summer," to *death's eternal cold;* "if the house does not survive this winter it falls for ever"; there is a contrast between these two opposite ideas and the two open, similarly vowelled, Marlowan lines that contain them, which claim by their structure to be merely repeating the same thought, so that the two notions are dissolved into both of them, and form a regress of echoes.

Sometimes the ambiguous phrase is a relative clause, with "that" omitted, which is able to appear for a moment as an independent sentence on its own, before it is fitted into the grammar.

> *Their images I lov'd, I view in thee,*
> *And thou (all they) has all the all of me.*   xxxi.

There is some suggestion that the first clause may be wholly independent, and that *I view in thee* means "I look for them in you"; but on the whole the device merely puts "which I loved" into special prominence.

> *My life hath in this line some interest,*
> *Which for memorial still with thee shall stay.*
> *When thou reviewest this, thou dost review,*
> *The very part was consecrate to thee,*   lxxiv.

Passing over the comma at the end of the third line, the object of *review* is *part;* stressing the comma, it says tautologically, with the emphasis on the second *thou,* "it is enough immortality for me to be remembered by you," and the fourth line becomes a separate sentence.

This fluidity of grammar is partly given by rhetorical balance, because since the lines are opposed to one another in regular pairs you still get some sort of opposition by opposing the wrong pair. Sonnet lxxxi. runs this principle to death:

> *Or shall I live your Epitaph to make,*
> *Or you survive when I in earth am rotten,*
> *From hence your memory death cannot take,*
> *Although in me each part will be forgotten.*
> *Your name from hence immortall life shall have,*
> *Though I (once gone) to all the world must dye,*
> *The earth can yeeld me but a common grave,*
> *When you entombed in men's eyes shall lye,*
> *Your monument shall be my gentle verse,*
> *Which eyes not yet created shall ore-read,*
> *And toungs to be, your beeing shall rehearse,*
> *When all the breathers of this world are dead,*
> *You still shall live (such vertue hath my Pen)*
> *Where breath most breathes, even in the mouths of men.*

Any two consecutive lines in this, except 2–3 and 10–11 for accidental reasons, make a complete sentence when separated from their context; I do not say that this makes it a good sonnet, or that I know how it ought to be read aloud.

Tongues can *over-read* as well as *eyes,* and this would leave either *being* the subject of *rehearse,* or both *tongues* and *eyes.* However, *tongues* is particularly connected with *rehearse,* because the contrast of *your being* with *to be* ("in order to be") shows the transient tongues *rehearsing* your ideal *being,* lapping up your blood as it were, and thus implies a sort of timeless Platonic existence for Mr. W. H., informing the examples of his type, but in no way dependent on them. These shadows of his perfection were once to have been his children, but Shakespeare's partly scoptophile desire to see him settled in love has by now been with a painful irony thwarted or over-satisfied, and they are now no more than those who read his praise.

The following Sonnet is more two-faced in idea ("a complaint in the form of an assertion that he has no right to complain"), but can be put in the second type so far as concerns the ambiguity of syntax, as it reduces to a single meaning:

> *O let me suffer (being at your beck)*
> *The imprisoned absence of your liberty,*
> *And patience tame, to sufferance bide each check,*
> *Without accusing you of injury.*
> *Be where you list, your charter is so strong*
> *That you yourself may privilege your time*
> *To what you will, to you it doth belong,*
> *Yourself to pardon of self-doing crime.*   lviii.

And patience tame expresses petulance by its contraction of meaning ("suffer tame patience"; "be patience-tame," as in iron-hard; and "tame patience," as in *bide each check*) followed by a rush of equivocal words, clinched with *belong,* which has for subject both *your time* and *to pardon,* and implies, still with sweetness and pathos (it is an extraordinary balance of feeling), "that is all I could have expected of you."

> *But wherefore do not you a mightier waie*
> *Make warre vppon this bloudie tirant time?*
> *And fortifie your selfe in your decay*
> *With meanes more blessed than my barren rime?*
> *Now stand you on the top of happie houres,*
> *And many maiden gardens yet unset,*
> *With vertuous wish would beare your liuing flowers,*
> *Much liker then your painted counterfeit:*
> *So should the lines of life that life repaire*
> *Which this (Times pencil or my pupil pen)*
> *Neither in inward worth nor outward faire*
> *Can make you liue your selfe in eyes of men,*
> > *To give away your selfe, keeps your selfe still,*
> > *And you must liue drawn by your owne sweet skill.*   xvi.

Lines of life refers to the form of a personal appearance, in the young man himself or repeated in his descendants (as one speaks of the lines of some one's figure); time's wrinkles on that face (suggested only to be feared); the young man's line or lineage—his descendants; lines drawn with a pencil—a portrait; lines drawn with a pen, in writing; the lines of a poem (the kind a Sonnet has fourteen of); and destiny, as in the life-line of palmistry—*Merchant of Venice*, ii. ii. 163.

This variety of meaning is rooted more effectively in the context because *lines of life* and *that life* may either of them be taken as subject of *repair;* taking the most prominent meanings, "lineage" and "the features of yourself and your children," *lines* is subject, and this is also insisted upon by rhythm and the usual sentence order; *that life* means "life such as your present one." But *that life* (*repair*) is given a secondary claim to the position by *this* (. . . *make*), which follows evidently in contrast, as subject in the next line. (Punctuations designed to simplify the passage all spoil the antithesis.) *This* has a bracket expanding its meanings: *time*, bringing old age that will pencil you with wrinkles, or a riper manhood that will complete your beauty; *this Times pencil*, firstly, the style of painting, or average level of achievement, of Elizabethan portrait-painters; secondly, the frame and "atmosphere" given to beauty by that age of masques and gorgeous clothing and the lust of the eye (so that we must look back to the second line of the Sonnet, where the same double meaning is hinting that beautiful courtiers in the wake of Essex came to bad ends); *my pen* that describes you, *pupil* as immature and unskilful: as *pupil* of that *time* whose sonnet tradition I am imitating; or of *Time* which matures me. A natural way to take it is *that life,* "your life," and *this,* "my life" (devoted to describing you), but the meaning of *this* opens out into all the transient effects which are contrasted with the solid eternity of reproduction, and by reflection backwards *that life* is made subject of its sentence, meaning "the new way of life I propose to you," that is, of matrimony, or of the larger extra-human life in your lineage as a whole.

Independently of whether *lines of life* or *that life* is subject and whether *that life* is "your present way of life" or "the way of life I propose to you," there is a double syntax for lines 11 and 12. Taking them together there is a main reading, "the age of Elizabeth is not competent to express you, either in your appearance or character" (of the two pairs one would naturally associate the artist's pencil with *outward fair,* and the playwright's pen with *inward worth,* but the order is the other way round, so that each works with either, or "I try to write about your beauty, but the hand of time, graving the lines of character on your face, tries to show your inward worth"). This, the main grammar, involves a rather clumsy change from *life* to *you* in the object, and this greater directness of address, needed after the sagging of grammar in the extraordinary complexity of the intervening two lines, leaves room for an alternative syntax. For, taking line 11 with 10 (and preferably

that life as subject), it is *this* which is not fair either in inward or outward worth; *make,* of the present age, which has produced out of its
worthlessness such a beauty as yours, is opposed to *repair* of the vege-
table life, capable of producing many such flowers, which I propose to
you; as if the greater durability given to a type by making it repeatable,
giving it to a noble house rather than a single person, was compared to
making it anew, as "risen a heavenly body," in the next world, or to the
placing of it timelessly among Platonic ideas, so that it need not be
anxious about its particular patterns on earth; *live* of line 12 then becomes an adjective, and the force of so many words in apposition, *you,*
live, yourself, is to express wonder at the production of such a thing out
of the dull world of line 11, and make the young man, by contrast, ideal,
heavenly, or worthy of being made into a general type. Line 13, separated from lines 12 and 14 equally by commas, is as a main meaning
cut off into the final couplet, "you are not less yourself because you have
had children," but in the minor sense has for subject *this,* "your present
life of pleasure and brilliance carries in it no eternity, and keeps you
only to give you away." *Drawn* of line 14 then may take an additional
echo of meaning, as "drawing back," dragging yourself out of your present way of life, which your lover has not power to do for you.[2]

Ambiguities of this sort may be divided into those which, once understood, remain an intelligible unit in the mind; those in which the pleasure belongs to the act of working out and understanding, which must at
each reading, though with less labour, be repeated; and those in which
the ambiguity works best if it is never discovered. Which class any particular poem belongs to depends in part on your mental habits and critical opinions, and I am afraid that for many readers who have the
patience to follow out this last analysis, it will merely spoil what they
had taken for a beautiful Sonnet by showing it to be much more mud-
dled than they had realised. This is a pity, but however wise the view
may be that poetry cannot safely be analysed, it seems to me to remain
ignoble; and in so far as people are sure that their pleasure will not bear
thinking about, I am surprised that they have the patience not to submit
them to so easy a destruction. The fact is, if analysis gets in your way,
it is easy enough to forget it; I do not think that all these meanings should
pass through the mind in an appreciative reading of this Sonnet; what
is gathered is the main sense, the main form and rhythm, and a general

---

[2] There may after all be misprints in the text. The doubt as to whether *that life* is subject
or object, I now feel, does not add anything important to the meanings deduced. Also one
should probably put a full stop at the end of the twelfth line to cut out the overrun syntax
for the final couplet, which is assumed to be a final summing up. The Christian paradox
of the thirteenth line could still be taken either way round.

   The stops of the first edition of the Shakespeare Sonnets of course do not deserve reverence; you sometimes even get a comma at the end of a sonnet. The claim for them is that
they always deserve consideration because they seem to be an inaccurate but unedited
version of what Shakespeare actually wrote. . . .

sense of compacted intellectual wealth, of an elaborate balance of variously associated feeling. . . .

[*In the fourth type the alternative meanings combine to make clear a complicated state of mind in the author.*]

An ambiguity of the fourth type occurs when two or more meanings of a statement do not agree among themselves, but combine to make clear a more complicated state of mind in the author. Evidently this is a vague enough definition which would cover much of the third type, and almost everything in the types which follow; I shall only consider here its difference from the third type. [*The condition for third-type ambiguity is that two apparently unconnected meanings are given simultaneously.*]

One is conscious of the most important aspect of a thing, not the most complicated; the subsidiary complexities, once they have been understood, merely leave an impression in the mind that they were to such-and-such an effect and they are within reach if you wish to examine them. I put into the third type cases where one was intended to be mainly conscious of a verbal subtlety; in the fourth type the subtlety may be as great, the pun as distinct, the mixture of modes of judgment as puzzling, but they are not in the main focus of consciousness because the stress of the situation absorbs them, and they are felt to be natural under the circumstances. Of course, different readers apply their consciousness in different ways, and a line which taken alone would be of the third type may become of the fourth type in its setting; but the distinction, I think, is usually clear.

> *I never saw that you did painting need,*
> *And therefore to your fair no painting set,*
> *I found (or thought I found) you did exceed,*
> *The barren tender of a Poet's debt:*
> *And therefore have I slept in your report,*
> *That you yourself being extant well might show,*
> *How far a modern quill doth come too short,*
> *Speaking of worth, what worth in you doth grow,*
> *This silence for my sin you did impute,*
> *Which shall be most my glory being dumb,*
> *For I impair not beauty being mute,*
> *When others would give life, and bring a tomb.*
> > *There lives more life in one of your fair eyes,*
> > *Than both your Poets can in praise devise.*
> > > lxxxiii.

Shakespeare is the writer upon whom ingenuity has most often been misapplied; and if his syntax appears ambiguous, it may be because the Elizabethan rules of punctuation trusted to the reader's intelligence and were more interested in rhetoric than in grammar. One must pause before shadowing with irony this noble compound of eulogy and apology. But one may notice its position in the sequence (Shakespeare seems to have been taunted for his inferiority, and is being abandoned for the rival poet); the mixture of extraordinary claims and bitter humility with which it is surrounded; and that the two adjacent Sonnets say: "Thou truly fair were truly sympathised In true plain words by thy truth-telling friend," and "You to your beauteous blessings add a curse, Being fond on praise, which makes your praises worse." It is not true that the feeling must be simple because it is deep; irony is similar to this kind of lyrical self-abandonment, or they relieve similar situations; by the energy with which such an adoration springs forward one can measure the objections which it is overriding, by the sharpness of what is treated as an ecstasy one may guess that it would otherwise have been pain.

Line 2, then, goes both with line 1 and line 3. Taking it with line 1, Shakespeare was only concerned for the young man's best interests: "I did not praise you in verse because I could not see that your reputation could be set any higher by my praise." Even for this, the primary, meaning there are two implications; either *never* "until you told me to praise you," an order accepted humbly but with some echo of *being fond on praise,* or *never* "until I found you out"; "At one time I had not yet discovered that your cheeks needed rouge, and your character whitewash"; "When I first loved you I did not realise that you had this simple and touching desire for flattery."

The first line may also stand alone, as an introduction, with these meanings, so that line 2 goes with line 3; for this version one would put a comma after *therefore;* "And so, when no painting had been set to your fairness" (paint to your cheeks or to a portrait, praise to your beauty or to your virtue, apology to your vices), "I found that you exceeded" (in beauty, in virtue, or in wildness of life); "And so, judging you simply, not foreseeing the defences I should have to build up against feeling harshly of you, it came to me as a shock to know you as your are." The first version is much the stronger, both because *I found* is parallel to *I never saw* and because *exceed* wants to pass over the comma and take the fourth line as its object; indeed, I put the second version down less from conviction than because I cannot now read the line without thinking of it.[3]

For the various senses of line 4 we must first consider the meaning of *tender,* which is almost wholly limited into its legal sense by *debt;* "offered payment of what is due." This is coloured, however, by "tender regard" (1 *Henry IV.,* v. iv. 49); also the meaning "person who looks

---

[3] One must, I think, either say that the comma after *exceed* is a misprint or that it is intended to attract attention to the word and suggest that W. H. exceeded in more ways than one. But the complexity of feeling is still there if it is a misprint.

after" may be fancied in the background. Taking the word as object of *exceed*, we have: "I found you were worth more than the normal compliments due from a poet hired to write eulogies of you," "I found that you exceeded what I could express of beauty in verse," "I found your tenderness towards me exceeded the barren tenderness I owed you as your tame poet," "I found that you were more to me than the person who would see to it that the hired poet wrote adequate praises." These assume the *poet's debt* is a debt owed *by* a poet. Taking it as owed *to* a poet, we have: "I have found that you gave me more than you need have done," "I found that you treated me more as a friend than as a hired poet," and "I found you felt for me more generously than I felt for you, when I merely looked after my job and wrote eulogies of you." I am being verbose here to show the complexity of the material; the resultant ideas from all these permutations are only two: "You were treating me as a friend, not as a poet," and "You were more than I could describe." Here *tender* is the object of *exceed*, but, stressing the comma after *exceed*, *tender* may be either, as a mere echo, a second object of *found*, "I found only the barren tender," "You did *not* treat me more as a friend than as a poet, so I stopped writing" (*or thought I found* is now a more generous doubt), or may be a comment in apposition to the whole first three lines: "This was merely my business; I thought your beauty and virtue so excessive because that was the proper thing; to be expected from a poet in love; to be expected from a professional poet trying to win favour at Court." Most people in reading the line only recognise the meaning, "You were more than I could describe," but they are made to feel also in the word *barren* a more dreary and more petty way of feeling about the matter, they know there is some bitterness which this wave of generosity has submerged.

Therefore in line 5 seems parallel to *therefore* in line 2, so that it could refer to *found* or *saw*. Or with a larger rhythm, the fifth line refers to the whole first quatrain and starts a new one. Alternatively, *therefore* may refer forward to line 6: "for this reason . . . in order that." *Report* is either what people in general say or what Shakespeare says, or what Shakespeare writes, about him; thus *I have slept in your report* means either "I have stopped writing about you," or "I have stopped contradicting rumours about you," or "I have bolstered up my faith in you by accepting the public's good opinion of you." *That* means "in order that" (you might show well), "the fact that" (I have slept, which your being extant well shows), or "for fear that" (your being extant might show how far a modern quill comes too short). *Extant* means visible, or successful and respected, or the subject of scandal. *How* and *what* follow *show* and *speaking* respectively, but for variations of grammar which leave them detached they may be regarded as introducing an exclamation and a question. The last line of the quatrain evidently refers backwards as its main meaning: "A modern quill comes too short when attempting to write of as much worth as is in you"; it can also refer forwards, but in trying to regard it in this way one is bothered by a modern usage which could take it alone; "and, talking of worth, *are* you worth anything, now, frankly?" This is not an Elizabethan idiom and was certainly not intended, but its coarseness is hard to keep out of one's mind, because the version which takes line 8 with line 9 is very similar to it: "I was describing all the worth I could find in you without the effort of flattery, and this amounted to the silences of which you, being fond on praise, have been complaining." If you like you may call this version ridiculous, and hurriedly place a colon at the end of the second quatrain; but please notice that the line may still be read as: "I was afraid that a modern quill might come short of a high standard of worth in describing all the worth that it can find in you."

This seems to me a good illustration of the difference between the third type of ambiguity and the fourth. Shakespeare was exquisitely conscious of such subsidiary uses of grammar and the jokes that could be made out of bad stops (if example is needed, consider Quince in Act v., scene i. of the *Dream*); but I do not think he was conscious of these alternatives (certainly I do not think that the reader who is apprehending the result as poetry should be conscious of these alternatives) in a clear-cut way as if they were jokes. They do not need to be separated out to give their curious and harrowing overtone to the quatrain; and once they have been separated out, they can only be connected with the mood of the poem if you hold clearly in mind the third quatrain which is their reconciliation. I might first paraphrase the second. "I have not written or talked about you fully, as the absence, or the particular kind, or the excess of scandal about you shows; *either* because your reality was already a sufficient expression of your beauty and virtue, *or* in order that you might still make a good show in the eyes of the world, as you might not if I were to describe you as I now know you, *or* for fear that the contrast between you and your description might be bad for the literary reputation of the Elizabethans, *or* for fear that the contrast between what this time and previous times could produce in the way of beauty and virtue might be bad for the Elizabethan reputation as a whole."

It would be possible to regard line 12, which clinches the third quatrain, as an antithesis: "When others would bring life, I in fact bring a tomb." This might be Shakespeare's *tomb;* "I do not flatter you but I bring you the devotion of a lifetime." More probably it is W. H.'s; "I do not attempt to flatter you at the moment; I bring you the sad and reserved gift of an eternal praise." We may extract from this some such meaning as: "I do not describe your beauty or your faithlessness, but my love for you." However, there are two other ways of taking the syntax which destroy this antithesis: "When others would bring life, I, if I wrote about you, would bring a tomb," and "When others would try to write about you, would try to give you life, and thereby bring you a tomb"; for both these the *tomb* must imply some action which would *impair beauty*. The normal meaning is given by Sonnet xvii.:

> *Who will beleeve my verse in time to come*
> *If it were fild with your most high deserts?*
> *Though yet Heaven knowes it is but as a tombe*
> *Which hides your life, and shows not halfe your parts.*

This first use of the word has no doubt that it is eulogy; the Sonnet is glowing and dancing with his certitude. But when the metaphor is repeated, this time without being explained, it has grown dark with an incipient double meaning; "I should fail you, now that you have behaved so badly to me, if I tried to express you in poetry; I should give you myself, and draw from my readers, a cold and limited judgment, praise you without sincerity, or blame you without thinking of the living man." ("Simply the thing I am Shall make me live"; Shakespeare continually draws on a generosity of this kind. It is not "tout comprendre," in his view, it is merely to feel how a man comes to be a working system, which necessarily excites a degree of sympathy.)[4]

A literary conundrum is tedious, and these meanings are only worth detaching in so far as they are dissolved into the single mood of the poem. Many people would say that they cannot all be dissolved, that an evidently delicate and slender Sonnet ought not to take so much explaining, whatever its wealth of reference and feeling, that Shakespeare, if all this is true, wrote without properly clarifying his mind. One might protest *via* the epithet "natural," which has stuck to Shakespeare through so many literary fashions; that he had a wide rather than a sharp focus to his mind; that he snatched ideas almost at random from its balanced but multitudinous activity; that this is likely to be more so rather than less in his personal poetry; and that in short (as Macaulay said in a very different connection) the reader must take such grammar as he can get and be thankful. One might apologise by saying that people have always read obscure meanings into Shakespeare, secure in the feeling, "If it means less, why is it so beautiful?" and that this analysis can only be offered as another mode of approaching so mysterious a totality, another glance at the effects of language. Or it may

---

[4] The *tomb* is formal praise such as would be written on a tombstone, whereas the real merits of the man are closely connected with his faults, which can't be mentioned in a formal style of praise. I am not now sure that the ambiguities of word and syntax add a great deal to what is clear enough as the theme. That the feeling behind the poem is ambivalent would not, I suppose, be denied.

Maybe I should explain that I put another complete analysis of a Shakespeare Sonnet (xvi.) in the second chapter [pages 128–131, above] on the ground that it has much less background of rudeness to W. H. than this later one.

boldly be said that the composition of feeling, which never falls apart among these ambiguities (it is, on any interpretation, pained, bitter, tender and admiring; Shakespeare is being abandoned by W. H., and stiffly apologising for not having been servile to him), rises and is clinched plainly in the final couplet; we are reminded of the references to the roving eye glancing round for new conquests; Shakespeare includes the whole ambiguity in his enthusiasm; the worth and sin, the beauty and painting, are all delightful to him, and too subtle to be grasped. . . .

ARTHUR MIZENER

The Structure of Figurative Language
in Shakespeare's Sonnets

IN *The World's Body* Mr. John Crowe Ransom has an essay that is pretty severe on Shakespeare's sonnets;[1] Mr. Ransom's strategy is to set Shakespeare up as a metaphysical poet and then to assail his metaphysical weaknesses. The late Shakespeare—the Shakespeare of *Measure for Measure, Antony and Cleopatra,* and the romances—had a good deal more in common with Donne than may sometimes be recognized, but even this Shakespeare was not, I believe, a metaphysical poet in Mr. Ransom's sense of the term. But whether Mr. Ransom is right or wrong, he has done the sonnets a good turn by raising in a serious way, for the first time since the eighteenth century, the problem of their figurative language.

In those distant days, some severe strictures were passed on this aspect of Shakespeare. Dr. Johnson remarked that "a quibble was to him the fatal Cleopatra for which he lost the world and was content to lose it"; Warburton laboriously explained that "he took up (as he was hurried on by the torrent of his matter) with the first words that lay in his way; and if, amongst these, there were two mixed modes that had a principal idea in common, it was enough for him"; Steevens roundly declared that "such labored perplexities of language, and such studied deformities of style, prevail throughout these sonnets" that he saw no reason to print them in 1793, since "the strongest act of parliament that could be framed would fail to compel readers into their service." These eighteenth-century critics were never answered. The usual remarks about this aspect of the sonnets ("An average Shakespeare sonnet comes dancing in, as it were, with the effortless grace of a bird, etc.") are not answers but ways of filling an embarrassing pause.

The original version of this essay appeared in *The Southern Review*, V (1940), 730–747. It is here reprinted, with the author's revisions, by permission of Louisiana State University Press.

[1] [See pages **86–105**, above.—Ed.]

Mr. Ransom, however, is not Steevens or another of those outspoken and outmoded eighteenth-century gentlemen, but a contemporary critic, less outspoken and as a consequence in some ways more devastating, and very far indeed from being outmoded. One can of course say that if we distill off the poetry of Shakespeare's sonnets, leaving in the flask only the bare "idea," that "idea" will be found not only familiar but, indeed, trite. Even the most ardent advocate of this view, however, usually gives his case away before he is through with some reference to the mystery of Shakespeare's language. Nor does this view meet Mr. Ransom's argument. The only way that argument can be met is by a description of the structure of the sonnets' figurative language which accounts for that structure without damning Shakespeare as, at his best, a metaphysical poet who lacks the courage of his convictions, and, at his worst, a manufacturer of trifles. If Shakespeare's sonnets are really metaphysical, then they are bad in the way and to the extent Mr. Ransom says they are.

Mr. Ransom's argument is that good poetry is always airtight extensively (to borrow a term from Mr. Allen Tate). He is willing to allow it to function intensively only within the limits set by a vehicle that is described with logical consistency. A poet, that is, must never be more in earnest about the tenor of his metaphor than about the vehicle, must never be willing to sacrifice the strict logic of his vehicle in order to imply something further about the tenor. This is a seductive definition of good poetry but an arbitrary one, which, if strictly applied, excludes from the category of good poetry all nonmetaphysical poetry. In the present state of our knowledge of the way language works, this consideration alone is enough to cast serious doubt on such a definition. It produces, in addition, some curious results. For instance, Mr. Ransom says of the opening quatrain of sonnet LXXIII ("That time of year thou may'st in me behold") that the metaphor here is compounded and that "the two images cannot, in logical rigor, co-exist." It is true that *choirs* can be looked on as a metaphorical extension of *boughs*,[2] but it is only by a pun that this extension can be maintained in the phrase "sweet birds" and Mr. Ransom cannot allow puns. Not even a pun, moreover, will bring "shake against the cold" within the limits of the figure, since by no stretch of the imagination can ruined cathedrals be thought of as shaking against the cold.

But it is plain before one reaches the end of this analysis that the success of Shakespeare's compound metaphor does not depend on the strict logic of its vehicle. His purpose is apparently to relate to his time

---

[2] By taking the boughs as the choirs and the trees as the cathedral. But "in logical rigor" Mr. Ransom's definition will not permit this ingenuity of Steevens; no metaphor is strictly logical—certainly this one is not—and the metaphorical extension of a metaphor's vehicle is therefore illegal.

of life, by some other means than the strictly logical elaboration of vehicle, both the boughs which shake against the cold and the bare ruined choirs. The age of Shakespeare's love, which is his life, is like the autumnal decline of nature, and thus natural, inevitable and, perhaps, only the prelude to a winter sleep rather than death; it is at the same time like the destruction of an artificial and man-made thing by man's wilful violence, and thus not inevitable, save as evil is inevitable, but regrettable as is the destruction of a building beautiful not only in itself but as a symbolic act. The fusion of these two meanings brought about by the compound metaphor is richer and finer than the sum of them which would be all the poem could offer if the two metaphors did not coexist.

The fusion is brought about by Shakespeare's slurring up from *boughs* to *choirs* and then down again. He gets up to choirs with the adjectival sequence "bare ruin'd"; "bare" modifies, primarily, *boughs,* and it is only through the diplomatic mediation of "ruin'd," primarily the modifier of *choirs,* that "bare" becomes intimate with *choirs.* He gets down again to *boughs* with the pun on "sweet birds"; in the phrase's secondary, euphemistic sense these are the choristers, but in its primary sense they are the quondam occupants of the now shaking boughs. The fact that this fusion gives the vehicle, not logic, but an ingeniously devised air of being logical really deceives no one (least of all, I suspect, Mr. Ransom) into supposing that Shakespeare's lines do rely for their power on the rigorous logical coherence of the metaphor's vehicle. Mr. Ransom's real point is not that he believes Shakespeare *did* intend them to, but that he believes Shakespeare *ought* to have intended them to.

Shakespeare's method is, then, fundamentally different from the metaphysical method: where Donne, for example, surprises you with an apparently illogical vehicle which can be understood only if its logic is followed, Shakespeare suprises you with an apparently logical vehicle which is understandable only if taken figuratively.

The position taken by critics like Mr. Ransom thus forces them to write down as a blunder one of the most essential features of Shakespeare's kind of poetry. A critic is of course free to dislike Shakespeare's kind of poetry, and I imagine Mr. Ransom does not mean to express admiration when he describes Shakespeare's poetry as the kind "which we sometimes dispose of a little distastefully as 'romantic.'" Probably a great many more people than profess to would dislike it were they not bullied by Shakespeare's name into accepting it. But the critic has not the right to treat this poetry as if it were of another kind, as Mr. Ransom does in discussing what he calls Shakespeare's "metaphysical" sonnets.

The characteristic feature of Shakespeare's kind of poetry at its best is a soft focus; a metaphysical poem is in perfect focus, perhaps more than perfect focus (like those paintings in which every detail is drawn with microscopic perfection). In a good metaphysical poem each figurative detail may be examined in isolation and the poem as a whole presents itself to us as a neatly integrated hierarchy of such details. Mr. Ransom suggests that the metaphysical poet shows a special kind of courage in committing his feelings in this way "to their determination within the elected figure"; probably no one will question this claim, or the implication that the special intensity of good metaphysical poetry derives from this self-imposed restriction. But the metaphysical poet shows also a special kind of perversity. He achieves a logical form at the expense of richness and verisimilitude; for the more ingeniously he elaborates his elected figure, the more apparent will it be that it is either distorting or excluding the nonlogical aspects of his awareness of the object.

Mr. Ransom, however, believes that the business of the poem is to express not the poet but the object, and draws a distinction between the poetry of knowledge and the poetry of feelings. This is a useful distinction, particularly in dealing with nineteenth-century poetry of the kind from which Mr. Ransom is such an expert in selecting horrible examples; but it does not go all the way. For whether or not the object has an existence independent of our awareness of it is for poetry an academic question; so far as poetry is concerned its existence is our awareness of it. That awareness may be more or less disciplined by what it thinks things actually are, more or less in control of its tendency to see them as it wishes them to be. But in either case, it remains an awareness. This awareness is what the poem presents; it never presents actual objects (even if poets could somehow present collages or *objets trouvés* the very process of selection itself would color the objects in such a way as to destroy their objectivity: objects are never just found; someone finds them). Expressing an object, giving to it, in Mr. Ransom's phrase, "public value," consists in "publishing" our awareness of it; and feelings are no less feelings for being a publishable, a communicable, part of that awareness. Mr. Ransom's very proper distaste for a poetry which presents a gross awareness, one which includes undistinguished or ill-distinguished feelings about the object, seems to have led him to try to eliminate the concept "feeling" from his definition of the best poetry. But to say that the best poetry expresses the object is to use a figure of speech which only apparently allows you to escape the fact that "speech as behavior is a wonderfully complex blend of two pattern systems, the symbolic and the expressive, neither of which could have developed to its present perfection without the interference of the other."[3]

---

[3] Edward Sapir, "Language," *The Encyclopedia of the Social Sciences.*

Since poetry is not the world's body but a verbal construct between which and the world-as-object the poet's awareness mediates, there are bound to be disadvantages to any kind of poetry which requires a definite distortion of that awareness for its intensity. It is this price which Shakespeare's poetry does not have to pay. There is, certainly, much to be said against his kind of poetry too. It is, for one thing, always wantoning on the verge of anarchy; and I think Mr. Ransom is right as to the unhappy effect of Shakespeare's example on such poets as Matthew Arnold, who brought himself to announce of Shakespeare's receding hairline that an assorted collection of painful sensations "find their sole speech in that victorious brow." But whatever may be said against it, much, too, must be said in favor of a poetic method which made possible the richness and verisimilitude of the best of Shakespeare's sonnets.

II

The only way to particularize this description of Shakespeare's method is to examine one of the sonnets in some detail. I have chosen for this purpose CXXIV (I have modernized the spelling but kept the punctuation of the 1609 edition):

> If my dear love were but the child of state,
> It might for fortune's bastard be unfathered,
> As subject to time's love, or to time's hate,
> Weeds among weeds, or flowers with flowers gathered.
> No it was builded far from accident,
> It suffers not in smiling pomp, nor falls
> Under the blow of thralled discontent,
> Whereto the inviting time our fashion calls:
> It fears not policy that heretic,
> Which works on leases of short numbered hours,
> But all alone stands hugely politic,
> That it nor grows with heat, nor drowns with showers.
>   To this I witness call the fools of time,
>   Which die for goodness, who have lived for crime.

This sonnet has at least two advantages in this connection: it is obviously a serious effort and it is not likely therefore that its consequences are unintentional; and it has that "excessive dispersion in the matter of figures" which seems to be characteristic of Shakespeare at his most serious and has annoyed others besides Mr. Ransom.

"If my dear love were but the child of state." The difficulty here is with *state,* which has a very complex meaning. It covers, in its general sense, the condition of those who live in this world and in time; in its specific senses, it includes most of the particular aspects of life which are touched on in the rest of the sonnet. I begin with the general sense.

If Shakespeare's love were the product of, had been generated by, the combination of circumstances and attributes belonging to the young man addressed and to the age, it might, as a subject of the kingdom of time and consequently "subject to" the whimsical decrees of Time's perverse rule,[4] at any time be "unfathered." The more specific sense of *state*—the metaphorical father of which Shakespeare's love would risk being deprived—touched on in the rest of the sonnets are: (1) Fortune, the deity who rules worldly affairs; (2) status; (3) wealth; (4) natural endowment (talent, beauty); (5) authority, pomp, display, the more obvious of the secondary characteristics of *state* in the previous senses; (6) the body politic; (7) statesmanship, "policy," the kind of maneuvering by which all earthly results, good or bad, are achieved. Of this complex father Shakespeare's love, were it the child of state, would run the constant risk of being deprived, either as the bastard of state in sense (1) or in order to make way for some other bastard of state as Fortune. In either case, Shakespeare's love, as a child of state, would be a bastard.[5]

Nothing, I think, could show more clearly than these three lines the difference between Shakespeare's figurative language and that of a metaphysical poem. For no single one of the meanings of *state* will these lines work out completely, nor will the language allow any one of the several emergent figures to usurp our attention; it thus becomes impossible to read the lines at all without making an effort to keep all the meanings of *state,* all the emergent figures, in view at once. That is, the purpose is to make the reader see them all, simultaneously, in soft focus; and the method is to give the reader just enough of each figure for this purpose. The figure of state as Fortune, for example, emerges just far enough to make it possible for the reader to see what this figure would have come to had it been worked out completely; and the figure of state as the body politic within which Shakespeare's love would be subject to Time just far enough to suggest what that figure would have come to. And so of the rest. If any one of these emergent figures had been realized in full, all the rest would necessarily have been excluded. They must then have been developed separately, and Shakespeare would have written a poem in which each of these figures appeared seriatim, perhaps a figure to a stanza, as in Donne's "Valedic-

---

4 The figure at this point is tending, on the one hand, toward a comparison to the court of an omnipotent prince, perverse, moody, shrewd, as Queen Elizabeth was; it is tending, on the other hand, toward the essentially medieval idea of Fortune, who rules everything on this side of the moon, and whose rule is wholly without order or meaning.

5 There seems to have been a close connection in Shakespeare's mind between bastardy and Machiavellian, policy-breeding, anarchic cynicism, as if this cynicism presented itself to his mind as the bastard of Time. See, for example, Edmund and Thersites ("I am a bastard begot, bastard instructed, bastard in mind, bastard in valor, in everything illegitimate"), or the cynicism of that strangely unfathered child of state, Hamlet.

tion; of the booke," which Mr. Ransom offers as an illustration of meta-physical structure.[6]

It is difficult to say how daring a venture "Weeds among weeds, or flowers with flowers gathered" is; it all depends on how familiar in Shakespeare's day were the associations of weeds and flowers he is using here. It is easy enough to show that they were familiar to Shakespeare, but I suspect they were also peculiar to him. Fortunately the line is carefully paralleled with l. 12; indeed, the primary sense-connection of l. 12 is to l. 4. From this parallel I think l. 4 gains enough support so that it will serve simply in its general sense: if Shakespeare's love were the child of state, so long as Fortune favored it, its every aspect would be a flower gathered with all the other flowers blossoming in the sunshine of Time's love; if Fortune ceased to favor it, its every aspect would be a weed, gathered with all the other weeds which rot noisomely in the damp of Time's hate. *Gather'd* carries out the personifications of the first three lines, and hints at a new one, Father Time (cp., the scythe in the final line of CXXIII); the flowers and weeds represent the specific consequences of Time's love and Time's hate.

But the particular value of this line as a summing up of the whole quatrain depends on our familiarity with Shakespeare's usual use of weeds and flowers; and it is not quite fair therefore to say that this value is communicated as well as expressed. In Shakespeare the contrast between weeds and flowers is most frequently applied to court life, society, problems of state, this-worldly affairs; figures of this kind are frequent in the history plays and in *Hamlet*. Weeds, particularly in their rankness (vigorousness, grossness, rancidity, indecency), are among the strongest of Shakespeare's images for evil.[7] Thus the gardener in *Richard II* ends his elaborate comparison of his garden to a commonwealth by saying:

[6] There is an interesting parallel between Donne's poem and the present sonnet which not only demonstrates the commonness of the "ideas" treated in both poems but also allows the very different methods of the two poems to be compared. Donne starts his sixth stanza as if he were going to take the other side of the argument from Shakespeare. Statesmen, he says, can learn much useful "policy" by studying the annals of his love, since in both love and statecraft "they doe excell/Who the present governe well,/Whose weaknesse none doth, or dares tell"; but then, just as Shakespeare implies that the "policy" of love is of a very different order from that of statesmen (see p. 148), so Donne adds that any statesman who fancies he finds love's methods like his is comparable to the alchemist who believes he finds authority for his art in the Bible.

[7] Caroline F. E. Spurgeon, *Shakespeare's Imagery*, pp. 154–155, 220–223.

> I will go root away
> The noisome weeds, which without profit suck
> The soil's fertility from wholesome flowers.[8]

Hamlet finds the world

> an unweeded garden,
> That grows to seed; things rank and gross in nature
> Possess it merely.

This sense of evil is primarily a result of his mother's sins; these are for Hamlet both weeds on which she is in danger of spreading compost "to make them ranker" and an "ulcerous place," the rank corruption of which may infect all within unseen. But Hamlet's sense of evil is not limited to its immediate cause; it is *all* the uses of this world which seem to him weary, stale, flat, and unprofitable, just as in the present sonnet Shakespeare distrusts Time's love as much as its hate. The "facts" of both the play and the sonnet are the vehicle for a feeling about the world as a whole. It is the essence of Shakespeare's success with this kind of figurative language that he never loses the individual "facts" in the perilously extended feeling.

With the association of rank weeds and spiritual corruption goes quite naturally the association of physical and spiritual decay which appears in Hamlet's "ulcerous place" figure. The ease with which Shakespeare bridged what may seem to the reader the considerable gap between the imagery of flowers and weeds and the imagery of disease can be demonstrated from a simple narrative passage in *Macbeth*:

> CAITHNESS: Well, march we on,
> To give obedience where 'tis truly ow'd:
> Meet we the medicine of the sickly weal;
> And with him pour we, in our country's purge,
> Each drop of us.
> LENOX: Or so much as it needs
> To dew the sovereign flower, and drown the weeds.

Here, quite characteristically, their blood, in Caithness's speech a medicine with which to purge the sick society, becomes the dew which makes the sovereign flower grow and drowns the weed. And, precisely as in

---

[8] There is the implication here and throughout *Richard II* that a proper gardener can put things right. The gardener himself specifically adds that "The weeds . . . are pluck'd up root and all by Bolingbroke," and it is only at the end and only from Richard that we hear:
> Nor I nor any man that but man is
> With nothing shall be pleas'd till he be eas'd
> With being nothing.
It is a very different matter in *Hamlet*—and in the present sonnet—where all the authority of Hamlet is behind the belief in the incurable weediness of this world and where the mere easement of death has become the only "felicity." Hamlet's authority is not of course complete, but the king is a distinctly lighter weight in the scale against him than Bolingbroke is against Richard.

the present sonnet, the fact that the ultimate referent of weeds is a group of human beings leads Shakespeare to use a verb (*drown*) which is more immediately applicable to persons than to weeds.[9]

The physical decay of this imagery may be either that of disease or that of death. It is the special horror of this aspect of life that the sun's breeding maggots in a dead dog and the son's breeding sinners in that living variety of good kissing carrion, Ophelia, are scarcely distinguishable. Both kinds of physical decay appear frequently in connection with the evils of human life, especially the evils of power and passion. Hamlet's mind is haunted by the smell of rotting flesh as well as by the imposthume that inward breaks. The king will be able to nose the corpse of Polonius as he goes up the stairs into the lobby; and Hamlet's final comment on the humiliating futility of Yorick's life is: "and smelt so? Pah!" But perhaps the most perfect collocation of all these images and their association is the close of sonnet XCIV:

> The summer's flower is to the summer sweet,
> Though to itself, it only live and die,
> But if that flower with base infection meet,
> The basest weed outbraves his dignity,
>   For sweetest things turn sourest by their deeds:
>   Lilies that fester, smell far worse than weeds.

Rain is closely connected with these images of corruption, too, for though it causes flowers as well as weeds to grow (but "sweet flowers are slow and weeds make haste"); it is also the cause of weeds' and flesh's rotting and stinking. The first gravedigger, after observing that "we have many pocky corpses now-a-days, that will scarcely hold the laying in," remarks that a tanner's corpse will last the longest because " 'a will keep out water a great while, and your water is a sore decayer of your whoreson dead body." And it is the rankness of nettles which lends the terrible dramatic irony to Cressida's reply to Pandarus.

> PANDARUS: I'll be sworn 'tis true: he will weep you,
>   and 'twere a man born in April.
> CRESSIDA: And I'll spring up in his tears, an 'twere a
>   nettle against May.

It is these associations of weeds and flowers (and of heat and showers too) which give such great force to l. 4.

---

[9] In the present sonnet, of course, Shakespeare is dealing directly with the mystery of loyalty and sovereignty which gave such limited perfection as it possessed to government, whereas in *Macbeth* that mystery is incarnate in the royal family and its loyal followers. Hence, in *Macbeth* the sovereign flower is ultimate earthly good, whereas, in the sonnet, it is only smiling Fortune. The overriding metaphor in *Macbeth* is such as to eliminate those impediments to the marriage of true minds the tragic reality of which so haunts Hamlet, Troilus, Othello, Lear, and the present sonnet. But apart from this distinction, the use of weeds and flowers is the same in *Macbeth* and the sonnet.

III

With the second quatrain Shakespeare starts another of his great metaphors for the destructive power of time, that of a building: "No it was builded far from accident" (where "waterdrops have worn the stones of Troy,/ And blind oblivion swallow'd cities up,/ And mighty states characterless are grated/ To dusty nothing"). This metaphor is then compounded in much the same way that the opening metaphor of sonnet LXXIII is; that is, the building is personified: "It suffers not in smiling pomp, nor falls/ Under the blow of thralled discontent." The figurative significances which may be derived from this compounded metaphor, taken in connection with the two metaphors of the first quatrain, are so many and so shaded into each other that a listing of them is neither possible nor desirable. The effect here, as in the first quatrain, depends on our being conscious of as many of these figurative significances as possible without bringing any of them exclusively into focus. They resist any effort to separate them one from the other; if the reader nevertheless insists on trying to force the lines to work for any one meaning alone, they will appear hopelessly defective. If this were not the case, they would be unable to function for all their meanings simultaneously.

The disadvantages of trying to bring any one implication of this complex of interacting metaphors into sharp focus are manifold. If the reader will oversimplify the problem by ignoring the metaphor of a building which intervenes between Shakespeare's love and the personification which suffers in smiling pomp and falls under the blow of thralled discontent, he will discover that there is a variation of meaning in these lines for every variation of meaning to be found in the first quatrain as a result of the multiple signification of *state*. But if he tries to bring each of these possible meanings of the second quatrain successively into focus he will find not only that the lines will not support any one of them alone, but that each of them tends to shade off into every other, till the possibility of bringing any one into focus becomes remote. There are certainly very real differences between *state* as status, as wealth, and as physical beauty, and it is certain, too, that one can associate a different kind of pomp and a different kind of discontent with each of them. But if the reader attempts to elaborate in detail each of these combinations, he finds in the first place that *suffer* and *fall* range from merely awkward to downright impossible, and in the second that the pomp of the young man's status and the pomp of his wealth begin to fade into each other, that the thralled discontent of status unrecognized, of talent unrealized, of policy unsuccessful begin to merge; and so it is with the rest of these distinctions which are perfectly satisfactory in a general focus.

But the reader cannot afford to ignore the fact that the *it* of l. 6 refers quite as clearly to that which was builded far from accident as to "my dear love." For unless he realize that ll. 6–7 retain the metaphor of the building he will miss the delicacy with which Shakespeare carries out the irony, obvious enough, in a general way, in the implications of the negatives. (*Unless* the young gentleman possesses all this state and is at least conceivably within danger of being victimized by it, and *unless* Shakespeare is capable of being hurt by such a development, it would never occur to Shakespeare to protest that his love is not the child of state.) Shakespeare does not say that the young man is tossed from success to failure and from discontent to satisfaction on the whirligig of time and that, in spite of this, Shakespeare's love remains unchanging. What he does say is that his love is like a building, a building which may be thought of most significantly as not like a courtier riding such a whirligig. The delicacy of the irony thus depends on the fact that this comparison is ostensibly chosen as the perfect description of the building and on the implication that Shakespeare would be surprised and dismayed were he to discover the young man taking it as a reference to himself. Shakespeare, that is, ostensibly and indeed ostentatiously disowns any responsibility for the coincidence of the young man's state and this figurative courtier's.

The insistence of Shakespeare's sonnet on generalizing the focus of the reader's attention will be quite clear, I think, if he will work out the simplest meaning for ll. 6–7 at each of the three levels, without considering either the remoter figurative significances, or the interaction of the various levels of meaning, or the interrelations of these lines with other lines. A courtier may be said to go about smiling and pompous in the conceit of his success; he may not be said to "suffer smiling and pompous." He may be described as wholly enslaved by discontent but only by some stretching of the figure as falling under the blow of his discontent. A building may be described as rich and elegant; it can scarcely be said to "suffer rich and elegant." It may fall under the blows of rebelling slaves; one blow, however, seems a little inadequate.[10] Finally, Shakespeare's love, not having been generated by anything that dwells in Time's kingdom, is beyond the power of either Time's love or Time's hate, both of which are spoken of in l. 6 as disastrous (the first causing suffering and the second discontent). The language of ll. 6–7 is directed just sufficiently toward each of these meanings to make it impossible for the reader to ignore any one of them. In no instance is

[10] My implication of dislike for richness and success and of sympathy for the discontented is, I think, in the lines. Notice that l. 8 tends to attach itself exclusively to "thralled discontent." This implication places Shakespeare, for all his brave show of living in the light, not of this world but of eternity, among the discontented and even, perhaps, among the approvers of violence. This implication may be a deliberate preparation for the irony of the final couplet.

it directed toward any one of them sufficiently to make it possible for the reader to contemplate that meaning to the exclusion of the others. The reader is thus forced to try to contemplate them all simultaneously. This procedure obviously permits an immense concentration of meaning within the particular passage. It has the further effect of almost forcing the poet to use the multitude of interrelations between the various passages which suggest themselves. This is, of course, the great danger of Shakespeare's kind of poetry. It is a danger over which Shakespeare at his best always triumphed but which has pretty consistently defeated his imitators.

"Whereto the inviting time our fashion calls." To such an existence this encouraging age calls us to fashion our lives as nobles, our relatively more permanent structures (both physical and social), our lives. (There is an ominous quality in "inviting" not represented by "encouraging." Perhaps, therefore, a less literal paraphrase would be more accurate; for example, "a way of life in which this easy age encourages us." But the point here is to bring out the metaphorical richness of the line.) But there is another important meaning here. It is impossible to keep this *time* from establishing relations with the *time* that loves and hates in l. 3; thus Time in its local and temporary manifestation, this age, calls on our fashion to become subject to King Time and thus calls on us to expose ourselves to its love and hate (smiling pomp and thralled discontent being the results of accepting).

IV

In the final quatrain Shakespeare draws together all his metaphorical themes. His love "fears not policy" since it is no child of state but was born in another kingdom than that of Time, in which policy operates.[11] Policy is a heretic by the familiar trick of transferring the vocabulary of the Christian worship of God to the lover's worship of the loved one. But it is also a heretic ("an indifferentist in religion, a worldly-wise man") because it is a child of state, worshipping the god of Time rather than the God of eternity. *Policy* is then said to be able to work only within the limits of human foresight, which is a space of short numbered hours compared to the eternity in terms of which those work who are subjects of God's kingdom. The line in question (10) is another

---

11 "Policy" here is a kind of metonym. That is, the figurative courtier of ll. 6–7 is a politic fellow. The substitution has the advantage of allowing the meaning of ll. 9–11 to extend beyond the courtier to the general philosophic attitude of shrewd, ambitious, and worldly people. The linking of this line to the figurative courtier of ll. 6–7 thus makes it an extension of the statement that Shakespeare's love, since it is not a child of state, is like a building built far from the kingdom of accident and chance and thus not subject to the alternate pomp and discontent of all which is subject to Time: not only does this love know nothing of the maneuvering of courtiers; it knows nothing of worldly policy in any form. It may be worth noting, as a part of the link, the very specific senses of "an indifferentist in religion, a worldly-wise man" which was given the noun *politic* in Shakespeare's days: "A carnal fellow, a mere politic." (N.E.D.)

one of those which says several things and works out without defect for none of them alone. That is, policy, personified as a heretic, may be said to work, but scarcely on a lease of any kind; on the other hand this same policy may *have* a lease on life of short numbered hours. A building in Time's world will presumably be held on a short lease, the duration of which is carefully measured; it can hardly, however, be described as *working* on that lease.

"But all alone stands hugely politic." With a slight stretching of "hugely politic" this line will work for the two immediate meanings involved, those of the previous line. That is, Shakespeare's love, as a building, stands all alone, perhaps like New Place with its orchards and gardens rather than like one of those speculative structures in London, crowded between other buildings, which were giving the authorities so much to worry about. It stands "far from accident," incredibly old and wise, (This is the stretching of "hugely politic." The Elizabethans used *politic* in this good sense regularly; as in the phrase "theyr polytycke wyt and learnyng in Physicke." [N.E.D.]) representing, as it were, the good old certainties of faith rather than the new-fangled values of shrewdness and calculation. Shakespeare's love, as person, stands apart from the human world of petty policy, dependent on no earthly devices, politic only in the infinite's craft, learned not in Machiavelli's but in God's book.

Thus Shakespeare's love is unlike the blooming favorites of Time's love and the rank and weedy creatures of Time's hate; it is unlike the worldly courtier who flourishes in the sun of prosperity ("For if the sun breed maggots in a dead dog . . . Let her not walk i' th' sun") and goes down in the floods of adversity ("Pulled the poor wretch from her melodious lay/ To muddy death");[12] it is unlike the house built upon the sand which shows in pomp in the sun and sinks to ruin in storms. "It nor grows with heat, nor drowns with showers."

Shakespeare calls to witness the truth of this statement those people who are made fools of by Time. In general in Shakespeare everyone is in one way or another made a fool of by Time; those who know enough

---

[12] The richness of Shakespeare's flood imagery has been emphasized by Mr. G. Wilson Knight, but the significance of his sun and light imagery seems to have been unduly neglected. Richard uses it in describing his earthly glory and ends with talk of the "brittle glory [which] shineth in this face" and of melting "before the sun of Bolingbroke." Hal, warning the audience that presently he will emerge as the perfect king, says that "herein will I imitate the sun. . . ." Juliet associates the "garish sun" with ordinary, worldly, daily living; it is the light by which Capulet and the nurse live; but the face of Juliet's heaven is made bright by the starlight of her love. For Hamlet Juliet's sun is not merely garish but a breeder of maggots, as Richard's garden is for him weedy not merely through carelessness but by nature, incurable. Angelo combines the sun imagery with that of flowers and weeds: "but it is I/That, lying by the violet in the sun,/Do as the carrion does, not as the flower,/Corrupt with virtuous season." This whole complex of weeds, flowers, carrion, sun and rain, seems, as the Variorum points out, to be derived ultimately from a speech in *Edward III*, but the beautiful and complex use of it in the plays and sonnets is Shakespeare's own.

try to escape its tyranny most tragically of all. For these discover, as Troilus did, that their fears are only too well grounded:

> What will it be
> When that the watery palate tastes indeed
> Love's thrice repured nectar! Death, I fear me,
> Sounding destruction, or some joy too fine,
> Too subtle potent, tun'd too sharp in sweetness
> For the capacity of my ruder powers:
> I fear it much; . . .

Troilus, Hamlet, Isabella, all in their ways tried to escape from the life of this world, and all discovered that they could not escape the human consequences of the fact that they were living in it. "Does your worship mean to geld and splay all the youth of the city?"[13]

I think these facts are necessary to an understanding of the amazing inclusiveness of Shakespeare's description of the fools of time. At the most obvious level this line (14) makes a distinction between martyrs and worldly-wise men. (*Crime*, not ordinarily a very strong word among the Elizabethans, is here roughly equivalent to "worldly success.") For though *who* certainly modifies *which*, the change of relatives tends to divide those which die for goodness from those who have lived for crime. And this division is reënforced by the ambiguity of *goodness*, which may mean what Shakespeare takes to be good or what the criminals take to be good. Those who die for goodness in this second, ironic sense may, like "Pitiful thrivers in their gazing spent," (Cp. the second quatrain of Sonnet CXXV) die physically for the sake of the "compound sweet" which they, "dwellers on form and favour," have devoted their worldly lives to seeking; it may be that they also die eternally, are damned, for lack of goodness in the serious sense and for living sinful lives. Those who die for goodness in the serious sense, who are martyrs, may die physically, because, like Richard, they failed to give enough attention to the worldly-wise man's kind of good, after living lives which, even at their best, were not without sin ("in the course of justice, none of us/ Should see salvation") and, at their troubled worst, offended against more than one of the world's canons, to say nothing of the Everlasting's.[14]

---

13 The thought is developed as early as *Richard II;* cp., 5.5. 45–49, where Richard, having mentally escaped from his prison into the timeless world of ideals, is reminded by the imperfect beat of the music that he still lives in this world:

> And here have I the daintiness of ear
> To check time broke in a disordered string;
> But for the concord of my state and time
> Had not an ear to hear my true time broke.
> I wasted time, and now doth time waste me. . . .

A moment later Richard, who has lived for crime, dies for goodness.

14 I omit the significance which may be derived from taking *die* less literally (i.e., desire deeply) which several editors have noticed, perhaps because they are so prominent in sonnet CXXV; they are remoter in this sonnet and my paraphrase is already overburdened.

The most astonishing consequence of this line is its inclusion among the fools of Time of the speaker of this sonnet, so that by a terrifying twist of irony Shakespeare offers his own failure—the unavoidable fact that for all he has been saying about it, his love cannot escape the consequences of his being human and not divine—as part of the evidence for the truth of his contention that his love is not "the child of state."

V

The pattern which one of Shakespeare's sonnets aims to establish in the reader's mind is not the pattern of logic aimed at by the metaphysical poem; his typical sonnet is rather a formal effort to create in the reader's mind a pattern, externally controlled, very like the pattern of the mind when it contemplates, with full attention but for no immediately practical purpose, an object in nature. Such a pattern is not built simply of logical relations nor does it consist simply of what is in perfect focus; it is built for all the kinds of relations known to the mind, as a result of its verbal conditioning or for other reasons, which can be invoked verbally. The building of a verbal construct calculated to invoke such a pattern requires the use of every resource language as a social instrument possesses, and it involves a structure of figurative language which at least approaches, in its own verbal terms, the richness, the density, the logical incompleteness of the mind.

No one can say how much the effect which a poem may fairly be said to produce can in the ordinary sense have been intended by the poet; apparently a good deal it does is not consciously intended. But unless the best of Shakespeare's sonnets are to be passed off as miraculous accidents, it is difficult to see what grounds there are for supposing that they are the result of following the path of least resistance in contrast to Donne's poems, which Mr. Ransom quite justly claims must be the result of stern intellectual labors. If the structure of figurative language in Shakespeare's sonnets is not an accident, and if its consequences are calculated, in so far as the consequences of any poem may be said to be calculated, then it seems more than probable that their making involved at least as great an effort of the intellect and imagination as the making of Donne's poems.

Mr. Ransom has it that in a formal lyric "the poetic object is elected by a free choice from all objects in the world, and this object, deliberately elected and worked up by the adult poet, becomes his microcosm. . . . It is as ranging and comprehensive an action as the mind has ever tried." It seems to me that Shakespeare's serious sonnets fail, as they do sometimes fail, not because they do not live up to this admirable description of the formal lyric but because they have tried to live up to it altogether too well.

WINIFRED M. T. NOWOTTNY

Formal Elements in Shakespeare's Sonnets
SONNETS I–VI

DESPITE SHAKESPEARE'S own description of his sonnets as being "far from variation or quick change," they have proved to be remarkably resistant to generalizations. It is, however, the purpose of this article to suggest that there is one generalization that can be made about them; one, moreover, that affords a point of view from which it is always helpful to regard them: namely, that the *Sonnets* reveal Shakespeare's strong sense of form, and that it is with respect to their form that the peculiar features or striking effects of individual sonnets may best be understood. There are in the *Sonnets* so many experiments with form that it would be difficult to lay down at the outset a definition of "form" at once comprehensive and precise, but the meaning of the term as it is used here will be sufficiently indicated by describing "form" as "that in virtue of which the parts are related one to another," or indeed as "that which manifests itself in the relationships of the parts." What is important for the purposes of this article is not the precise definition of form, but rather the indication of elements which commonly contribute to the manifestation of form. At the present day, the most illuminating criticism of individual sonnets is characterized by its concentration on imagery, and though it is true that imagery in the *Sonnets* is of great importance, it is not of exclusive or even of paramount importance. In this article I shall try to show that in Shakespeare's sonnets imagery is subordinated to the creation of the form of the whole and that imagery itself is at its most effective when it supports or is supported by the action of formal elements of a different kind.

Sonnets I–VI of the 1609 Quarto afford illustration. Shakespeare is often praised for his power of using imagery as an integrating element, yet in these sonnets it is evident that he has sacrificed the integration of the imagery of the individual sonnet to larger considerations of form; this sacrifice has features which show that it is in fact a sacrifice and not the ineptitude of a novice in sonnet-writing. In Sonnet I, the de-

Reprinted from *Essays in Criticism*, II (1952), 76–84, by permission of Basil Blackwell, publisher.

gree to which the images assist the organization of the poem is slight indeed. Almost every line has a separate image, and these images are heterogeneous (for instance: "Beauty's rose"—"heir"—"contracted"—"flame"—"famine"—"foe"—"herald"—"buriest"—"glutton"). The relation between the images is, for the most part, a relation *via* the subject they illustrate; it is not by their relations to one another that the poem is organized. This, however, it not ineptitude. The separateness, the repetitiveness (in that there is no increasing penetration of the object, but only an ever-renewed allegorization) and the regularity (a single new image in each of the first twelve lines) give this sonnet the character of a litany. If Sonnet I is indeed in its rightful place, there would seem to be here a recognizable decorum of form in the poet's electing to open by a litany of images[1] a sonnet-sequence which makes extended use of each. Further, the hypothesis that in Sonnet I there is a decorum of form which to the poet seemed more important than the congruity of images within the individual sonnet, is borne out by some features of Sonnets II–IV. The imagery of Sonnet II falls into two distinct parts connected by a modulation. In the first quatrain there is a group of images all referring to the beauty of the face; in the third quatrain a very different group, not visual like the first, but moral or prudential, relating to beauty considered as treasure, inheritance, and a matter for the rendering of accounts; the intervening quatrain is entirely devoted to a modulation from one type to the other:

> Then, being ask'd where all thy beauty lies,
> Where all the treasure of thy lusty days,
> To say, within thine own deep-sunken eyes,
> Were an all-eating shame and thriftless praise.

(In this modulation the visual and the prudential—"beauty" and "treasure"—are formally balanced, and the "deep-sunken" unites the eyes and the treasure in a single imaging epithet.) This careful four-line modulation suggests that Shakespeare was well aware of the virtue of relating images one to another as well as to the object they convey; yet the very necessity for a modulation here derives from the remoteness from one another of the two types of imagery. Here again the discrepancy finds its justification in larger considerations of form: namely, in the relation of Sonnet II to Sonnets III and IV. Sonnet III takes up and expands the first quatrain of Sonnet II, turning as it does upon the beauty of the face ("Look in thy glass, and tell the face thou viewest . . ."), and Sonnet IV takes up and expands the third quatrain of Sonnet II, turning as it does entirely upon beauty as treasure, inheritance and a matter for the rendering of accounts. It is further to be observed that Sonnets V and VI

---

[1] The litany of images is at the same time a litany of considerations or arguments, for in these sonnets the image is often an emblem of an argument.

repeat this pattern, V dealing with visual beauty in visual terms, and VI dealing with "beauty's treasure" in a long-sustained conceit drawn from usury. Would it be fanciful to suggest that the infelicity of the usury conceit in Sonnet VI reflects the difficulty the poet found in bringing this little sequence to a formally symmetrical conclusion?

In each of these six sonnets, features of the individual sonnet are illuminated by a consideration of the design of the whole group. But since we have no external warrant of the correctness of the 1609 order, the case for Shakespeare's sense of form must further be argued on grounds affording independent corroboration. This is found in Sonnet IV where, though the imagery chosen relates the sonnet to its fellows, the development of that imagery within the sonnet is a self-contained exercise in abstract form. The sonnet must be quoted and discussed in full.

> Unthrifty loveliness, why dost thou spend
> Upon thyself thy beauty's legacy?
> Nature's bequest gives nothing, but doth lend,
> And, being frank, she lends to those are free.
> Then, beauteous niggard, why dost thou abuse
> The bounteous largess given thee to give?
> Profitless usurer, why dost thou use
> So great a sum of sums, yet canst not live?
> For, having traffic with thyself alone,
> Thou of thyself thy sweet self dost deceive.
> Then how when nature calls thee to be gone?
> What acceptable audit canst thou leave?
>   Thy unus'd beauty must be tomb'd with thee,
>   Which, used, lives, th'executor to be.

Here we have a sonnet in which, patently, there is a high degree of organization. Firstly, the imagery of financial matters is sustained throughout. Secondly, there is within this integrated scheme a number of strongly marked subsidiary systems. The most immediately striking, which may therefore be cited first, is the ringing of the changes in lines 5–8 on "abuse"—"usurer"—"use," which is taken up in the couplet by "unus'd," "used." Another marked system is that of the reflexive constructions associated with "thee": "spend upon thyself"—"traffic with thyself"—"thou of thyself thy sweet self dost deceive," taken up in the couplet by "thy . . . beauty . . . tomb'd with thee." That these are deliberate systems, not inept repetitions, is proved by the way in which they interlock in the couplet: "unus'd" is, in the first line of the couplet, linked with "thy beauty . . . tomb'd with thee," and this contrasts with the second line of the couplet, where there is a linking of "used," "executor," and "lives," to produce the complete formal balance in thought, diction and syntax, of

> Thy unus'd beauty must be tomb'd with thee,
> Which, used, lives, th'executor to be.

This formal balance is of course closely related to the thought of the sonnet: Nature, which lends beauty in order that it may be given, is contrasted with the youth, whose self-regarding results in a usurious living on capital alone, which is a negation of Nature and of life; these paradoxes of the thought make possible the correspondences and contrasts of the verbal systems. What is remarkable is the way in which the poet evolves from this material an intricate and beautiful form which is very close to the art of fugue. Like the fugue, its effect resides in the interaction of the parts; critical analysis, which cannot reproduce the simultaneousness of the original, must labour heavily behind, discussing first the development of each part and then their interaction. We may note, then, that "Unthrifty loveliness," with which the sonnet opens, is, as it were, a first blending of those two distinct voices, "why dost thou spend upon thyself" and "Nature's bequest." The second quatrain blends them again in "beauteous niggard," which is itself an inversion, formally complete, of "unthrifty loveliness," and moreover an inversion which leads on to the extreme "profitless usurer"; further, the movement towards the judgment represented by "profitless usurer" has all the while been less obtrusively going on in the verbs as well as in the vocatives ("spend"—"abuse"—"yet canst not live"). Then, with "yet canst not live," the sonnet brings out the second voice, that reflexive (and self-destructive) action announced in "spend upon thyself," but kept low in the first eight lines, maintaining itself there only by the formal parallels of "why dost thou spend"—"why dost thou abuse"—"why dost thou use." This voice now emerges predominant in "For, having traffic with thyself alone," and this voice in turn reaches its extreme of formal development in the line "Thou of thyself thy sweet self dost deceive." The remaining lines bring the two voices to a sharp contrast with "nature calls thee to be gone" (where "nature" and "thee" achieve a syntactical nearness embodying a conflict of opposed concepts, and this conflict-in-nearness is fully stated in the complete formal balance of the couplet). In this rough analysis of the blending of the voices in this sonnet, much has had to be passed over, but now we may go back and point to the incidental contrast and harmony of "beauteous niggard" with "bounteous largess"; to the transition, in the pun of "canst not live," from usury to death (which leads on to the contrast in the couplet); to the felicity of "audit" in line 12, which is relevant not only to all the financial imagery that has gone before, but also to the rendering of an account when life is at an end; to the subtle conceptual sequence of "unthrifty loveliness" (the fact of beauty), "beauteous niggard" (the poet's reproof), "profitless usurer" (the youth's own loss), and finally, "unus'd beauty" (the whole tragedy—of beauty, of the poet, and of the youth—in the hour of death). Thus this sonnet, which in its absence of visual imagery has little attraction for the hasty reader, reveals itself to analysis as having an intricate beauty of form to which it would be hard to find a parallel in the work of any other poet.

Though Sonnet IV is a *tour de force* in the handling of form, Sonnet V is even more important to the critic who would make much of formal elements, in that it has a quality which sets it apart from the preceding four: a quality the average reader might call seriousness or sincerity. Here Shakespeare deals with Time and Beauty (and for the application of these to the particular case of the youth requires Sonnet VI, linked to V by "Then let not . . ."). The evident artifice of Sonnets I–IV (emblematic imagery, conceits, punning and patterned word-play) gives place in Sonnet V to language which, though it is of course figurative, derives its figures from that realm of common experience in which processes conceived philosophically by the mind have in fact their manifestations to the senses: from the seasons which figure Time, from the flower and its fragrance which figure Beauty and Evanescence. In short, the poem appeals to us in that realm of experience where we are all, already, half poets. Yet despite this change from the "artificial" to the "sincere," this poem too derives much of its strength from its formal designs. The design is simple but perfect. The easy continuous process of Time is stated in lines themselves easy and continuous:

> Those hours that with gentle work did frame
> The lovely gaze where every eye doth dwell,

and in the next two lines, which suggest that this process implies a coming reversal, the reversal is still a thing of the future and is indicated not by any change in the movement but only by the verbal contrasts between "gentle" and "will play the tyrant" and between "fairly" and "unfair." So the continuous movement flows uninterrupted through these lines and on into the fifth:

> For never-resting time leads summer on

but in the sixth line,

> To hideous winter and confounds him there

the reversal so casually foretold in the first quatrain becomes, by the violence of "hideous winter" and "confounds" and by the change of tense, a present catastrophe, and the movement of the fifth and sixth lines taken together perfectly corresponds to the sense: the running-on movement of summer is checked by "hideous winter" and again by the heavy pause at "there." The next two lines embody perfectly, by sound and imagery as well as by sense, this checking and reversal:

> Sap check'd with frost and lusty leaves quite gone,
> Beauty o'ersnow'd and bareness everywhere.

(Particularly subtle is the way in which the alliteration of "lusty leaves" gives place to that of "beauty" with "bareness.") Now in the remaining six lines the poet in his turn attempts a reversal, and the beauty of the form is to be seen in the way in which he now uses the two kinds of movement already laid down in the sonnet (the one of flowing, the other of checking). What he does is to *transfer to Beauty* the flowing movement of Time, and then to *arrest* Beauty in a state of permanent *perfection;* this he does by the long flowing movement, ending in arrest and permanence, of the line,

> Then, were not summer's distillation left . . .

This triumphant transfer to Beauty of the movement formerly associated with Time, is of a piece with the imagery of the next line ("A liquid prisoner pent in walls of glass"), where Beauty's distillation is at once arrested ("prisoner," "pent") yet free ("liquid") and visible ("glass"); this image of course reverses the implications of the earlier images of winter, where the sap was checked with frost and beauty was o'ersnow'd. Thus the movement of the first eight lines proves to have been designed not merely to make the sound repeat the sense, but rather to lay down formal elements whose reversal enables the poet to reverse the reversal implicit in Time. Similarly, the image of distillation is seen to be not merely an illustration of the concept of preserving Beauty, but also an answer to the image of winter's freezing of the sap and obliteration of Beauty. Clearly, the formal elements of Sonnet V are part of the poetic logic: the movement, as much as the imagery, is a means of poetic power. It is because of this that the study of formal elements in the Sonnets is not an arid academic exercise. Such a study can help one to arrive at a fuller understanding of Shakespeare's means of communication and a fuller possession of those poetic experiences with which the Sonnets deal.

This article has dealt only with the first six sonnets of the 1609 Quarto. These six sonnets are not exceptional in their successful handling of forms; from the whole range of the *Sonnets* many examples more subtle and more striking might have been chosen but it seemed to me best, in order to argue the case for Shakespeare's interest in form, to make no arbitrary selection, but simply to begin at the beginning and scrutinize what is to be found there. The findings warrant a much greater attention to formal aspects of the *Sonnets* than is at present customary. The result of such an attentiveness to Shakespeare's handling of form is the discovery that the greater the immediate effect of a sonnet, the more surely does it prove, upon examination, that the effects rest no less upon the form than upon the appeal of the sentiments or of the imagery (as, for instance, in the famous Sonnet CXVI, "Let me not to the marriage of true minds . . ."). Again, it will be found that many of the sonnets which are not commonly held to be of the finest, reveal an unsuspected depth and strength when they are, after scrutiny of their form, revalued. It is upon this last point that particular stress may well be laid, for it is here that one becomes aware of new possibilities for the interpretation of Shakespeare's language, not only in the poems but also in the plays. A close study of the language of the *Sonnets* makes it clear that, great as was Shakespeare's ability to use imagery not only for its beauty but also for its integrating power, he possessed in even greater measure the power to make the formal elements of language express the nature of the experience with which the language deals. No doubt a knowledge of rhetoric, which must direct attention to verbal patterns, did something to develop this power. Of the early plays it may be true to say that sometimes the rhetorical forms are empty, that they have little virtue beyond that of providing a ready-made mould for the flow of what is thought and felt. But Shakespeare's rejection of rhetorical forms of the over-elaborate and merely self-regarding type was coupled with an increasing awareness of the expressiveness of those forms he did retain. Thus in the language of the great plays the recurrence of a marked form is not fortuitous, nor is it, in cases where a recurring form is associated with a particular speaker, merely a device for adding body to a character; that is to say, these features of the style are rarely, if ever, designed to contribute merely to the creation of a "character part"; they are almost always an expression of something essential in the speaker himself considered in his relation to the play as a whole. Pope in his preface to his edition of Shakespeare commented on the highly individualized styles of the characters. It still remains for the interpreters of Shakespeare in our own time to discover to what extent these styles are expressive as well as characteristic. And further it may be said that the expressiveness of formal organizations in Shakespeare's language is matched by the expressiveness of form in all his dramatic structures. Every age rediscovers the genius of Shakespeare. It is open to ours to discover and to show the working of his genius in the realm of forms.

C. L. BARBER

The Sonnet as an Action

To READ through the sonnets at a sitting, though it is useful for sur-
veying the topography they present, does violence to them and to the
reader—it can produce a sensation of hothouse oppression. Each poem
needs to be dwelt on; each requires the kind of concentrated attention
which could have been given when they were received singly or in small
groups. To read and reread is essential if we are to enjoy the way each
moves, the use it makes of the possibilities of the sonnet form, the particular development in it of a design of sounds and images. The sonnets
ask for a special sort of attention because in them poetry is, in a special
way, an action, something done for and to the beloved. Indeed sometimes the activity of the poetry alone makes endurable the passivity of
the attitudes expressed by the poet.

Many of the sonnets are wonderfully generous poems; they *give* meaning and beauty. The generosity is at once personal, a selfless love, and
impersonal, the glow upon the world at the golden moment when
Shakespeare began to write. The poems create a world resonant with
the friend's beauty:

> Thou art thy mother's glass, and she in thee
> Calls back the lovely April of her prime;
> So thou through windows of thine age shalt see,
> Despite of wrinkles, this thy golden time.　　(3)

The curious theme of the first seventeen sonnets, which urge a friend
to marry and have children, works partly because it provides occasions
for saying simple things beautifully: how lovely April is; how fine it is
that age, in spite of wrinkles, has windows through which to see its
golden time renewed. The poet's vicarious interest in the young man's
sexual fulfillment is not queasy because it is realized by evoking the
creative power generally at work in nature:

> Those hours that with gentle work did frame
> The lovely gaze where every eye doth dwell . . . (5)

The phrase "gentle work" is typical of the direct cherishing of the processes of life. The feeling about the destructiveness of death is equally direct:

> For never-resting time leads summer on
> To hideous winter and confounds him there . . . (5)

There is no holding back from obvious words or metaphors: the sun's light is gracious, music is sweet, the buds of May are darling; death is winter, darkness, Time's scythe; beauty is all the usual things, for example a flower. But the meaning of the usual things is renewed:

> Since brass, nor stone, nor earth, nor boundless sea,
> But sad mortality o'ersways their power,
> How with this rage shall beauty hold a plea,
> Whose action is no stronger than a flower?   (65)

That a flower is a fragile thing is familiar enough. But that a flower has its own kind of power too—this comes as a poignant realization. It often happens that the metaphorical vehicle in which Shakespeare conveys the tenor of his love absorbs our chief attention, so that the love itself is left behind or fulfilled in what it is compared to. We dwell on the fact that "summer's lease hath all too short a date," that the earth devours "her own sweet brood," that the morning flatters "the mountain tops with sovereign eye," that black night is "Death's second self," and "seals up all in rest." Consider, as a summary example, the direct descriptions of the seasons in 97 and 98, "old December's bareness every where," "teeming autumn big with rich increase," "proud-pied April, dress'd in all his trim," and summer when we "wonder at the lily's white" and "praise the deep vermilion in the rose." The world is full of value that can be looked at front-face. Shakespeare could get more of this gold into his poetry than anyone else in the golden age because he had the greatest power of admiration.

To quote isolated phrases or lines from the sonnets is unsatisfying, because every line or phrase is, in the act of reading, part of a single movement: when you know a sonnet well, an individual line, quoted alone, rings with the sound that it has in its proper place. Each sonnet is one utterance. Shakespeare's use of the form is simple and forthright and also delicate and subtle. He never varies from three quatrains followed by a couplet, *abab, cdcd, efef, gg*:

> Why write I still all one, ever the same,
> And keep invention in a noted weed,
> That every word doth almost tell my name . . . ? (76)

Other Elizabethan sonneteers showed more technical restlessness. Shakespeare not only uses nothing but the Shakespearean form (it *does* tell his name!), but for the most part he uses it straight. He does not run his syntax against the line endings or rhyme scheme. There are exceptions, but normally the sentences close with the close of each quatrain, or else are balanced symmetrically within the four-line unit. Within sentences, grammar and thought typically pause or turn at the end of the line; where they do run over, the enjambment is rarely emphatic. Shakespeare does not exploit the more outward forms of variation because within the pattern he is making astonishingly beautiful designs with sound and syllable and cadence. He is like an accomplished figure skater who sticks to the classical figures because what he cares about is what he can make of each evolution. (Shakespeare had, after all, unlimited opportunities in the plays for free-style improvisations, swoops, spins, leaps.) Each sonnet is different, but the difference is achieved not by changing the framework of form but by moving in fresh ways within it.

It seems clear that Shakespeare wrote by quatrains. In coming to know a sonnet by heart, you find yourself recalling it one quatrain at a time and often getting stuck trying to move to the next, for lack of a tangible link. The imagery does not regularly carry through; what does carry through is the momentum of the discourse. The movement from quatrain to quatrain is usually a shift of some sort, though it can be simply a continuing with fresh impetus. The figure skater starts each evolution by kicking off from an edge, and can move from one evolution to another either by staying on the same edge of the same blade, or changing from inside edge to outside edge, or from left foot inside to right foot outside, and so on—each of these technical moves focusing a whole living gesture of the balancing, moving body. People praise Shakespeare's sonnets because each one is about one thing: one should add that each is *one motion* about one thing, the motion normally being composed of three large sweeps and the shorter couplet. (The very different serial movement of 66 is a revealing exception to prove the rule.)

It is important to recognize that in most of the sonnets the couplet is *not* the emotional climax, or indeed even the musical climax; where it is made so, either by Shakespeare's leaning on it too heavily, or by our giving it unnecessary importance, one feels that two lines are asked to do too much. This let-down or over-reach in the couplet is the most common defect in the sonnets, though with tactful reading it usually can be kept from being troublesome. One needs to attend to the motion and the imaginative expansion which the sonnet achieves in the quatrains, realizing that the couplet is often no more than a turning around at the end to look from a new vantage at what has been expressed.

The main line of the sonnet as Shakespeare writes it is the patterned movement of discourse, not the imagery. The voice rides the undulation of the meter, gaining remarkable power and reaching out in ardent or urgent or solemn gestures defined by rhythmical variations. The criticism of our time has been fascinated by the way poetry can explore experience by carrying out the implications of a metaphor or conceit, as notably in Donne's work. Shakespeare in the sonnets occasionally does something like this—most perfectly in the three paralleled metaphors of 73: "That time of year . . . the twilight of such day . . . the glowing of such fire." But the progression by extending metaphors in 73 is most definitely not typical. He is responsible to rhythmical, not metaphorical consistency. The sonnet often starts with something like a metaphorical program, but usually it is not carried through; metaphors are picked up, changed, mixed, dropped *ad lib* while the sonnet runs its strong course as an utterance.

One often finds, as one penetrates the poetic texture of a particular poem, that it holds together by determinate rhythm and sound several almost independent strains of meaning, or a cluster of ambiguities which, worked out logically, are almost mutually exclusive. A case in point, which also will be of interest to us in considering the relationship of Shakespeare to the friend he addresses, comes in 16, where the poet urges that children can provide reproductions of the friend "much liker than your painted counterfeit," and then goes on with an extraordinarily rich use of the word "lines":

> So should the lines of life that life repair,
> Which this Time's pencil, or my pupil pen,
> Neither in inward worth nor outward fair,
> Can make you live yourself in eyes of men.

The suggestiveness of "lines of life" appears in the variety of commentators' paraphrases recorded in the Variorum edition: the "lines of life" can be the lines life etches on a face, or the lines of descent in a genealogy, or the lines of the living pictures presented by children, or the lines of children as living poems (as opposed to the mere written lines of the "pupil pen"), or even perhaps, as an echo at the back of the mind, what one commentator defends in urging unconvincingly that "lines of life" is a misprint for "loins of life" (compare the sonnet's conclusion: "And you must live, drawn by your own sweet skill"). Shakespeare had a supremely wandering mind! To ravel out such associations can of course be misleading. In an actual, live reading of a sonnet such clustering ideas as these are felt together, not sorted; they are the opening out of mind and heart into the plurality of the world's riches. What keeps us from coming to a standstill in wall-eyed contemplation is the flow of the poem's movement as it gathers in meaning in the service of the poet's love.

One can instance even more dramatic places where the poetry makes a thick harmony out of wool-gathering multiplicity—the most famous is "Bare ruin'd choirs, where late the sweet birds sang," thanks to William Empson's discussion at the outset of his *Seven Types of Ambiguity*.[1] What criticism now needs to stress, I think, is not the interplay of imagery but the interplay of sound. (A case in point is the chord of vowels and of "r's" in "bare ruin'd choirs," sounded in three successive long, slow syllables—the mystery of the line comes from this music as much as from the wonderful complex of metaphors it holds in solution.) We need to consider, not a special case like 73, but the much more common case where there is great richness of metaphor but metaphorical consistency is not regarded:

> O how shall summer's honey breath hold out,
> Against the wrackful siege of battering days,
> When rocks impregnable are not so stout,
> Nor gates of steel so strong but Time decays?   (65)

These are splendid lines—but it is the design of sound that chiefly carries them, the open-breathing *o* and *u* sounds and flowing consonants of "how shall summer's honey breath hold out" followed by the battering lines, with "wrackful" and "rocks impregnable." One can understand summer's honey metaphorically as provision for a siege—but one cannot carry the metaphor further, one cannot "batter" honey! And the summer-winter opposition, as well as the battering, have been lost by the time we get to "Time decays."

Sound and rhythm again and again give life to statements or figures which might otherwise be banal: so in a quatrain from 97 selected almost at random:

> How like a winter hath my absence been
> From thee, the pleasure of the fleeting year!
> What freezings have I felt, what dark days seen,
> What old December's bareness every where!   (97)

A rich use of various *e* sounds emerges: the poignant sense of absence from "thee" is developed as we encounter the same sound in "fleeting" and "freezings"; the open *a* sounds in "What dark days" feel cavernous against the prevailing *e* tones; "December's bareness" includes the three vowel sounds present in "every where," so that the bareness seems to spread out "every where"—and the meter makes "every where" larger than it would be in prose by stressing two of its three syllables. Consonants of course are also put to work reinforcing the meaning, for example by linking "fleeting and freezing" to "felt," "old" to "December," "December" to "bareness." One can go on and on in this fashion, once

---

1 [See page 124, above.—Ed.]

one starts looking for such tangible patterns—and though it is not always possible to know where to draw the line between cases that really matter and cases that are farfetched, such texture of physical relations among words is clearly fundamental to the beauty *and* the meaning of the poetry. When we shift from quatrain to quatrain, turning to lean into a new evolution, part of the newness is often the sound of a fresh set of dominant vowels; or again, we sometimes recognize a set of sounds carried all through a sonnet to give it its distinctive tune.

The sonnets often would be "witty" if it were not that the wit in them goes along with sound and cadences that hold feeling—the wit is rarely isolated to be felt separately, as Donne's so often is, but enters into the whole motion. If we read them in isolation, we would be amused by the virtuoso alliteration and assonance in lines like

> And with old woes new wail my dear time's waste. . . .
> And heavily from woe to woe tell o'er
> The sad account of fore-bemoaned moan.   (30)

But when we read them as an integral part of the lovely sonnet "When to the sessions of sweet silent thought," the huddled sounds serve to convey the pressure of the past on the present as a thickening or troubling of speech. Where we feel a twinge of amusement, it is usually in combination with feelings dictated by the underlying rhythm, as with the ruefulness of "But ah, thought kills me that I am not thought . . ." (44). It would be wrong to suppose that the sonnets are without humor. There are places where Shakespeare positively romps, but the fun is almost never unmixed with serious feeling:

> Let not my love be call'd idolatry,
> Nor my beloved as an idol show,
> Since all alike my songs and praises be
> To one, of one, still such, and ever so.
> Kind is my love to-day, to-morrow kind,
> Still constant in a wondrous excellence;
> Therefore my verse to constancy confin'd,
> One thing expressing, leaves out difference.
> Fair, kind, and true, is all my argument,
> Fair, kind, and true, varying to other words . . . (105)

This gay whirl is an extreme example of the repetition common in the sonnets, the same words rolled round, each time with added life because they fall differently each time within the poem's progress. In 105 this sort of fun is indulged in almost by itself, in celebration of a moment's carefree confidence. But even 105, which is as near to a *jeu d'esprit* as we come, has its serious side, for it raises a question about idolatry which it does not settle.